Resurgent

Resurgent

New Writing by Women

Edited by   Lou Robinson and

Camille Norton

University of Illinois Press
Urbana and Chicago

© 1992 by the Board of Trustees of the University of Illinois
Manufactured in the United States of America

1 2 3 4 5 C P 5 4 3 2 1

This book is printed on acid-free paper.

Library of Congress Cataloging-in-Publication Data

Resurgent : new writing by women / edited by Lou Robinson and Camille
Norton.

   p. cm.
  ISBN 0-252-01835-4 (cl).—ISBN 0-252-06203-5 (pb)
   1. Literature, Experimental—Women authors.   2. Women and
literature.   3. Feminism and literature.   I. Robinson, Lou.
II. Norton, Camille, 1954–
PN6069.W65R4 1992
808.8'99287'09045–dc20   91–8297
                                                                CIP

For Theresa Cha

Contents

1 Introduction

I. Transmission/Translation

13 Melpomene Tragedy
THERESA CHA

20 Ultrasounds
NICOLE BROSSARD

33 About Flight
DÔRE MICHELUT

36 this.notes.new year.
KATHLEEN FRASER

39 Lily, Lois & Flaubert:
The site of loss
KATHLEEN FRASER

42 The decision
KATHLEEN FRASER

44 Five letters from one window,
San Gimignano, May 1981
KATHLEEN FRASER

49 Love Pain and the
Fading of Orchids
ANNE-MARIE ALONZO

52 Dune Wild Sands
ANNE-MARIE ALONZO

58 The Blue Door of Detroit
JANET KAUFFMAN

59 from The Reproduction of Profiles
ROSMARIE WALDROP

66 Small of the Year
TOBEY HILLER

69 from Harvest of Ghosts
NINA CROW NEWINGTON

74 Liszt or Schumann
LOUISE DUPRÉ

82 Perfection and Derangement
FANNY HOWE

88 litter.wreckage.salvage
DAPHNE MARLATT

92 from *The Arab Apocalypse*
ETEL ADNAN

98 Main Bride Remembers Halifax
GAIL SCOTT

111 The Hour of Pan/Ama
NUALA ARCHER

116 Blue Mosque
ANNE WALDMAN

II. Collaboration/Spectacle

127 from *The Wide Road*
CARLA HARRYMAN AND
LYN HEJINIAN

134 from *Sex and Other Sacred Games*
KIM CHERNIN AND
RENATE STENDHAL

153 Four Pairs
CAMILLE NORTON AND
LOU ROBINSON

158 Reading and Writing Between
the Lines
DAPHNE MARLATT AND
BETSY WARLAND

165 Rewire//Speak in
Disagreement
ABIGAIL CHILD AND
SALLY SILVERS

173 from *Black Holes, Black Stockings*
JANE MILLER AND
OLGA BROUMAS

183 from *Life, After All*
SUZANNE JACOB

194 A Motive for Mayhem
ABIGAIL CHILD

198 from *Surname Viet Given Name Nam*
TRINH T. MINH-HA

209 La Luta Continua
NTOZAKE SHANGE

214 The Sofa Is Black
ANNE WALDMAN

216 Laments
JENNY HOLZER

230 A Barrel of Her Own Design
ELLEN ZWEIG

241 Acknowledgments

245 Contributors

Introduction

Everywhere in these prose pieces I find that unpredictable element in the language which forces consciousness to leap a gap where other writing would make a bridge of shared meaning (shared, at least, to an assumed 'we')—a sense of something so urgent in its desire to be expressed that it comes before the words to say it, in the interstices, in the rhythm: Marina Tsvetaeva's "song in the head without noise." A spirit that sees dislocation, displacement, not as disorder but as rich complexity. A voice too head-strong and insistent for the bounds of story, poem, novel, yet bearing the revolutionary fervor of poetry, the evidence of story, the window on a soul of a novel. This is writing that swings out over a chasm, that spits.

The chasm opened between words and their meanings in the last three decades with radical developments in linguistic and literary theories. In this reverberating space—at the intersection of poststructuralist ideas of 'difference' as relational, constructed, and feminist concerns with 'difference' as plurality of experiences—a surge of innovative writing by women has been produced.

As the terms are invented to describe the cultural contributions of our age, it seems crucial to gather the creative writing itself, make it available, lest individual women writers be lost to a monolithic idea of the postmodern, as modernist women writers were obscured in their own time. The debate continues about what, exactly, is *postmodern*. Sometimes the term describes a continuation of modernist methods, sometimes a reaction to modernist forms that have become conventional. Whether the term will be useful or not, it is in the air wherever innovative writing is discussed.

Resurgent brings together prose by contemporary women writers engaged in literary experiments with language. The anthology represents the variety of nuances within postmodern expression: writing that breaks formal limits, dismantles conventional notions of genre, merges poetic

I

line with prose sentence, shakes up hierarchical relations within syntax, and dissolves the boundaries between self and other, narrator and author, writer and reader.

Some of the writers collected here work from the tradition of such early modernist women writers as Djuna Barnes, Mina Loy, Violette Leduc, H.D., and Gertrude Stein. Others make use of futurist, surrealist, and other avant-garde techniques. Their work shares concerns with the new French feminist philosophies, psychoanalytic literary criticism, the decolonization movement, the language poets, postmodern film theory—the writing cannot be described by a single approach.

What is influence? Where does a thought originate? Readers, writers, philosophers, scientists, critics, filmmakers, computers, mad voices in the street infiltrating the page, animals signing resignedly to earnest human trainers, a pen writing without a hand in a box in Rolla, Missouri. Writing respects no authority. Many things contribute to the state of language today, the layered meanings through which we read. I can say what holds my eye, stops my breath, arouses that acute writing frenzy, but how can I be sure what moves another woman to write? Does this matter? Not so much as being able to read the writing.

There is always a risk of forcing a false unity by generalizing about a selection of work. How do you collect writing that is powerful and important without reducing it to ideology? Writers lumped together do not necessarily share intentions or see connections among their works. How do you identify new work and yet avoid setting up an avant-garde dependent on a rear-guard? More traditional kinds of writing by women coexist, serving different ends, making their own discoveries.

The works in this book were chosen for their reach, for the risks they take, and for their sublingual, visionary, poetic heart, which can't be fully grasped by critical analysis, although analysis lets us speak to one another about what we feel shifting, opening, in women's writing today.

For me, the impetus behind this book has to do with what makes me write, slantwise and fast, in spite of the censor and the canon-maker. The overheard fragment crosses the air, transcribing itself into another kind of narrative. I am interested in writing as an act of transmission between those who might not otherwise necessarily speak to one another, between Québecoise feminist writers and U.S. language poets, between innovative black women playwrights and Korean and Vietnamese writers devising a language of cultural translation. When I began to think about this book, I visualized a web of language, of countertradition, of influence.

I had been deeply influenced by the events of the Third International Feminist Bookfair, a kind of feminist U.N. of writers and publishers that convened for five days in June 1988, at the University of Montreal in Québec. In workshops that were for the most part simultaneously translated into English, French, and Spanish, and organized within the topic of memory, power, and feminist thought, the ideological struggles waged around women's writing produced in me a completely new understanding of difference. There could be no one way of writing as women. There could be no one feminist poetic. And yet at no time in history has the confluence of writing by women seemed so urgent, fierce, or critical. Out of this central paradox came the title for this book. Res*urgent*, evoking a groundswell of urgent material.

Then, in 1989, I began collaborating with Lou Robinson on a series of prose fragments that crossed and recrossed between Boston, Massachusetts, and Ithaca, New York. These transmissions through geographical space subverted assumptions about my life as a writer, not the least of which was the pressing isolation involved in the making of fiction. Our work together led us to ask, What makes you write? What do you read? Where do you find what you read?

These questions initiated a series of conversations about the publishing situation facing the serious woman writer of experimental prose. We discovered that innovative work by women was scattered in publications of small presses, in some Canadian feminist presses, and in university presses (the latter usually only isolated work in translation). In Canada, largely because the Québecois movement takes to heart some of the same questions regarding the politics of language as do Canadian feminist writers, innovative writing is more accessible.

A number of magazines and journals have focused on women's experimental writing in the past few years—*f(Lip)*, *How(ever)*, *Trivia*, *Poetics Journal #4/Women and Language*, *Big allis*, *Mirage*—nowhere, however, has women's experimental writing appeared together in one book where various writers might be read in light of other writers who were charting similar courses or breaking similar rules. There has been, on the one hand, a growing theoretical interest in innovative writing by women and, on the other, no collection of this contemporary creative prose. We took seriously Kathleen Fraser's warning that writing that remains uncollected and disregarded by its own generation faces certain oblivion.

In gathering the material for this book, innumerable packets flew between our two houses. I began to think of this collection as an occasion for what Catherine Clement called "the foreseen, unforeseen spectacle," an ensemble at odds with its own collectivity, shouting down the notion of what it means to be experimental. When we proposed this project to our potential contributors, the response was overwhelmingly encouraging. Other women, including writers, academics, and teachers of creative writing, told us to hurry with this book, that it was necessary to them in concrete ways. Why do you write? What makes you write? To me, these questions seem urgent.

What makes you read, think? What overcomes despair, restores you to an engaged curiosity? This writing helps release the kink in the hose, as Maureen Brady calls that thing which chokes us, made of stories of damage to women and resistance to words like *damage*. As deep inside muscles a memory of strength and stretching resides, so the writing speaks with the energy released by imagining possibility from the syllable level outward. Because of its stretch, its reach, it is not easy or comfortable reading. It also speaks from our fragmented, dislocated lives, from the very conditions necessary for subversive thought.

This book is organized in two sections that track a possible trajectory for the writer's voice as it moves through shifting textual and auditory frames. Part 1, "Transmission/Translation," collects a number of individual texts, some of them excerpted from longer works, that represent the writer working autonomously. The writing gathered in Part 1 lives primarily on the page; print is its primary medium. Part 2, "Collaboration/Spectacle," presents several works of collaboration between women writers, as well as a selection of experimental writing that moves toward spectacle—performance art, installation art, theater, and film. The divisions between these two sections, however, are arbitrary. Some writers in Part 1—Nicole Brossard, Daphne Marlatt, and Etel Adnan—have worked collaboratively on many occasions. Marlatt, for example, appears again in Part 2, in collaboration with Betsy Warland. Anne Waldman publishes poetry and fiction and also performs her texts on the stage. Almost all of the writers in Part 2 have published work that does not require a theater, a camera, or a gallery. Nevertheless, by designing the book in this way, we hope to suggest that there is an engagement among the word, the text, the conversation, and the world. The writing here is airborne; the letter, to quote from Brossard, is "aerial."

Part 1 begins with Theresa Cha's "Melpomene Tragedy," a chapter excerpted from her novel *Dictée*. In referring to Melpomene, the muse who presides over tragedy, Cha links the horror of the Korean War to the narrator's struggle to make a narrative of "replication, a war memorial" constructed out of a child's firsthand experience of war. Cha suggests that exile from one's homeland results in a series of linguistic dislocations that break apart the writing of history. Melpomene herself must make do with the severed utterance, just as the narrator must make do with "another tongue, a second tongue." The process of translation invoked here is the result of political necessity covering the tracks of a national nightmare. Korean is the language of the dead, English the tongue of the survivor. Cha, then, introduces translation as a condition framed by power and underscored by loss.

Brossard's "Ultrasounds" is the first of several actual translations into English that appear in this book. For Brossard, who writes out of a Québecois culture charged by the politics of bilingualism, the language of the creative imagination exists as an erotic interchange between two women. Half lyric, half essay, "Ultrasounds" takes up language as an effect of lesbian desire, which precedes the text and forever marks it. Dôre Michelut's "About Flight" recasts writing as a heroic encounter with myth, an encounter that requires sexual seeding by the male lover.

Some of the work here addresses the presence of the auditor, who is at once intimate and "other." As Kathleen Fraser writes, "Dear other, I address you in sentences. I need your nods and I hear your echoes." How does this need reshape the epistolary form, making of it a fiction, a fantasia for the writer? For Anne-Marie Alonzo, it is the absence of the other that provokes not only the form but also the natural tongue of "Love Pain and the Fading of Orchids": "This text came to me in English. Dedicated to N. who speaks reads mostly French. As if. The lover had ordered the choice of language. As if. Pain had to be sad written in translation of the mind heart. To hurt less." For Tobey Hiller, the presence of absence, the spirit of the dead, filters through the spaces of "Small of the Year." Louise Dupré's intimate other is addressed in the mind through a series of letters to the mother: "You are no longer just a little girl devoid of eloquence." What is it like when one's own body is "other," as in Rosmarie Waldrop's *The Reproduction of Profiles*? "The body is useful. I can send it on errands while I stay in bed and pull the blankets up to my head." In Gail Scott's story, "Main Bride Remembers Halifax," a woman rides the trains between Kingston, Toronto, and Montreal, following her officer/lover. She seldom meets him but writes about him obsessively in various hotel rooms.

Much of the writing here has to do with place, with shifting geographies that call into question standard defintions of 'nation' in a culture already moving toward global meanings. Place in conflict, place in flux, displacement, all resound on the level of language, on the level of the subject whose very identity is called into question. Nuala Archer: "She is told she is not where she is—*Place of many fishes*—Panamá. She is told she lives on the Isthmus, in the Canal Zone, in the U.S.A." Janet Kauffman: "Guess where you are. It is impossible to be a stranger to the climates of seven continents." Anne Waldman: "This is many lifetimes from the capital of India speaking." Etel Adnan: "Beirut wallows in misfortune HOU! HOU! HOU! Beirut bleeds. . . ." Daphne Marlatt: "Steveston . . . your women are invisible, your men all gone." "Is G-d a place that it should move with me in my car?" Fanny Howe asks in "Perfection and Derangement." The fractured selves of women in shelters and institutions have escaped into colors, oak trees, cello sounds, words overheard—signatures. Nothing that can be read is lost. Like music and painting, Howe's words arrange and help us bear our fears and griefs.

When women write together, the notion of text as property, author as owner, is questioned, further dismantling traditional ways of reading. What happens when you cannot tell who wrote what or visualize a creator, an artiste, occupying a heroic place in literature? What happens when the text divides and argues with itself? The space we create when we write together is like the space we create when we come together to talk about writing—fragile, unresolved, sustaining, charged.

Part 2 begins with six collaborative pieces by twelve women. Not surprisingly, many of them are about writing and about the erotic—language and sex, our most basic drives to connect, not just with each other, but with meaning, and with the universe outside our separate bodies. Everything we say must be forced through states of wants. Say them, write them down. Then there is a you that is in motion; then identity becomes a vehicle not of personality but of the process of writing and reading.

Traveling together, Lyn Hejinian and Carla Harryman are writing The Wide Road, a "picaresque novel containing views of contemporary erotic life." The excerpt published here for the first time is a humorous unwinding of the sacred mummy of authorship. "Their shadows wandered away from the word 'I'." Writing as "we" they prod at the tenuous boundaries that separate personalities. Their quest is an investigation of the nature of the erotic and how it relates to women writing. They locate the man, known as the Whimsical Male Sexual Appetite (WMSA) on the other side of the keyhole. Inside are the "we" who write, their new friend, "the third person pronoun, she," and "us," that is, their public, who, unlike the man outside, are all made privy to everything. We (two women) take us (readers) along the wide road, ourselves at the center, the opposite of marginal, our meaning "surliminal," exposed, the opposite of subliminal. We inclusive of women writing and reading confound woman as object or woman as too subjective. Meanwhile, "we eroticize our earthly situations and conditions and likewise they eroticize us."

In *Sex and Other Sacred Games*, Kim Chernin and Renate Stendhal each take on a fictional character, Claire Heller, an American, and Alma Runau, a European, to write a book about two women who meet, separate, correspond, and meet again in an ongoing unresolved conversation about sexual roles, an attempt to redefine female sexuality. A play on Plato's Dialogues, their discourse takes place on many levels, moving among mythological, psychoanalytic, and feminist points of view. Writing alternating chapters, they attempt to bridge the geographic space and the cultural difference of their characters by allowing the censored thoughts to emerge.

I, too, listen for things heard under and through ordinary language. The escaping thought, sound, is what became compelling in my collaborative work with Camille Norton. The *Pairs* project was to write for five to fifteen minutes at a time, rapidly and without any censorship or shaping, and with full concentration on a shared phrase or term selected at random from whatever text happened to be at hand. The writing was to be mailed in a sealed packet that the receiver was not to open until she had completed her part of the assignment. Immediately, words seem to flow with authority, unequivocating, unsoftened, and often, unwelcome. Often syntax led sense. I would feel tricked, caught out revealing not just unexpected thoughts or feelings, but voices I didn't know I had. The pairs became a way to subvert the ordinary use to which we must put words, revealing ironic contradictions between what is felt and said, a fissure for change. In the way they sometimes overlapped, mirrored, paralleled each other, they became a demonstration of the unexplainable, the mysterious, the element in writing that is to me the most motivating.

Writing together is for Daphne Marlatt and Betsy Warland "a reciprocal subversion of the definitive." In "Reading and Writing Between the Lines," they play off the military association of the word collaboration, which implies that the one collaborated with holds the power, to explore the nature of writing as negotiation, seduction. Asserting that all writing is collaborative, they, like Harryman and Hejinian, question the delineation between the collectivity of conversation and the individual's ownership of the written.

Sally Silvers is a dancer and choreographer. Abigail Child is a writer and filmmaker. "Rewire//Speak in Disagreement" is an essay they wrote together about making art, or about "girls and modernism." This manifesto exhorts women to "defeat coherent subjectivity on which capitalism, idealism is based—point up multiple contradictions. . . . do, rather than apologize. . . . fracture the social conditions. . . . Speak in disagreement, enter the discourse." Enacting this directive, they dispute, they argue strategies. What is clarity? And what is adherence to a convention that blunts the complexity of a piece of writing? What is the goal? An unsolved work that satisfies.

In *Black Holes, Black Stockings*, Olga Broumas and Jane Miller set out to write together each day during their travels, and then to "take out all the ego we could identify." A review in the *Village Voice* calls the book "the record of a journey, a strange and luxurious trip through unnamed Mediterranean countries in which characters appear and disappear with the authority of dreams."

All these works assume a collective process between writers and readers. The following pieces also involve actors, audiences, and take the text off the page into the world through performance and installation art, video, and film—the spectacle. Anne Waldman performs her poems in the United States and throughout Europe and is known for her unique harmonic oratory. She works collaboratively with musicians, composers, and dancers, and on radio and television, and her prize-winning video *Uh-Oh Plutonium!* was one of the first to unite poetry with New Wave music. Suzanne Jacob is a singer, composer, and performer from Québec who believes that "things can never be seen in other ways than by the fictions that organize them." Therefore, "to *be* is an activity of fiction."

In "La Luta Continua," Ntozake Shange, best known for her work in theater, develops a monologuist's voice as a counterpoint to Candace Hill-Montgomery's mixed media panel "Glimmering Through the African Brush." The story is from Shange's *Riding the Moon in Texas*, in which each story is a textual response to a visual medium. The narrator in "La Luta Continua" speaks from the woman artist's appetite—for sex, for kiwi and melon, for Stevie Wonder and Shirley Cesaire, for her own canvases. The subject is synesthesia and desire, the voice who is always wanting what she has experienced.

Trinh T. Minh-ha's script for *Surname Viet Given Name Nam* uses different typefaces to stand for the five places from which women speak in the film: folk poetry is sung in Vietnamese, interviews are conducted in English and Vietnamese, and a text is read on screen. "The story never stops beginning or ending. It appears headless and bottomless for it is built on differences. Its (in)finitude subverts every notion of completeness and its frame remains a non-totalizable one. . . . Difference undermines the very idea of identity."

Performance artist Ellen Zweig takes on the identities of forgotten women adventurers. "A Barrel of Her Own Design" is the script of a 1988 installation/performance at the ArtPark near Buffalo based on the diary of the first woman to go over Niagara Falls in a barrel. Using a camera obscura built into a large wooden barrel to project images, and with music and words piped in, Zweig tells the story of Annie Edson Taylor, who wanted to make her mark, and did in 1903, before dying in poverty and anonymity.

Playing with the idea of anonymity, Jenny Holzer leaves her works unsigned. A graphic artist whose primary medium since 1988 has been language, she seeks to make her art accessible to a wide public, infiltrating the everyday with her cryptic messages. Her trademark medium has become writings programmed on L.E.D. (light-emitting diode) signs. Holzer's open-ended questions and poetic monologues—which challenge economic and political institutions and notions of gender—blink across gallery and museum walls, light up the streets, and flash against city skylines. "Laments" concerns the psychic effects of daily urban violence.

Forward desire, a combination of heart and momentum, was our chief criterion in selecting these works. We hope they will incite debate and analysis by the many means now available, and catalyze new writing that makes words say more than they do say.

The initial inspiration to do this project came from the energy of the Third International Feminist Book Fair in Montreal and for that spark we thank the women who organized it and came together there. Credit is due also to Irene Zahava, who urged us on in the early stages. The work of assembling such a volume as this, we found, can often threaten to overwhelm even the most ignited spirit, and for helping to sustain us throughout, in ways tangible and intangible, we thank Jane Picard and Carol Betsch.

The project benefitted from the comments and suggestions offered by the two readers for the University of Illinois Press, and we thank in particular Elizabeth Meese for her enthusiastic support. Our thanks are due also to our editor, Ann Lowry, for her encouragement and help along the way.

Lou Robinson
Camille Norton

I. Transmission/Translation

Melpomene Tragedy

THERESA HAK KYUNG CHA

She could be seen sitting in the first few rows. She would be sitting in the first few rows. Closer the better. The more. Better to eliminate presences of others surrounding better view away from that which is left behind far away back behind more for closer view more and more face to face until nothing else sees only this view singular. All dim, gently, slowly until in the dark, the absolute darkness the shadows fade.

She is stretched out as far as the seat allows until her neck rests on the back of the seat. She pulls her coat just below her chin enveloped in one mass before the moving shades, flickering light through the empty window, length of the gardens the trees in perfect a symmetry.

The correct time beyond the windows the correct season the correct forecast. Beyond the empty the correct setting, immobile. Placid. Extreme stillness. Misplaces nothing. Nothing equivalent. Irreplaceable. Not before. Not after.

The submission is complete. Relinquishes even the vision to immobility. Abandons all protests to that which will appear to the sight. About to appear. Forecast. Break. Break, by all means. The illusion that the act of viewing is to make alteration of the visible. The expulsion is immediate. Not one second is lost to the replication of the totality. Total severance of the seen. Incision.

April 19
Seoul, Korea

Dear Mother,

4. 19. Four Nineteen, April 19th, eighteen years later. Nothing has changed, we are at a standstill. I speak in another tongue now, a second tongue a

foreign tongue. All this time we have been away. But nothing has changed. A stand still.

It is not 6. 25. Six twenty five. June 25th 1950. Not today. Not this day. There are no bombs as you had described them. They do not fall, their shiny brown metallic backs like insects one by one after another.

The population standing before North standing before South for every bird that migrates North for Spring and South for Winter becomes a metaphor for the longing of return. Destination. Homeland.

No woman with child lifting sand bags barriers, all during the night for the battles to come.

There is no destination other than towards yet another refuge from yet another war. Many generations pass and many deceptions in the sequence in the chronology towards the destination.

You knew it would not be in vain. The thirty six years of exile. Thirty six years multiplied by three hundred and sixty five days. That one day your country would be your own. This day did finally come. The Japanese were defeated in the world war and were making their descent back to their country. As soon as you heard, you followed South. You carried not a single piece, not a photograph, nothing to evoke your memory, abandoned all to see your nation freed.

From another epic another history. From the missing narrative. From the multitude of narratives. Missing. From the chronicles. For another telling for other recitations.

Our destination is fixed on the perpetual motion of search. Fixed in its perpetual exile. Here at my return in eighteen years, the war is not ended. We fight the same war. We are inside the same struggle seeking the same destination. We are severed in Two by an abstract enemy an invisible enemy under the title of liberators who have conveniently named the severance, Civil War. Cold War. Stalemate.

I am in the same crowd, the same coup, the same revolt, nothing has changed. I am inside the demonstration I am locked inside the crowd and carried in its movement. The voices ring shout one voice then many voices they are waves they echo I am moving in the direction the only one direction with the voices the only direction. The other movement towards us it increases steadily their direction their only direction our mutual destination towards the other against the other. Move.

I feel the tightening of the crowd body to body now the voices rising thicker I hear the break the single motion tearing the break left of me right of me the silence of the other direction advance before . . . They are breaking now, their sounds, not new, you have heard them, so familiar to you now could you ever forget them not in your dreams, the consequences of the sound the breaking. The air is made visible with smoke it grows spreads without control we are hidden inside the whiteness the greyness reduced to parts, reduced to separation. Inside an arm lifts above the head in deliberate gesture and disappears into the thick white from which slowly the legs of another bent at the knee hit the ground the entire body on its left side. The stinging, it slices the air it enters thus I lose direction the sky is a haze running the streets emptied I fell no one saw me I walk. Anywhere. In tears the air stagnant continues to sting I am crying the sky remnant the gas smoke absorbed the sky I am crying. The streets covered with chipped bricks and debris. Because. I see the frequent pairs of shoes thrown sometimes a single pair among the rocks they had carried. Because. I cry wail torn shirt lying I step among them. No trace of them. Except for the blood. Because. Step among them the blood that will not erase with the rain on the pavement that was walked upon like the stones where they fell had fallen. Because. Remain dark the stains not wash away. Because. I follow the crying crowd their voices among them their singing their voices unceasing the empty street.

> There is no surrendering you are chosen to fail to be martyred to shed blood to be set an example one who has defied one who has chosen to defy and was to be set an example to be martyred an animal useless betrayer to the cause to the welfare to peace to harmony to progress.

It is 1962 eighteen years ago same month same day all over again. I am eleven years old. Running to the front door, Mother, you are holding my older brother pleading with him not to go out to the demonstration. You are threatening him, you are begging to him. He has on his school uniform, as all the other students representing their schools in the demonstration. You are pulling at him you stand before the door. He argues with you he pushes you away. You use all your force, all that you have. He is prepared to join the student demonstration outside. You can hear the gun shots. They are directed at anyone.

Coming home from school there are cries in all the streets. The mounting of shouts from every direction from the crowds arm in arm. The students. I saw them, older than us, men and women held to each other. They walk into the *others* who wait in *their* uniforms. Their shouts reach a crescendo as they approach nearer to the *other side*. Cries resisting cries to move forward. Orders, permission to use force against the students, have been dispatched. To be caught and beaten with sticks, and for others, shot, remassed, and carted off. They fall they bleed they die. They are thrown into gas into the crowd to be squelched. The police the soldiers anonymous they duplicate themselves, multiply in number invincible they execute their role. Further than their home further than their mother father their brother sister further than their children is the execution of their role their given identity further than their own line of blood.

You do not want to lose him, my brother, to be killed as the many others by now, already, you say you understand, you plead all the same they are killing any every one. You withstand his strength you call me to run to Uncle's house and call the tutor. Run. Run hard. Out the gate. Turn the corner. All down hill to reach Uncle's house. I know the two German shepherd dogs would be guarding one at each side, chained to their house they drag behind them barking. I must brave them, close my eyes and run between them. I call the tutor from the yard, above the sounds of the dogs barking. Several students look out of the windows. They are in hiding from the street, from their homes where they are being searched for. We run back to the house the tutor is ahead of me, when I enter the house the tutor is standing in front of him. You cannot go out he says you cannot join the D-e-m-o. De. Mo. A word, two sounds. Are you insane the tutor tells him they are killing any student in uniform. Anybody. What will you defend yourself with he asks. You, my brother, you protest your cause, you say you are willing to die. Dying is part of it. If it must be. He hits you. The tutor slaps you and your face turns red you stand silently against the door your head falls. My brother. You are all the rest all the others are you. You fell you died you gave your life. That day. It rained. It rained for several days. It rained more and more times. After it was all over. You were heard. Your victory mixed with rain falling from the sky for many days afterwards. I heard that the rain does not erase the blood fallen on the ground. I heard from the adults, the blood stains still. Year after year it rained. The stone pavement stained where you fell still remains dark.

Eighteen years pass. I am here for the first time in eighteen years, Mother. We left here in this memory still fresh, still new. I speak another tongue, a second tongue. This is how distant I am. From then. From that time. They take me back they have taken me back so precisely now exact to the hour to the day to the season in the smoke mist in the drizzle I turn the corner and there is no one. No one facing me. The street is rubble. I put my palm on my eyes to rub them, then I let them cry freely. Two school children with their book bags appear from nowhere with their arms around each other. Their white kerchief, their white shirt uniform, into a white residue of gas, crying.

I pass a second curve on the road. You soldiers appear in green. Always the green uniforms the patches of camouflage. Trees camouflage your green trucks you blend with nature the trees hide you you cannot be seen behind the guns no one sees you they have hidden you. You sit you recline on the earth next to the buses you wait hours days making visible your presence. Waiting for the false move that will conduct you to mobility to action. There is but one move, the only one and it will be false. It will be absolute. Their mistake. Your boredom waiting would not have been in vain. They will move they will have to move and you will move on them. Among them. You stand on your tanks your legs spread apart how many degrees exactly your hand on your rifle. Rifle to ground the same angle as your right leg. You wear a beret in the 90 degree sun there is no shade at the main gate you are fixed you cannot move you dare not move. You are your post you are your vow in nomine patris you work your post you are your nation defending your country from subversive infiltration from your own countrymen. Your skin scorched as dark as your uniform as you stand you don't hear. You hear nothing. You hear no one. You are hidden you see only the prey they do not see you they cannot. You who are hidden you who move in the crowds as you would in the trees you who move inside them you close your eyes to the piercing the breaking the flooding pools bath their shadow memory as they fade from you your own blood your own flesh as tides ebb, through you through and through.

You are this
close to this much
close to it.
Extend arms apart just so, that much. Open
the thumb and the index finger just so.
the thumb and the index finger just so.
That much
you want to kill the time that is oppression itself.
Time that delivers not. Not you, not from its
expanse, without dimension, defined not by its
limits. Airless, thin, not a thought rising even
that there are things to be forgotten. Effortless. It
should be effortless. Effort   less   ly
the closer it is the closer to it. Away and against
time ing. A step forward from back. Backing
out. Backing off. Off periphery extended. From
imaginary to bordering on division. At least
somewhere in numerals in relation to the
equator, at least all the maps have them at least
walls are built between them at least the militia
uniforms and guns are in abeyance of them.
Imaginary borders. Un   imaginable boundaries.

Suffice more than that. SHE opposes Her.
SHE against her.
More than that. Refuses to become discard
decomposed oblivion.
From its memory dust escapes the particles still
material still respiration move. Dead air stagnant
water still exhales mist. Pure hazard igniting flaming
itself with the slightest of friction like firefly. The loss
that should burn. Not burn, illuminate. Illuminate by
losing. Lighten by loss.
Yet it loses not.

Her name. First the whole name. Then syllable by
syllable counting each inside the mouth. Make them
rise they rise repeatedly without ever making visible
lips never open to utter them.

Mere names only names without the image not hers
hers alone not the whole of her and even the image
would not be the entire
her fraction her invalid that inhabits that rise
voluntarily like flint
pure hazard dead substance to fire.

Others anonymous her detachments take her place. Anonymous against
her. Suffice that should be nation against nation suffice that should have
been divided into two which once was whole. Suffice that should diminish
human breaths only too quickly. Suffice Melpomene. Nation against nation
multiplied nations against nations against themselves. Own. Repels her rejects her expels her from her own. Her own is, in, of, through, all others,
hers. Her own who is offspring and mother, Demeter and Sibyl.

Violation of her by giving name to the betrayal, all possible names, inter-
changeable names, to remedy, to justify the violation. Of her. Own. Unbegot-
ten. Name. Name only. Name without substance. The everlasting, Forever.
Without end.

Deceptions all the while. No devils here. Nor gods. Labyrinth of deceptions. No enduring time. Self-devouring. Devouring itself. Perishing all the
while. Insect that eats its own mate.

Suffice Melpomene, arrest the screen en-trance flickering hue from behind
cast shadow silhouette from back not visible. Like ice. Metal. Glass. Mirror.
Receives none admits none.

Arrest the machine that purports to employ democracy but rather causes
the successive refraction of her none other than her own. Suffice Melpomene, to exorcize from this mouth the name the words the memory of
severance through this act by this very act to utter one, Her once, Her to
utter at once, She without the separate act of uttering.

Ultrasounds

NICOLE BROSSARD *Translated by* LUCILLE NELSON

NAVIGATING AT NIGHT BY MEANS OF
MILKY ARMS AND IGNITERS OF SYNTAX,
I THOUGHT ABOUT THE TUMBLES AND
BEAUTIFUL SOMERSAULTS THAT IN CHILDHOOD
WE LOVED TO SHARE ON THE GRASS

The perspective that enters into the composition of words perturbs every radical woman who wishes to draw nearer another woman with a sexual act in mind. A sexual act between two women requires prose beforehand, text long after. A sexual act between two women supposes the encounter of the parts, called sexual, which are in fact few in number, and constitute only a tiny area of the geography of the body. To draw nearer a woman is one thing, *with a sexual act in mind* another, which requires vast deeps within the eyes.

Prose, as word given, occupies a large place between two women mutually interested in engaging in a sexual act, because she engenders narratives that allow the multiplication of the sexual parts of both one and the other, while respecting the singularity of each (perfume, scar, childhood in the urban jungle, tattoo, blank page). Prose stimulates tiny glints of recognition deep in the eyes, glints which in turn ignite the senses. Sense is sometimes nomadic—one then thinks that syntax zaps into desire in search of sexual parts that in daily life are inaccessible to the eye, or even to the imagination.

The truth of prose lies in the filth of cliches, its essence in a sudden opacity that awakens our sleeping meanings. That being so, prose offers its epochs like so many mirrors, scripts and generations to ease the reading of the values and emotions that enter into the composition of our sexual parts. It is therefore used for various purposes, the main ones being to recover the memory of childhood, to observe the slow motion, movements and folds of feeling, and to shape the desiring self. *Prose says that nothing really dies.* Prose absorbs the shadow of our tears, absorbs part of our lives, the better to offer them to us in the munificence and spareness of our first visions.

Prose, prose, here is the essential word of a happy liaison between the abundant nature of the I and the copious imagination that enters into the composition of the real. Beautiful liaison, to which many women are indebted for a glimpse of the possibility that their sexual parts are more numerous than is usually thought. Prose, prose, starting with the ear, that sexed pearl (the ear being sensitive to a very wide variety of sounds, it easily welcomes the most strange propositions, the most bold words, provided they are accompanied by certain images known for the pleasure they provoke) where the secret leaning of our assertions takes over from the thread of narratives. Prose is tenacious, little comes together without her.

THUS, one day in May, while sitting in a cafe in Coyoacan (Mexico), exchanging some casual remarks about the effects of high altitude with a woman at the next table, the woman said "me too" with a shaped intention that disturbed me there where life is so intimate that we say it is invisible to earthly eyes. "Me too," then she proceeded to unroll before me a giant historical fresco of red-framed windows, big game, military costumes, piles of skulls, sumptuous stairways, mirrors in which her voice against her will, she said, always drew the same self portrait and its syntax, the same syntax, she said, because of this: "We were walking, my daughter and I. One evening in July, as beautiful as my mother. Dead at twenty-five. My pain, later. Since then I tremble easily but I paint. I love painting. Sometimes my diary." She paused, asked the waiter for some lemon and I continued to listen: "No one writes without piling up silence. Each time a word is beautiful or a fresco, alive in my breast, it diverts my attention to what is without memory. I am brave as the Frida of my red and orange Mexico. We will always have a childhood at the tips of our fingers to make us search through the vocabulary. I am a woman lover of words." Me too I replied very close to her ear and her hair, in the free zone of the spoken and a narrative that came to me in the form of paintings, water colours and etchings, all signed by women. I told how several years ago there had been a huge exhibition of the works of Emily Carr, Marcelle Ferron, Georgia O'Keefe and Frida Kahlo. I described in detail the light, the texture, the milkiness, the volume of the breasts, then, at a certain point, I don't know why, I ordered a mango and prose, prose, spoke at length of Montreal, unaware that most of the words I had used could have a sexual connotation. "Me too," because prose occupies a large place in my life, brings me nearer, I tell you, to women. That's the way it is, there's nothing I can do about it. I associate so many happy and unhappy events with our bodies that to understand them, I must always call upon my imagination. This seems contradictory to you, doesn't it, that to understand what is real, I have to make use of what we call fiction. But that's how it is. And you and stories? I like them short, but there should be no shadow of doubt about death. We will need long stories. And you and theory? There is no theory without representation, though abstraction sometimes nourishes my decisions. So from prose to prose we continued talking, so well that I could now make out, in the area of her face alone, the sexed number of character and mental traits which— not counting the voice, which had not ceased to trouble me since the first words exchanged about the lack of oxygen at high altitudes—invited me to introduce, into the composition of words, shapes and sounds of a nature other than narrative.

NAVIGATING AT NIGHT, BY
PURE FERVOUR OF AURAS
I ARRIVED THERE AHEAD OF
THE NIGHT AND HER BAROQUE FOLDS,
THE MILKY SHAPE OF INAUDIBLE THOUGHTS
FAR OFF, FLUENT.

The cerebral design that enters into the composition of words quickens any radical woman who wishes to draw nearer a woman with a very lyrical sexual act in mind. A sexual act between two very lyrical women requires of them that their voices project, high fidelity, very beloved nuances. A lyrical sexual act supposes the repeated encounter of the parts, called lyrical, that are in truth numerous and varied, as experience teaches us about beauty.

The poem does not have to carry the burden of proof that meaning, informed by a plural usage between two women envisaging a sexual act, leads to the steady erasure of the lie and its thrusts scattered throughout culture and the imaginary. The poem is desirable in itself, because it shelters a soul said to be sensitive to the light of loving bodies. Without the poem, neither the one, woman, nor the other, desirable, would have in the depths of their eyes that expression that ignites metaphors, that ignites pleasure and recognition, that expression where life will, within the so-called flow of laws, take stock of its vastness.

From beauty that plunges us into astonishment, it follows that a tear or embrace that can favorably be compared with eternity will find its song or offer itself to thought like a linguistic resource that can transform the sexual act into an extended exploration of the cerebral design and its complex curves.

Then, prose slowly reappeared like a new consignment of precious goods. Playful prose, whirlpool of fiction, labrys prose, gateway to dreams, see how before my eyes you come, three times changing your name, evoking the long struggles and she-loves of the tangled contours of narratives and utopias, see how you come, between the lines, bringing the poem closer to my lips still hot from the repeated question of urgency. Prose, seeing you so close up walking into the afternoon, I hear (right by my ear and hair) *any radical woman wishing to draw nearer a woman with a sexual act in mind.* Ultrasounds of the sexual parts. Silent prose, breastfed with images and landscapes, moist, pink, juicy. See how at last silence navigates at peace between the absolute yes of the resting body.

Thus, WHILE SEATED IN A CAFE ONE DAY IN MAY, I was working ON AN AESTHETIC ARGUMENT to justify MY EARTHLY SHOULDERS AND my SEXED intentions, I COULD, LOOKING AT HER, AVOID CERTAIN DESCRIPTIONS SUCH AS my life, OR EVEN THAT OF THE ROOM THE TWO WOMEN WITHDREW TO. I COULD, while looking at her, INVENT SHAPES THAT BRING TOGETHER SIGHS AND question THE CRAZY IMBALANCE OF DESIRE AND reality.

HENCEFORTH, I COULD, NAVIGATING BY DAY AND NIGHT AMONG
MILKY VOWELS AND THINKING MATTER, ADMIRE LIFE PERFORM-
ING HER TAI CHI, GREAT LEAPS IN THE GRASS, IN THE FLUSH OF
DAWN AND THE CORTEX

About Flight

DÔRE MICHELUT

I tell her to watch the bees. She sees them die when their wings wear out. She feels her wings wear out. She stares at the sounds of exodus.

Icarus wakes up on a beach: a shoebox filled with sand. All its life it pleads for life—is anchored by the breezes, absorbed by burden, shifts, is restless, answers to the power of judgment, is menaced by the facts. It is deaf for purity, speechless for truth, alternative by birth. It sighs by instinct only. "Hush, love. Do not create more gods."

My arm is a vacuum cleaner, an enemy to the dust that clumps and tumble-weeds into the open, sucking the alchemy of those winds dry, squeezing like a wine-press, transforming dustballs into molten coal. Pressing time is slow. It erupts now and then. I burn. I take it all back to the filtered queen who says she does not take returns. *Hollow out my bones with air. Keep the indrawn breath drawing until the whole world turns inside out. Porco Giuda.*

By chance, I find a space high in the tundra where I plant cork, and water it with the wine I thirst to drink. Pre-mephistophilian, I think. And there, in the barren cold, I nurture my porous, twisted plants with hot ash until they grow gnarled and strong and develop hunter roots that can penetrate hell for just a drop. I rarely think of happiness. I keep a clean house and run a small business where I age cork to prevent new wine from exploding. *The market is active today. Trading is brisk. The Commodities index is up.*

We have no value for rocks: they sit there, wanting nothing. In a moment of distraction, when the face of the world is turned, a rock reaches out and She is smitten. Before She knows it, She subsumes it in one great swallow and is rock-absorbed: suspended at the point where food and love and death congeal. As far as eternity is concerned, She is still—although She prefers the term objective. To remain fixed takes excruciating dreaming, holding the breath as weight until interiors solidify, concentrating in order to exacerbate the point and turning often to exchange views. For inspiration, She compares Her girth to relics and eats only earth. She cries often to expel moisture and uses deodorant all over, for the smell of food and love and death repel Her. The burden is heavy, but you can find Her where it really matters: underneath, in small Classic print, if you squint, you can read the label: *Artifact.*

All rise for Judgment Day. Pew upon pew of you. Up, spread out: touching obscures. Hands behind the head to be shorn of all bodily needs. What cannot be hidden under the fig belongs to the devil.

I do not reproduce without you. I am innocent of forgery.

Women, your breasts are damned. Men, the devil is ravenous. Think awe. Sing if you must. She who bleeds goes; he whose eyes fall, fails. Hear ye.

I do not take on unnatural forms. I am innocent of reason.

Has every iota been accounted for from conception? Have the by-products originated from the original? Have you undone in others what others have undone in you? Have you killed your child for me recently? Indicate the scars with crosses.

I love. I am innocent.

Those of you as yet unfelled. Those of you not turned into pillars of salt. Those of you who are still able to tread with the others. Those of you left, cower and rise. You are forgiven. Now levitate.

Do not swim in this pond. It smells of quick blood here. Maintain a good stance. Feel yourself heavy like a good stone arrow. Wait. The pond moves. It measures the length, breadth, diameter of your tears. Be silent. It determines the gravity of joy, the depth of relief, the width of the smile, the weight of the coin. Be still. Do not walk on coals here. This is not the place for the hungry dream. The water is not good. Do not stay to drink the reflections. Kill. Eat. Go. Sacred places are not for resting.

O Angel. Shades of neon surround you. Your penis: a camera. Probe my womb in depth. Report on my hidden crevices. Expose the fact that I am always with pregnancy.

this. notes.
new year.

KATHLEEN FRASER

Dear other, I address you in sentences. I need your nods and I hear your echoes. There is a forward movement still, as each word is a precedent for what new order. You can hear a distant habit. The sound of a low gas flame discharging. Even a hiss is only soothing because it is dark and nearing the shorter perimeters. When I run into boredom, I shift into another's past.

(She was "in a fury" and she wept in spite of herself. His letter told the usual stories in all the old ways. She swallowed them whole. Then came the nausea. She wanted a "flow" she thought, but in the translation it was corrected, displacing the o and substituting a. She could give herself to an accident. She was looking out the window.)

This is the Year of Our Lord. Every year we always have these difficulties. The sound of water splatting from the bathroom, heard through the kitchen, the clank of a soap dish. "I'm going to take a shower," David bragged, striding through the room on his twelfth birthday.

I tried to protect myself especially well. I had time to play at domesticity this year. Three-quarters cup of bourbon in the chocolate-covered bourbon balls. There were many occasions and I was there in a different skirt. I went to the sales with her. She believed in that and built up her vocabulary like a wardrobe purchased during ten different years, but only on December 26th.

One man said of another that he was committed to the sentence. I sentence you. I could hear the terseness of his sentences and how seductive it seemed to move the words always towards a drop in the voice. What did it mean to be flat? Was there a principle of denial? Of manipulation? I'm worried. He is embarrassed.

The French workers often raised their voices on the Blvd. des Minimes and along the tiny alleys of the Ile St. Louis. You could hear questions rising to the windows of the sixth floor of the Hôtel St. Louis, although the bathroom, if you wanted to take a tub bath, was on the fourth floor. Voices raised at the ends of sentences, as though all were in question. It made you want to look out the window. You could sniff the momentous occasion. The bakery opening its door each morning to a view of *pain au chocolat* on trays. *Entrez, s'il vous plaît.*

I wanted, suddenly, to speak French because of certain French women thinking about layers, thinking in layers, but as yet not translated. They had moved ahead but not in a line. It occurred to me that growing up inside of, yet opposing, a tradition peculiarly French and masculine appeared to give them a certain authority because the tradition itself assumed a dialectical plane and invited the next position, while echoing "I baptize thee in the name of the father and the son."

(She questioned the wistful half-truths he gained solace from, using a certain Rapidograph pen with its fine black lines. He gave the boy a very thick pen. He said it was for art. The boy's face broke open and filled with light. Enlightened. Boyish and tender.)

I question these wistful half-truths and why I sink into silence around them. Now that I've made the decision to attempt a separation from their hold on me, I am released into sentences. The gas heater is a constant I could compare.

I change my mind every day. I think of my mother's love. The antique bracelet she gave me with dozens of flowers etched into the tarnished brass. A line from Kunitz surfaces from the year I was twenty-one. "A single color oversweeps the field." That is all my memory provides of it. But to understand truly, you'd need the lines before it, building up to that crescendo that thrilled me. A vast field of scarlet poppies in the south of France . . . a movement in front of one. As a season. In a second. The forward movement of slow motion. Even then, the field. Of many flowers moving at their own speeds. Not forward. Not one then two then three. But moving. Split. Second. Rushing into petals.

That was a peculiar passion I do not often encounter in the poetry of the late '70s, but do not want to deny. That urgency we call romantic, but which might actually be, in part, the willingness to be told lies. That rush. How I've wanted it. His romance.

(He tried to deflect her anger. He tried to mystify her by leaving half of everything out. He made her laugh. He knew what she wanted. In her "worst moments" she wanted obliteration of choice.)

You are against confession, because it's embarrassing. I want to embarrass you. To feel your confusion. Someone's rhythm sneaking in again. Sharing a language. The osmosis of rubbing up. Communing.

I'll never make candy again. It is a relief to write this music. Who does it belong to? "Who can I turn to?" Las Vegas crooners with their soft, slimy hair styles. Feel the lyric hit, anyway. As soft as sniffing it. Where's the kleenex?

Christmas is over and "I'm glad," I said to David. "It's such a pressure building up." He smiled, being twelve now, and not satisfied, even though we tried to cover all the branches with icicles and double strands of lights. Next year, it's snowing.

12/26/78

Lily, Lois & Flaubert: the site of loss

KATHLEEN FRASER

for Robert Glück

"How is she?" I asked.

"She is well. She is just fine," he said. "My Lily is back. I have my family back. I can take the sitter home now. Would you like me to do that? The tires are bad, so I go up hills slowly. But Lily doesn't mind."

Who is Lily? I think. I try to remember which one Lily is. I feel she is probably one third of his nuclear family. The other third is his Aunt Cora, sitting in an airplane above Los Angeles. She hovers—a thin trail of white smoke drifting always above and behind him. One can almost hear the gossamer command of her voice in his childhood, filtered like light falling perpetually upon him. Her shadow is a light jacket, his little coat from the third grade.

Listening to him speak of Lily, I decided that he must be speaking of his lover. I thought I understood him. That is, I immediately provided a set of images from which to identify this object of his affection. To my ear, his all-embracing acceptance of Lily sounded romantic and excessive. I felt a bit jealous. I compared his feeling for her to a cloud of dust escaping from a vacuum cleaner. Yet as the dust cleared, things took on their true shapes. I understood that Lily was his dog. "White Lily of my family," he called her. "I wanted a family," I once heard him say to himself.

His voice was a kind of scenery behind the scrim one sees at the front of the stage, at the apron of the stage where Lily was forever wagging her tail. Lily, who had been lost, was now back in his arms. There existed among us a scenario, stitching together our lives at intervals: this tin can of dogfood he opened and spooned into a dish for her, linked Lily's love of dogfood to his love of Lily to my romantic projection of his "other life."

•   •

Phillipe S. has a dog called Lois. From the beginning of our friendship, this fact has been clearly established. Phillipe feeds Lois *blanquette de veau* to gain her trust. He likes to think of Lois as something sacred, a sacrament as only the French know it. He likes to lick his chops when he thinks of the pure prosody of life with Lois, the sheer grammar of Lois when she gushes her dog speech—often a series of sharp barks, as though a ribbon of sound were emitted spontaneously.

Phillipe often imagines Lois ordering a five course meal with all the correct wines. Her commanding use of the vernacular provides him with clear directives, a perpetual reassurance of order in his otherwise muddled life.

Lois gives him vigorous argument as well as propriety. And her wag assures him, even in those hours alone, when he feels the subject falling away from the predicate and that odd chill rise up to drench his solar plexus, when the sentence, as he's known it, begins to dismantle itself.

•   •

We have a dog at our house. His name is Rover. He's hardly ever around. Sometimes we call him Flaubert, to introduce a second possibility—as, for instance, on a greyish day when you pull up the shade on waking, with the hope of orange emerging somewhere among the cloud layers—just a small gash, even, as when my friend's old work pants developed a rip and you could see his muscular thigh showing through, a bit of tawny skin, though the trousers were loose and not normally the kind of garment you'd attribute to sexual arousal.

Flaubert, as a nickname, provides an immediate source of imagery. A guest walking in and hearing you call out "Flaubert . . . Flaubert???" might enter a different context than he thought his steps were leading to—a configuration of narrow lanes and dark doorways opening onto courtyards, or an acknowledgement of certain social issues he had hoped to dismiss as buried.

The wine you serve at dinner takes on an entirely different bouquet, a brickier color, haunted by an aftertaste of vineyards in the Dordogne. It hardly matters that Flaubert does not come in, wagging his tail and per-forming the set of tricks his former master taught him. His name is enough.

"Flaubert . . . Flaubert?" Now the guest begins to ease toward that seam where the stretch of his former life is stitched to this room, where Flau-bert's remembered barks form a discourse that still perforates the common silence.

The decision

KATHLEEN FRASER

Today a package at my door. Brown wrapping paper, imprinted three times with the same foreign currency—a golden cow with herringbone wings and tail, the number 20 under its belly and the word EIRE stamped in white against a marine blue background.

•

I was looking through my collection of black silk beauty marks. *Mouches pour bal* cut from a black field of silk at 42, *Rue de Chabrol*. A horse. Two horses pulling a carriage. Star. Heart. Star, heart, half-moon. A gentleman in a top hat. Dashing off, as they say. I was looking for a mark. A sign to place abruptly there, on the white field of the paper. To hold your attention for an instant only. Then to set free the threads which would loosen themselves from the interior. You thought you were somewhere else. This would move the prediction you had made for yourself. Now you would be riding, either on the bare back of the horse or inside the carriage where you wouldn't be seen but could look out from the gold leaf casements. As you like.

•

She had been occupied. As in "occupied zone." She had gone to see the Peruvian gold exhibit at the Hall of Science. She decided to wear her gold, imagining how to dress for the event. Gold circles through her ears. The twisted gold strands, always now on the middle finger of the right hand; she did not want to encourage misinterpretation. Also the gold chain, given her by a lover who had handed it to her in a tiny scarlet bag drawn shut with silk threads. But the chain was not around her neck when she felt for it. Nothing would stay in place in her memory, looking for the chain as through pages in a magazine. What she could remember of the last two days and on what occasions she took it off, the only occasions being swimming and making love. She pulled the blanket halfway off the bed and found nothing.

·

After looking at the Peruvian gold, they were filled with the idea of simplicity. They tried to remember who sacrificed so many live victims from their own source, the Aztecs or the Incas? That night, while he undressed, instead of watching his body she hunted again for the gold chain. She found it at the very end of the bed where the sheet tucked in. She placed it on the white dresser without comment. Then she made love to him.

·

I wanted to send you one of the three stamps from Ireland because of the field of marine blue which might suggest water and how deep it has been known to travel below the surface. There was a lake, for instance, at the bottom of some caves near Alt Aussee, where an enormous European art treasure had been hidden by members of Hitler's S.S. troops. Secured boxes of treasure had been dropped into the lake. Gold and jewels. They thought to drain the bottom of the lake at the end of the war and recover the treasure. Divers were sent down and did not come back. Four died. Separately. There seemed to be no bottom to the lake. And yet they know the treasure is still there. There are several who cannot let go of this thought.

·

She feels somewhat safe in the water. She knows he doesn't care for it much. She needs to know how deep it is. She looks for the markers at the side of the pool, although she has swum in lakes and has felt their muddy bottoms on the soles of her feet. It is an alarming experience and thus difficult to give in to the sensuality of this physical surprise. But on that day, she wanted to turn her back on her fear. They took off their clothes at the edge of the water. She put the gold chain in a little heap on top of her folded blouse, where she could see it. His wife was watching them but she didn't want to come in. They had never seen each other's bodies. Something passed between them in the water. They looked beyond each other, as if there were no mystery. She swam to the other side. It was a warm, late afternoon and the moon was already out, very white and pared down. A flicker, or was it a mockingbird, lit in the topmost branches of the only tree at the lake's edge. It was then she began to imagine she understood the gestures of birds. She watched them closely during the following year and was able to make several startling decisions with split-second timing.

Five letters from one window,
San Gimignano, May 1981

KATHLEEN FRASER

Dear Michael,

A car, sky-blue, is rolling as easily as a marble across the two middle panes of my studio window. It follows the road to Certaldo. Call the left and right sides of my window Points A and B. Point A is a tree still leafing out in the grassy green brightness of April, though May has just entered its fourth week. A small-bird-flying completes the third line of a triangle begun by the upper left corner of the window frame. I can hear a steady stream of tractor motors up in the vineyard puttering their threads and knots of sound through the gauze of nightingales, who seem to make no distinction between sunlight and moonlight. They sing their notes in separate clear quizzical trails. Point B is a house at the edge of the road to Certaldo, at the top of the hill in front of me. The house is longer than tall; its roof of brick-red tiles breaks into three sections. The blue car has traveled from Point A to Point B with the soft momentum of gravity. Now a white car takes the same path but moves out of sight, behind a patch of trees quite particular in their varying height and cut of leaf yet dominated, finally, by the shape made from their overlapping differences. Shadows are moving to the left. Boccacio was born in Certaldo. How long is the life of a bee?

. Dear Steve,

I have not written before this because language has become less urgent. I pick up your book sometimes and remember the past. There are certain luxuries in my life. Iris grow wild on the hill outside my window: they are pale lavender or the richer purples often seen in Chinese scroll painting. The red poppies appeared first in Sicily, in April. (We were walking among the Greek temples in Agrigento . . . broken columns, stone and lava lying randomly in stretches of green wheat . . . then, suddenly, a fling of red poppies.) Now their dark centers are springing up in the fields around our house. In the presence of such history, the urge to be original diminishes. One hears one's childhood and it is ancient. When I think of you, it is at work not at rest. I do not know how to explain this leisure without the learned habit of apology, yet that would be false. Ambition still makes static, but the air is often clear. I write to you out of affectionate attachment and severe doubt . . . and some memory of another life not quite surrendered. I never wanted to make choices. You are able to, each time you change body positions or deliver a line. You turn on the radio and it's your own voice falling to the left of you. You are slim and of medium coloring with an often droll expression hovering near your mouth. You are living a life I know nothing of, except through your description and the dream of the black car. Love has always been the motivating force in my life. Someone asks if you've heard from me and you haven't.

5:30 P.M.

Dear Sue,

I am worried, I haven't heard from you, are your teeth still hurting? I never found the perfect thing to wear with the grey silk scarf you gave me for traveling. Thank you anyway. I have discarded half of everything; nothing is as planned.

When I last saw you, you were confused and miserable, yet in less than a year everything seems to have changed. You are looking out different windows and your bathrobe matches another's, hanging next to it on the back of the bathroom door. I have never required explanations and this is not one. I am voiceless much of the time, although a running dialogue is there whenever I shut the door.

A huge bee died on our kitchen windowsill—still perfect, shiny and black, with soft fuzzy leggings. Its little opaque wings reflect surfaces much like the northern lights on August nights in Vermont, the same shifting mallard blues and violets caught in mother-of-pearl. Arturo said we should save it. Whatever he finds, whether it's the white stem of a garlic head or a discarded seed pod, he places in the one space where it can best be seen for exactly what it is. Now we share the bee; it is in the light of the kitchen window on the red brick ledge. But in September, we return to separate houses. This plunge forward into the pulling apart of our present delight is a thought I want to push away. I am waiting to understand how I can protect myself from sadness and a return to the past. You understand, then, that when the second bee appeared, resting for a moment on the window ledge in the living room, I wanted it for my own. I confess this to you, trusting your knowledge of human fallibility and your accepting nature.

When I touched the bee's foot, its whole body seemed to stir slightly. Was it reminded of life in the air? I wanted it to be dead. I wanted to bring it home with me and remember this house, the Tuscany hills with their snows of cottonwood, their rolling vineyards as tidy as herringbone tweed, their slumbrous yellow and pink roses with the black bees nosing and lurching from blossom to blossom. I got the shot glass from the kitchen cupboard and put it over the bee, like a clear dome. It immediately started to struggle, feeling the sides of the glass with its front legs. It wouldn't stop, but something in me wouldn't let it go free. How can a person know what she wants or how she will act until a thing happens? The bee was bold, it had the beauty of some absolute, primary form. I walked away, knowing it was trapped alive but hoping to find it lying quietly whenever I passed through the living room and glanced casually in its direction. But it still frantically pawed at the glass. By evening it appeared to be motionless, all its legs perfectly positioned and its wings poised as if for flight. I lifted the glass. Apparently the sudden draft of oxygen began to revive it. I wanted to trap it again. I stood there, caught in the cool curiosity of the child, whose need to possess is absolute. Finally I decided to leave it alone, hoping it would naturally exhaust itself. By the time I finished cooking supper and had time to look again, it was gone.

Are you happier, now that you have what you wanted? Write me at the Florence address by the end of June.

6:18 P.M.

Dear Andrea,

The view beyond my window is divided almost equally between green hills and a Della Robbia blue sky. In the last hour the blue has been suffused with a paler, thinner stuff, maybe mist, soothing the landscape with a calm evening light. Having a horizon to measure by alerts one to change. Only fifteen minutes ago, when I looked up from my work table, big puffs of white cloud were creeping swiftly over the edge of the buildings fronting the road at the top of the hill. Cloudrise, like sunrise speeded up. I thought, for a minute, the earth was tipping backwards. Now there is nothing but skim milk color and a few crowing roosters scratching the evening air. What happened in those brief moments, when I looked down, absorbed?

Arturo (as they call him here) has just put a Mozart violin concerto on the record player. I can hear it drifting up the stairs and down the hall to me, a signal that the evening has formally begun and he would like my company. He is cooking some wonderful rabbit thing in mustard sauce, flamed with Stravecchio Branca (the local brandy). Last night, when I was cleaning squid bought at the morning market, I remembered you cooking it for my birthday. You stuffed their white bodies, and then we watched them swell up, one by one, as you turned them in butter . . . you'd just returned from Italy (we'd never been), and you kept comparing them to men's "private parts." But I didn't *really* understand until these last months, surrounded by so much Italian sculpture. All the hugely muscled bodies of Michelangelo and Bernini, with their boy-size genitalia . . . is this a point of view, a metaphor or a biological fact? Can we hold art historians responsible for this sort of information? Does Comparative Literature include the language of the body?

The record has just been turned over. A flute concerto. In Firenze we bought some of those inexpensive, second-press recordings they sell at newsstands, because there was an old record-player here in the farmhouse. Two Charlie Parker albums. What bliss, to begin the morning with "Moose the Mooche" turned up loud . . . like being at home, almost. We are happy. Arturo often sits outside in the sun to study Italian, in a little alcove just under my window. I can hear him muttering his verb conjugations.

My studio is upstairs. I chose it for the proportions of the room and its eastern light, which seems conducive to concentration and expansiveness. My writing is changing. One might sometimes think I was returning to the style of work I did twenty years ago, except that my line is surer and my eye more exacting. Still, I am just as uncertain and resistant, at the beginning of each work attempted, as I ever was. In fact, my bursts of confidence are fewer, my self-doubt greater. I'm trying to find a way to include these states of uncertainty . . . the shifting reality we've often talked about—fragments of perception that rise to the surface, almost inadvertently, and come blurting out when one has lived in intense desire and frustration. We need to be able to map how it is for us, as it changes . . . but are often half-choked by awkwardness in the face of the mot juste. But why deny this partialness as part of our writing? Why not find formal ways to visually articulate its complexity—the on going secret life—without necessarily making it a candidate for the simple-minded "confessional?" Writing is, in part, a record of our struggle to be human, as well as our delight in reimagining/reconstructing the formal designs and boundaries of what we've been given. If *we* don't make our claim, the world is simply that which others have described for us.

I've pinned my favorite Wittgenstein quote to the wall just above my typewriter: "The world is everything that is the case."

7:39 P.M.

Dear Bob,

There is a small green insect (do 3 pairs of legs and 1 pair of antennae equal insect?) crawling across a hand-set, letterpress version of "The Heights," by Louis Zukofsky, propped up against my window.

"The sun's white in the high fog."

(The bug's green on the white Fabriano)

I began this letter wanting to tell you of yesterday's peculiar events, because something *did* happen. But I'm not yet sure of its significance or whether my story has "a point." I have discovered the stories of Martha Gelhorn (once a wife of Hemingway, and too often remembered for that instead of for her extraordinary travel book and her finely-tuned prose works) . . . anyway, one of her characters—a male novelist—says: "It was too much trouble, he wanted to follow no one through the planned deviousness of a story." Her anti-hero has been writing successful, well-plotted novels all his life and is tired, finally, of pre-fabricating significance in human events.

One of the things that attracts me about the story you just sent me is the way you begin with the end of a thread and wind it as you go, following it with the curiosity of a metaphysician.

The sun is gone from the white Fabriano.

(The bug is green in the falling dark)

Love Pain and the Fading of Orchids

ANNE-MARIE ALONZO

I

to hold seek   remembrance   and to show heart not knowing why or
what it might confuse   holding as in a desert where you   mostly I   await
night and day and night to pass without wind nor sand cries mostly and
sighs as to say thighs thinking of yours hoping for whispers in stride forgetting time absorbing it gently and you say: truce! ask for some while I vanish
while I do.

II

please don't leave me but if   and you might   I'll shiver and die I'll certainly not live for I find my breath in you   only there   and the mist covers
the orchids from your body so overwhelming in the light   you choose
candles light a fire as I beg to see you and in you where pearls lay   my hand
vaguely my lips tongue and hand   somewhere the cry   do you say pleasure or should I when tears submerge you (or I! do we know)   I   let me
repeat myself I do love you   infinitely there are no more words as I search
for you find you lose you please don't leave me not yet not as the candles are
still melting your heart pounding against yours my body all around there is
my face mouth tongue lips nose eyes   there is   and the unique scent of
you on my neck   I was there hurt there you heal me   warmth runs thru
me we are   you I as I you   you'll disappear I'll stop breathing will breathe
no air that smells of saffron and spice.

III

somewhere   the cities have changed resemble each other as I search for
your eyes your lips so dark like some parts of you I wait say nothing wait
silently or cry nobody hears or listens it is you and I   the distance unbearable the miles and days nothing to approach you when you ask for peace

and to be left   alone   you forget try desperately to leave me! the words are hidden and your eyes how can I   not knowing seeing you   agree say yes to the pain accepting death wanting it at all costs without you life is life nothing else so much less   but I stop do not speak lay in bed tears are scarce the heart has died every day night and day   while you stay silent.

IV

silver and gold around my neck never to be taken off then you'd leave I'd die or be terribly sick for the loss of you   the chain is off (you've left me) put back on begging you to stay   within   caress embrace kiss gently as if you   and not I   had the power to survive the leaves have been stricken by gold   you were the jeweler I the poet what have we saved.

V

chasing you away keeping you the swords have crumbled please allow me to scream no sorrow should be kept silent no sadness so intense my tongue refuses to talk ever whisper!   as for her standing there closer than life begging holding me to stay! not leave (for or because of you)   tears this time hers   her eyes wanting she pleads says please as I leave her and you   I renounce   what is there she says   me   kissing my eyes lips and tongue grasping it what is there if not the scent of you always within the eyes of you the dark ships to follow distance fades the trees linger as I do never to call you   again.

VI

the strength the trees I look up to my legs arms grasping   you're impossible to find   running and you know I don't refuse to   the body is yours mine has been dead do you prefer asleep!   to awaken only by your touch feeling as if nothing has happened I have walked with you played jumped dove never fear nor pain clinging to your eyes dark as nights of love and lust never ending eyes prolonged by khol fine lines of laughter your neck resembles your mouth so soft under my tongue impeccable as I watch remember   your picture has gone I can't won't look at you pray not to forget the features fading or is it the memory so terribly soon   I love you that has been said thought desperately believed in where are you at three o'clock this sunday afternoon.

VII

I hate   you not being here my body has gone astray is not reacting the hurt
pain my hands bleed cut my fingers seek you the phone your lips thighs
hold me   I   have nothing left lay in bed sick (some say because your
leaving!)   and I desert the body do not care to live your breasts forget me I
never them   do you still remember the nights mornings the hours never
ending the light licking your back and mine   who are we or are we   other
than ourselves torn as you chose and choose again without me saying yes
or die in peace.

VIII

look   open your legs to hear feel the aching from one to one side of the
bed you buy a car to come to me for a day hour minute to share never more
you are taken as you know and she takes all never lets you out of grip sight
    she says love without blinking says hate when speaking of me in terms
always certain grinning can't stand as you say no and manipulates you and
refuses to see hear you burst in anger order me to stop as I stop naturally
you love her what else is there to say.

IX

months pass you go come go again there's no end to your travels and always
as far from me as possible you call write say love words as songs as I wait
once again   not knowing you have left me will leave and leave the pain is
too strong brutal your eyes you cry for the loss of her I for yours afar we
become estranged so much away from each other   you   don't love me
you say not in the same way you say that as truth while I fall to the ground.

X

I don't see the phone keeps ringing my eyes are dead to the world   I have
not found a dying way your picture is watching over me you are the jeweler
mold me I won't say take me back will not speak words of love nor beg
as you propose friendship I won't hear need your thighs around my waist
need your scent to breathe   I love you   not moving while my body aches
moans from the definite loss of you.

Dune Wild Sands

ANNE-MARIE ALONZO *Translated by* LUCILLE NELSON

It is not over. I remember you. When I cannot. I starve.
And my dream dwindles in some dark mouth.
—Dôre Michelut
   The Wolf Runs Through Me

She had broken off resumed broken off that was year one! the seasons saw them anxious she had returned from travelling had seen love leave in turn! (while) the one hidden in the heart of the tent did not move said nothing stopped eating wept lamented threatened to leave did not this tent belonged to her and love having lived there with her for ten full years belonged to her and to her alone love's favours.

She understood that no woman nor she herself would attempt to carry off steal love without waging battle and fighting to the death this was unquestioned could in no wise be questioned.

She did not look for a war to win or lose she saw love when seeing her happened she waited for a sign without faltering wrote letters that love read only at her side never mailed those letters knew the rage of the one who lived in the tent knew her enraged! did not wish trouble on the nights of her love knew herself banished hidden took it as that.

She had no other choice chose to live like that and lived like that love shared (herself) spent second-long hours with her lied told stories invented but arrived on foot or by horse always arrived once promised arrived out of breath said: forgive me! enveloped her in caresses ran her tongue along her cheeks held her in her arms gave her body to drink from without a word or reproach being said.

So she put her letters in a notebook and kept them for what would follow told herself that love would read better like that awaited visits gentlewomen callers received them sometimes and sometimes not love tried to call or come by they had to be careful were but she never again opposed her she spent so much time waiting that her eyes reddened with lack of sleep yet love called! then did not the horsewomen brought her messages of hope and sometimes not it seemed to her that her time belonged mostly to the one guarding the tent and her love.

She sitting somewhere she who cannot call herself love without enraging! she says repeatedly: I love you want you want only you! explodes again this sun lacerates the eye hides in the centre of this world hides explodes this sun without light or brightness the earth is dark and dark the sky no star survives the grief.

She whispered: so you! seated before her like a pharaonic goddess or noble sultana with eyes of shadows she said: you watch smile weep also and her tongue does not quit her mouth licking her love's cheeks until salt her tongue falls silent as her eyes fall silent now dead inert and cold faceless.

She said: we have broken off resumed broken off have called a truce no winners or losers you remain there and I! distance hurts us distance is necessary she said again for herself alone said: I want to touch caress embrace you you rise lean over me brush against me embrace me love does not answer her lips take her again that alone counts should count.

She thought: this is mine! did not want to tame anything left wisdom to the wise and moved on because moving on brought back into play the parts of her that slipped away she thought of childhood saw it pass beseeched it missed it sought it with a magnifying glass then remembered so much she abandoned it with a glance she had love could only choose non saying she wrote another long letter a letter of understanding she wrote then began to laugh and laughed at so many tears since tears abound and make puddles then lakes and seas to swim in she added: I swim you know very well I inhabit the uninhabitable (body).

She knew how to write without laughing aligned each and every sentence of ceremony and circumstance became an author of service seated scribe she took notes returned them asked questions and questions of use received no answer worried wept or smiled the result was the same fragile and frail she tried to flee said: watch me leave! also said: flowers survive in lukewarm water.

She thought of the one who lived in the tent her blood circled her heart three times then thrice more then she cried out.

She understood that today was a dark day and a sombre day she would not see the eyes like ships would not see anything good would feel so terribly alone would feel alone walking would find the desert again and the dune wild sands would not understand that this also was said in three keys: today is a dark day and a sombre day.

She brought a letter to the feet of the one who lived in the tent she carried her letter gave it to the weapon's mistress gave it to her without speaking bowed three times backed away to the donkey saw the guard enter the tent heard her give the letter to the one who reigned there and went away.

She imagined the rage of the one reading the letter she imagined and this rage gave her no pleasure or joy her love would suffer but she had not seen her love for three and three days times three had not spoken to her nor written had waited in vain had hidden in the dunes to wait had washed herself had darkened her eyes with kohl had put a necklace around her neck had adorned herself perfumed herself had changed her dress rubbed her palms and the soles of her feet with henna had started afresh each morning and night to come she told herself she was not a woman of hope yet hoped (for) much.

She had not written anything in her letter that could hurt she knew only that writing could enrage had written it with tears had inscribed three words renouncing forewarning the one who reigned of her departure had written that to the one so she would know and would tell her love had written it hastily so she would not change or alter her mind had done it on the run without flinching or trembling had written: sleep I'm leaving! had never left.

She began to dream of departure wanted to leave invented trips to foreign countries invented saw her eyes open thought about cities thought especially about the little-known women who live in them dreamt about them so much that she forgot love in her absence did not think of her.

She took out the maps spread them out there were so many countries to cover she closed her eyes pointed a finger let it fall on the land of h then the land of n she pointed again found herself elsewhere in the land of l lay down across the maps stretched out her arms her legs spread herself across the maps as if she were enveloping the world pretended she was swimming swam on the sheets of paper buried her head in this city here then that one there sought the city of water the city of bridges sighed turned toward the city of ice and the city of sand then chose the city of age as a place to begin.

She did not move remained spread out over the maps yet she felt her body rise being raised softly taken up by the fingers the neck the eyelashes everything seemed drawn upwards everything pulled upwards stretched she saw the maps move away from her body saw the earth dwindle beneath her become small distant she did not feel alone she believed she heard voices called to them to find out who they were recognized the voice of h then that of n and the softer one of l recognized these voices spoke to them listened to them took them onto her to protect herself wrapped them around her like sheets of silk and satin wrapped them on/under her enveloped herself in them so she could fly away.

She so let herself be carried away·that she flew over the tent circled it three times blew it three times three kisses told herself that she had to stay refused to leave looked into the distance to see her quartered body spread out over the maps she saw it told herself that she had simply taken a holiday she buried the body buried it in bits and without slowness buried herself lost a part here and there in this way scattered she saw her arms leave her legs her eyes her head fly away saw everything in pieces then whistled like she whistled for the donkey and her arms her legs her eyes came back to their positions she found herself intact recognized herself and flew away.

She felt herself weaken   leaving was not simple   nor departing never having any news sometimes hearing vicious words or words of love pierce the veil of the tent no one came out she counted ten and three as they say thirteen felt her heart give way rose from the maps fell back her head was caught her arms weak her breathing ragged without understanding she fell did not see herself falling fell on the maps crushing cities.

She spent days and nights like that without tears without dreaming or awareness felt herself light and alone sometimes wept no water touched her cheeks she moaned while sleeping the donkey approached her sniffed smelled her recognized her smell moved off in this way she spent three days and as many nights and on the third day awoke rose and walked toward the tent rose and slowly walked.

She had circled the tent so many times had walked run wept had lamented so much had three times three cried the names of her love had screamed then breathed had let her voice rise and fall had seen it rise had listened to the sounds had understood had not recognized herself did not want to recognize herself told herself it was another's voice became sad to hear such moans weeping and moans became sad then thought she was losing her mind.

She told herself that she had no malice did not thank herself for it wanted to be violent desperately crazy saw herself hitting killing tearing apart counted the arms the legs the eyes made piles of jumbled bones gathered members and pieces sharpened knives thrust withdrew thrust again she imagined carnage and great death saw herself as a warrior at the front slaughtering the enemy saw herself alone in the fight fought without faltering felt herself grow heavy and light no longer felt anything new her head drooped she bent over tried to sit had walked so much these past days tried to sit then get up got caught in the heap of bones and wounded flesh saw the piles could not believe her eyes rubbed them to make it go away saw herself falling into the bones saw herself did not fall continued forward into the dunes touched sand no longer crushed powdered bones crushed everything did not know where to put her feet injured the soles of her feet injured herself continued walking until exhausted.

She did that for days did not keep her rage locked up did not keep it in cried out spat felt herself expand with rage felt herself aroused saw her arms tremble saw her legs and her feet saw her belly her breast saw her fingers her body tremble strong fast and strong could not be calm or slow felt herself boiling told herself she was boiling water oil that by such trembling she would spill over would burn (herself) would burst into flame would leave ruins and calcified bodies would leave nothing in this desert would die here.

She lived did not die of grief love had disappeared leaving a letter saying: I'm gone! had left it when she vanished she had read wept and read had stretched out on the sand covered herself with sand in burial had watched the sky waiting for non-life saw nothing the donkey approached her sniffed her looked at her saw she was still breathing settled by her side.

She knew herself alone! did not call out or weep the tent was gone the desert belonged to her from far off she heard the voice singing she raised her eyes saw the woman sitting asked her to sing and sing again spoke in Italian to change the tune and loved language she said: *lasciatemi morire** whispered the words very low remembered her singing classes tried to rise felt weak so rose on the voice of the seated woman rose and sang filled the air with her deepest voice her breath swept the dunes caressed her in her tomb of sand brushed against her then held her she closed her eyes listened ceased calling sultana in her heart and left.

She no longer moved felt her legs become sand felt them burrow into the dunes to die there felt her arms plumb the sand pulling engulfing catching wearing her away worrying her with delight she had ceased to defend herself love was gone she no longer had paper nor turquoise ink she said to herself: *e che volete che mi conforte in cosi gran martire?* she smiled or pretended to her lips mouthed the words made the movements tried to sing along only able to cough swallowed sand while coughing and fell silent.

---

*"Lasciatemi morire," from the opera *Ariana* by Claudio Monteverdi (1567–1643).

The Blue Door of Detroit

JANET KAUFFMAN

Indoors, the outgoing door opens in. As a usual thing. Outdoors, the ingoing door opens out. And in a house of many doors, such as the city, the distinction, inside to out, may be difficult, an habitual mystery, what with the trees and jungle paraphernalia of tattoo shops and the concrete bedding and awned walkways under the air. Guess where you are. It is impossible to be a stranger to the climates of seven continents. And others. There are several others. The forearm registers low-lying air, off the chocolate pecan tub; and the various underground weathers rise, usually visibly, against the knee, the thigh. There is the underarm atmosphere, too, air of your swamp-ridden self—dank, creaturely, hair sweet. Temperature and steam and aroma, these ephemera, forewarn the way advertising forewarns: by assertion, mild haste, dispersal. It slips by. But if you could open a door, out or in, to look at an advertisement—that would be another story. If you could open a door, flat on the ground, to look at a subway, a grotto—that would be another story, too. Consider the number of doors. It is morning in Detroit. You can open a door and see sixteen bolts of hand-woven purple fabric. You can open a door and see the wooden step and the marigolds. You can open a door and see a woman pull at her own nipples. It is mid-day. You can see the man in the green hat on the sidewalk. You can see brickwork. The sky is there, plain as a cake. The blue ceiling. The blue floor. The blue door.

from The Reproduction of Profiles

ROSMARIE WALDROP

I

To explore the nature of rain I opened the door because inside the workings of language clear vision is impossible. You think you see, but are only running your finger through pubic hair. The rain was heavy enough to fall into this narrow street and pull shreds of cloud down with it. I expected the drops to strike my skin like a keyboard. But I only got wet. When there is no resonance, are you more likely to catch a cold? Maybe it was the uniform appearance of the drops which made their application to philosophy so difficult even though the street was full of reflection. In the same way, fainting can, as it approaches, slow the Yankee Doodle to a near loss of pitch. I watched the outline of the tower grow dim until it was only a word in my brain. That language can suggest a body where there is none. Or does a body always contain its own absence? The rain, I thought, ought to protect me against such arid speculations.

2

The body is useful. I can send it on errands while I stay in bed and pull the blue blanket up to my neck. Once I coaxed it to get married. It trembled and cried on the way to the altar, but then gently pushed the groom down to the floor and sat on him while the family crowded closer to get in on the excitement. The black and white flagstones seemed to be rocking, though more slowly than people could see, which made their gestures uncertain. Many of them slipped and lay down. Because they closed their eyes in the hope of opening their bodies I rekindled the attentions of love. High-tension wires very different from propensity and yet again from mirror images. Even if we could not remember the color of heat the dominant fuel would still consume us.

3

Androgynous instinct is one kind of complexity, another is, for example, a group of men crowding into a bar while their umbrellas protect them against the neon light falling. How bent their backs are, I thought. They know it is useless to look up—as if the dusk could balance both a glass and a horizon—or to wonder if the verb "to sleep" is active or passive. When a name has detached itself, its object, ungraspable like everyday life, spills over. A solution not ready to be taken home, splashing heat through our bodies and decimal points.

4

I tried to understand the mystery of names by staring into the mirror and repeating mine over and over. Or the word "me." As if one could come into language as into a room. Lost in the blank, my obsessive detachment spiraled out into the unusuable space of infinity, indifferent nakedness. I sat down in it. No balcony for clearer view, but I could focus on the silvered lack of substance or the syllables that correspond to it because all resonance grows from consent to emptiness. But maybe, in my craving for hinges, I confused identity with someone else.

5

Way down the deserted street, I thought I saw a bus which, with luck, might get me out of this sentence which might go on forever, knotting phrase onto phrase with fire hydrants and parking meters, and still not take me to my language waiting, surely, around some corner. Though I am not certain what to expect. This time it might be Narragansett. Or black. A sidewalk is a narrow location in history, and no bright remarks can hold back the dark. In the same way, when a child throws her ball there is no winning or losing unless she can't remember her name because, although the street lamp has blushed on pink the dark sits on top of it like a tower and allows no more than a narrow cone of family resemblance.

6

I learned about communication by twisting my legs around yours as, in spinning a thought, we twist fiber on fiber. The strength of language does not reside in the fact that some one desire runs its whole length, but in the overlapping of many generations. Relationships form before they are written down just as grass bends before the wind, and now it is impossible to know which of us went toward the other, naked, unsteady, but, once lit, the unprepared fused with its afterimage like twenty stories of glass and steel on fire. Our lord of the mirror. I closed my eyes, afraid to resemble.

7

Is it possible to know where a word ends and my use of it begins? Or to locate the ledge of your promises to lean my head on? Even if I built a boundary out of five pounds of definition, it could not be called the shock of a wall. Nor the pain that follows. Dusk cast the houses in shadow, flattening their projections. Blurred edges, like memory or soul, an event you turn away from. Yet I also believe that a sharp picture is not always preferable. Even when people come in pairs, their private odds should be made the most of. You went in search of more restful altitudes, of ideally clear language. But the bridge that spans the mind-body gap enjoys gazing downstream. All this time I was holding my umbrella open.

Small of the Year

TOBEY HILLER

So fine is sometimes always. This of course was provisional with us. That fall we tried it, night after night, under the covers, and so far, so fine.

It was his certain gaze and way of yes that did it, actually. And he could make such a yes of me—he had a handsome method, pioneer. Outside the moon waxed and waned in a very shiny way. Simply white sheets. I noticed everything about him I could. It went the other way, too; he called himself a fine toothed comb.

Then always was not the point. The point was always then and again. I forgot to think, I think, though my mother had tried to prepare for this by packing in a certain thought like same sardines, over and over, in the oil of bored evenings and drilling lectures. "Don't forget your head's upstairs," she'd say. "Don't try to think with what's downstairs, it's by and large an idiot." So I didn't think with any idiots, but dreamed with handy skin. "Here," he'd say, "try this." The habit of trying came quick, because trying often came out well, and long.

It was not summer, and in addition I was not eighteen or any bumpkin or budnut. I was well into high noon, that median strip, and my job, and of course my father.

My father's ungrateful future had crept into his spine, 3rd and 4th lumbar vertebrae, and started a spreading gnaw. Out the ribs, jumped to pelvis. The doctors looked sharkish, though wearing a bedside manner. Legions and militia marshalled minor Punic wars inside me, mostly daytime. I was trying a lot. On the phone my father kept at it, warning me about the wrong time to eat mussels, Oxalis in the grass, forgetting flowers for my mother's grave. A long November lessened slowly but listed toward December.

I tried and tried through familiar days. Also and with regular intermittence, the fine nights cradled me. Awakening was often evening.

My father was telling me about Oxalis and a ghost. "It's impossible to root out," he said, "once it gets started." He ignored the tubes and straps and all the fierce white and waved his arms, signifying roots, perseverance, danger. "It's incredibly well adapted, strong root systems, little bulbet things that winter over and multiply like crazy. Once it flowers you've had it, so I'm telling you, buster, get it out of your lawn." Buster's not my name or even my gender, but that's my father for you.

"Don't worry about the Oxalis, Dad," I said, "for god's sake." "It's as good as anything, don't you think?" he answered. "Answer me that one. Oxalis is as good as the next worry, I myself would certainly say, I don't know about you, and anything's possible if you catch it in time." Arguing was of course, but off coursed. I tried not to.

The ghost appeared in the evening he said, it was moon timing. As soon as things got blue he could expect a visit. "Oh you don't know what I mean really because ghost isn't the word, but that's what it is. There's nothing wrong with me. Don't move that, I want it right there. It's Barbara, of course. She doesn't have much to say, and I wish she'd speak up when she does. She mumbles, I'm deaf." He poked at the bed controls. "You need a pilot's license nowadays to be sick. What are you making for Thanksgiving? Pecan, or raisin?" Year after year, I made pecan pie, because they all liked it. I like raisin. "Dad," I said, "are you always going to hold it against me, that I can't see the superiority of the pecan over the raisin?" It must have been my tone. "I don't know," he said, and gave me that look. "Maybe you know about always, if you're so smart. Not me."

Best I could do was one thing after another, counting this and that the way they lined up. Night and day breathed in different directions, like Siamese twins, but between them only one heart. The body's not a narrow thing when you think how far, through what, it stretches, and as a continent it carries sweep. My father was in the dismissing stage. "Take this," he'd say.

"I don't want it any more." His hands folded easily, dropped down out of motion with thankful wrists. "I enjoy these evening talks," he'd say, "even though she mumbles."

After all Thanksgiving was pecan, as usual. As usual may be as always as you get.

Dad and Jackson never met. Dad said now was not the time for him to start something new, the trip home for the meal was just about as far as he could stretch it, God knows he wished me luck, and Jack said yeah never mind cranberry was the least of it. Dad and Stevie and Justin and Trina ate the turkey and the pie and watched the blue begin. To me blue announced either Barbara or Jackson. These exits, they're revolving doors.

When you know something's going to happen it surprises you when it finally does. Because you're always waiting which fools you into thinking you've prepared when you've merely fidgeted around trying to get settled in a place you know is only temporary. Now, pecan pies are something I miss, not because I like them. After all the all seems larger, at least in this case. He never mumbled, and I miss it sometimes.

In the small of the year ghosts come, small after years. This, along with the usual raisin, adds to the festivities. Jack regrets now not meeting Dad because he says then he could better unpick the many strands. The long nights always remind me, and the moon. In the small of the year so fine's not always but still usual with us.

from Harvest of Ghosts

NINA CROW NEWINGTON

Trousers

I hear footsteps in the hall. I lie with my arms by my side and my eyelids don't move. I am asleep. Bill went to sleep a long time ago. The door opens. She turns on the light.

"Goodnight," she says. Her voice is thin.

I won't look. She walks to the chair. My father is away. He's away. He isn't here. He went away. He went away to look at war. The war. He's away. She picks up something. She's in the middle of the room. I want to go away. Everywhere in my body I want to go away. I want to go away anywhere. I want to go. She's standing still. She's looking at me. I won't look. I can feel her eyes sucking on my cheeks.

"If you want to be a man, you have to learn to fold your trousers properly. Look at this, a crumpled mess."

I won't. She knows. I won't. I won't look.

"If you want to be a man you have to learn to fold your trousers properly. IF. YOU. WANT. TO. BE. A. MAN. YOU. HAVE. TO. LEARN. TO. FOLD. YOUR. TROUSERS. PROPERLY."

I open my eyes. Bill will wake up. She is standing by the chair. She is holding my jeans in front of her. She holds them upside down so the belt buckle dangles down. She pinches together the two legs so the seam is on the side. Her eyes don't have anything in the middle. I feel sick. She shouldn't know. I don't want her to know anything. I live on an island.

"LOOK. AT. ME."

She is still holding them by the bottom. Now she flips them up over her arm. They lie over her arm with the seam facing me.

"There," she says. "There." She smiles at them. "Do you see? DO. YOU. SEE."

"Yes."

"Yes what?"

"Yes thank you."

"Yes what thank you?"

"Yes Mum thank you."

She goes to the closet and gets out a hanger. I can't breathe. She hangs up the jeans and she slides the closet door shut. I close my eyes. I am asleep. I think she can hear my heart.

"Goodnight." She is near the door.

"G'night." I mumble it. She shuts the door. The light is still on. She's gone. I think about her fingers on my jeans. It makes me sick. It. Makes. Me. Sick. Bill hasn't moved at all. I don't know if he is asleep. I wish Dad would come home. I send him a thought in the air. To Biafra. He's flying in a plane with Prince Richard. It is dark except for the green light of the instrument panel. They are sitting close together in the little airplane. Prince Richard is steering. It is too dark to see except when a gun fires and then the ground is covered in dead bodies and the animals are taking legs and arms away in the bush to eat and the animals' eyes are green and shining. Prince Richard and my father fly back and forth. Nobody can shoot them. I get up and turn out the light.

Mask

My father is reading the Times, Prince Richard is wearing the crocodile mask. It has a long red and yellow checkered snout and black teeth. He brought it from the war as a present. After he takes it off he says to my mother, "She has your eyes, my dear. She'll be quite a beauty when she grows up. Just like her mother." I feel my mother squirm. She smells like seaweed. He crouches down in front of me, his face sweaty from dancing around the room, and on his cheeks there are red lines where the mask pressed down. His eyes grow big. "Little Anna, if I wait for you will you marry me?" I can't stop looking at the marks on his face. His lips are wet. "Say yes, beautiful Anna, say yes." Everything smells green and slimey. He turns his eyes away for a moment. He looks at my mother. I do too. The middles of her eyes are big and black.

"I'm not going to get married," I say to her and my voice comes out loud but I can't move.

"I'll wait for you," he says, "you'll see, I'm patient."

"No," I say, "I'm not going to get married." I can feel the tears in my throat and my belly hurts.

"Don't be silly," my mother says, "a prince just proposed to you." She is still looking at him. My father turns the page of his newspaper.

Christine says, "It's time for the child's bath, Madam."

I didn't hear her come in. I turn and walk with her upstairs. She has run the bath already but I have to ask her a question. "Christine, I don't have to get married, do I?"

"Girl," she says, "when your time is ready you will be wanting a husband. I too was like you. I wanted to stay in my father's house. When the fruit is ripe it fall from the tree. How is a woman without children?" In her eyes is the far away. I don't say anything.

Beach

On the beach she lies with her mouth open. Her lips are wet, as if she has been licking them in her sleep. Bill and Dad are far down the beach. I can see the kite, a red diamond in the blue sky with a yellow tail. I know the string I can't see leads down into their hands. I can't see them either. My father ran down the beach on his long hairy legs, the kite stumbling behind him till it swung up into the air, and Bill ran too. I can hear the waves, I can hear her snoring, the breath catching in her throat. The hairs on her lip are pale yellow. One arm is behind her head, the skin in her armpit is pale and naked like a chicken skin. Her eyes are very still under the eyelids. She smells sour and heavy, like milk that's gone off. She doesn't know I'm here. Her breasts point in two different directions. They lean away from each other. Her legs are covered in short sharp hairs like little spines and there are long blue-green knots which are her varicose veins. Her nipples are the color of liver. Her belly shivers when she breathes. Hairs climb out of her bikini bottoms. They are black and hard. I'm going to hit her. I see my fist above her, ready, my fist going down into her belly, sliding in and in, up to my elbow. I have to pull it out but I can't. She is sticking to my skin. I pull and pull and then there's a sucking noise and it comes out and I fall over in the burning sand. She'll swallow my hands if I hit her. I can see a piece of chicken in between her teeth. After meals she takes a piece of cotton, wraps it around two fingers, pulls it tight. She saws in between each tooth. I feel sick. My fists are clenched so tight they hurt. She's a whale and her belly's the mouth. She swallows everything. All the food in the ocean goes into her mouth. She puts her mouth over the whole ocean and sucks and there isn't anything left in the sea, the water is thin and empty. "You're disgusting," I say to her belly, "you're dirty. I hate you." Her eyes flicker.

I am running down the beach. The kite is laughing at me, high in the sky turning circles and figures of eight, the tail trailing behind like someone in a boat dangling their arm over the side. My feet sink in the sand. It burns me. I run until my feet touch the wet sand. I run. Each time my foot touches the ground, it pushes me forward and up into the air. My feet are running, I am standing still. The wind is in my hair, the roar is in my ears. I run until my stomach hurts then I dig a hole in the ground and I lie in it. I pile the sand back over my body. My toes stick out. When I wriggle them the sand crumbles. I want the sand to look smooth, as if nobody is there but it doesn't. I run again in the opposite direction. I feel something sharp in the sand. I look behind me. There's blood in the sand. I run looking back, there's more blood, there's blood everywhere I run. It's my blood. Everyone can see where I've been, like a map of an expedition, a line of stitches in the sand, they lead right up to the umbrella.

My mother is sitting up. She is wearing her bikini top. Dad and Bill are there. I stand on the edge of her towel.

"Where were you?"

"I just went for a walk."

"What's that on my towel?"

"What?" I want to hear her say "blood." It's my blood.

"That."

"Oh." I look down. The blood on the edge of her towel is a dark flag. "I must have cut myself."

Seeing

I screw the cap back on the tube. My hands are greasy. I wipe them on my thighs. Sand sticks to my hands, my thighs. I can't get it off. In the sky the kite is turning and turning.

"Thank you, darling," says my mother. Her voice is muffled. She's lying on her belly. The sand is white under her head. Her hair is black and the sand is white. It is like a cloud, thick, moving, the sand, like steam. I can't stop looking. Something's happening to the sand. I have to see. I see the dark in between the grains, thousands and thousands of dark pores in the sand. It's breathing, swelling and sinking, the whole beach a skin, hot and salty, the waves breathing harder. Dada dada. Come home. Dada come home. Dada dada went away in the car, greeney grey vroom vroom dada bye bye. Mummy in bed warm mummy salt smell mashed potatoes belly big and warm. Mummy moving, laughing, playing castles, rocking, rocking. Mummy's hands hold tight. Mummy let me go. Mummy moving me up and down, her legs tight around me, hairy scratch on my tummy. She is crying funny. My hand hits on her belly, fists on her belly, fists. Mummy let me go go drown pulls me down down drown breathe her skin Mummy in. My fists in her belly. Help. Help. She cries out. She lies still. She lies dead. Mummy. Mummy. Dirty. You dirty. You dirty girl. You dirty. Dirty.

She's picking me up. Her hands are melting into my skin. I'm cold and heavy her hands are melting through my skin they're going into my bones I'm getting smaller she's carrying me into the thundering the thick white billowing through the door the dragon lives there guarding his treasures he has scales like armor green and gold she holds me over the steaming pit he keeps his food there I look down into the steam it breaks into colors red and pink and purple and gold crimson and emerald a shining pile changing and changing there are knights in bright armor perfect as seahorses their chargers and grooms and pennants snapping in the breeze damsels with gold hair weeping silver tears tiny shining enamelled models and the dragon smelling like hot tar flames licking out of his snout his breath thundering watches like a bird on her nest I'm being lowered into the shining moving colors and the hands let go and in the holes they leave the burning rushes in it gets inside my skin I shrink in and in a scream begins to twist out from in a dark spool unwinding in my chest her hands are hitting my head "Stop it" she hisses "You're dirty. You have to get clean."

I run across the burning, heaving sand, dive into the sea, swim until I catch a wave, scramble free, dive in again, over and over until my skin is puckered, my eyes raw from the salt, and all the noise in my head is the sea. The sand is clean and white as new snow.

Liszt or Schumann

LOUISE DUPRÉ *Translated by* JUDITH COWAN

I

Perhaps it takes some special stance for a shard, a splinter to deflect the glance, slanted thereafter to the wetness of images, while you wait for words to come. You say *words* and suddenly there is nothing left to connect you to the tumult of November, so you write, a rain falling after victories, nothing but falling rain to stave off for a little while the moment when your lips will close upon their own clapping.

You write to her.

2

You wish that your letter could take on the garden and the urine smells, like the first words you copied out with her holding your hand, your black nails, stubborn and childish, and she says, *do you remember, the blots and mud-pies under your fingers*, and now you line up these characters on the page because the days count, the intensity of the days for the first time, her weariness, her vertebrae slumping, little by little. A new urgency to avoid speaking of more than the immediate future. Life ceases to be the centre of life, a woman looks towards eternity, and soon it will be your turn to take her hands. You are no longer just a little girl devoid of eloquence.

3

She says to you *we always love our children more than we love our mothers*, as if this were obvious. And on that day, you cannot write.

4

You remind her about the tulip beds, the bald dolls that you used to bury in the earth, disposing of childhood, at the age of ten your lips caught at the miracle, you would say to her *play a sonata for me, Liszt or Schumann, real things are not enough for me*, and silently you would watch her, fascinated by the notes she read so well, her shoulders tensed over the yellowed keys, the A which was never quite in tune any more. Sometimes you would start to sing. Already you were seeking a voice for your own passion.

And at the age of ten, the body of wetness that you found in yourself on certain spring evenings. But there was her reserve, her prudery, and yours.

5

You have stopped telling her your troubles. Instead you invent happinesses to make her forget upheavals in the landscape. Detail takes over, detail absorbs, and you catch her smiling. The slightest anecdote becomes an event. She says *you haven't been so tormented lately*. You would like to reply that it is now up to you to welcome her into your fiction.

You look down at the first brown spot on your left hand. You wonder if you will get used to her absence.

6

From the window, she watches you walking away under your dark umbrella. For an instant the universe is contained in her eye, fresh thyme, lavender, the familiar strides of a woman tearing herself away. She says *I'll write to you*. A veined hand finding its landmarks through the African violets and the old melodies, simple phrases which unsettle the images of the poem, and you will have to read these living affections, the skin of days without glory.

But you answered saying *write to me, oh yes, do write to me*.

7

And last of all she says *you know, I've kept all my mother's letters.* Then silence, blankness, while she asks for nothing.

So you type on a card *so do I, I keep all your letters.* You would like to add *religiously.* But you stop there, with your fingers on the keys, waiting for your muscles to respond. And the moment passes.

8

You say write with a wounded hand. You would have wished that she had never read your books. Between you the ordeal of what must not be mentioned, the barbarity of certain images. In her dream you are still a little girl and she is making tender gestures towards you, while you respond with phrases full of holes, holding back the panic, landscape of music, Liszt or Schumann, the glance too quickly clouded, mourning, sometimes you no longer know how to imagine silence.

And yet you do not write November to her, its outbursts, alarms and passions, November or this purple-red rupture of the voice.

Perfection and Derangement

FANNY HOWE

Dirt road, down a slope. In spring the trees are spackled with white blossoms, some flecks of pink. The branches look like long bones; the white has returned to them in the form of snow. Pinker berries dot the thinnest branches and thorns, and a spray of same lies across the rotted porch. If you look through the boarded-up windows you will see a contraption for restraining someone too sad to move.

Where can I rest? Satellites circle this snow-covered flatland. Orchards are bare by the reservoir, the green benches bent from cold. Under the ice I can see a leaf, a can, a tire, a fish, something from outer space. Then the water hardens like gelatin, swollen into lumps where old leaves are inlaid. An interior, destroyed by mismanagement.

Suffering is how the world informs the human mind that it is there. Suffering proves to the mind that it is exposed to alien substance, like it or not. If you can't act even while you suffer, you can only suffer and sink. Nonetheless a person has a right to protest and complain and to yearn bitterly for release.

May for one rejects any absolute dualism. She has it that past, present and future exist simultaneously. All time is the ONE's creation. Then police from Rhode Island call and want to know her status. They say they found her walking along the highway in shirtsleeves with no money, on her way to New York. They have brought her to the Cranston Medical Center and she can be picked up there.

Women are like roaches, they survive so much. They seem to grow tougher with each succeeding generation. I think the evolution of material things came before the entrance of women onto this earth, but they followed almost immediately. The first one was last seen through a hole in the clouds, going down through the top. A kind of intergalactic storm reviewer, she jumped directly for the heart and support.

Where are you that you don't invite me in, turning your hand out and over? Do you know which room I inhabit, the bed among beds and under stone joinings? That none of these belong to me?

To confabulate is to conceal your mental retardation. To confabulate is to be a fool filling in the gaps in your memory with detailed accounts of false events.

What do you dream about in the facility? Will you ever wake up to the facts and this way give up HOPE?

Your hands, like ten virtues, can only do so much. I have noticed, since coming here, that each person in this world is chasing his or her self at all times. Some people just move slower getting from the past person to the present or first one. Those who wail they want to go home are referring to a community where justice prevails and they get their mail. Though they are certainly sociopathic, they're not in prison, are they? They were never violent, but more likely terrified. Look into their oceanized eyes.

Our primordial metaphysical and religious experience begins in terror. This produces a modesty whose secret is only revealed through certain sacraments and only to those participating in them. This transaction is called THE DISCIPLINE OF THE SECRET.

I had just figured out how to live correctly when I realized it was too late, I had taken too long figuring it out.

Before on-rushing time I experience total helplessness. Like the words, "You shall see my back but my face shall not be seen," the loneliness in a human face belongs to the ONE.

Likewise for every one fact there's a second one to counter it. If therefore I knew all the facts, I would be paralysed—on wheels again at last.

The hidden countenance is one countenance worth contemplating. There a felicitous light swells into substance which sees as you see and breathes as you breathe; it even kisses where you kiss. Whisper your prayers if you want to call it out of the dark.

You asked me what I know about G-d and coincidence. I walk through you to tell you, the place where you stood like an opening in the form of an offering.

The soul originates in fire, cooperative and quick. It deteriorates into a self by becoming stiff and slow-moving. Now a place becomes a space suitable only for walking and the self often trails behind the body like a shadow. Better to feel your soul is rushing ahead of you than that your self is limping behind.

Colors return and scandalize the objects that were happily hidden. My position has changed. I've moved back to make room for the whole view, but still it's from that corner I see the space that held you.

I have failed to view my actions as having any importance, have spread myself thinly across the tops of things. I have resisted change, a new way of doing or thinking about the world. I have not lived up to the hopes anyone had for me. It makes me sick.

It's true that May had escaped in the morning and was returned by guards in the afternoon, saying *Because I had nowhere to go.* Now she is just sitting down in a dazed state. Inappropriate laughter as usual. She was very upset about the commitment proceedings. Her sister really hates her.

Why all the emphasis on lobbies, Paul asked me. I told him that they can be shortcuts to streets. I didn't want him to know that every lobby is private, so the homeless have one less place to congregate. The Department of Mental Health should have a terraced waterfall cascading down the stairs to show visitors how it feels being scared.

Come here and fill the space waiting.
May I lick your lips?
Any opinion on the defense budget?

Come here, never. You can rest there in the open door.
Three songs—refrigerator, birds and a trolley start at 5 a.m.

Bend to get the hint: there have been advances in cruelty since Oliver Twist.

Poor Paul called the sky Tubby. Snow, Tubby, he would say.

Anyone ordering restraints in this place has got to be familiar with the way
it feels on the other side. I carry a little glass ball on a thread as my refuge
and my joy. I do the lights, or did, every year on the facility green. I put the
spotlight on dogs. It was often foggy in December. And I bet Christmas Eve
wouldn't have eaten that apple if it had been that foggy. She wouldn't have
been able to see it in the first place.

What will you give me to leave you since I haven't begun to die yet? I'm
sorry. My mother would always say, "You get more excited by Christmas
than any child I know." That showed how much she loved me before she
left me in Valley Forget. We had a duplex with all the amenities, including
hardwood floors, central air conditioning, fireplace, private roof deck, a
Euro-style kitchen and a ranch-style livingroom. It was amazing. Ma kept
a table set and waiting all day every day. When I had time I'd grab a hot
dog and cola and sit right down in front of a display of china and silver.
No matter if I wolfed down my lunch. I appreciated every bite in that
environment.

Tonight the ward is quiet. People have a zombie attitude and seem only
inwardly hostile. Sam oiled his hair with toothpaste before bed. I had seven
vacancies and fourteen beds. Some of these people are ready for another
redeemer, I tell you. Every event is packed with hidden meaning.

I said we won't accept a lenient sentence since evil is built into our system.
Sustained, said Your Honor. I can't help worrying, though, we're so broke.
No awnings, no boat hulls or sails, no automobile panels, no water skis, no
beverage bottle carriers, no covers for cushions or appliance handles, to
name just a few.

No family, no friends.
In the shelter hot meals are liable to clang. Eyes are like primitive telescopes

facing the sea. I've been in that trick fortress too long. Someone is always fucking following me. There's no safety.

May is now acting very strangely, staring at the ceiling rigidly, tongue in cheek. She saw two red nails in a door that gave her a sign of Christ. Later when she was staring at the ceiling she said the holes in it looked as though they were breathing!

Now the snow is going up and down, now it is waving to the side. The branches seem to lift into zebra-snakes asking for food from the cloaked fir trees. The sky is solid white. A full moon will be rising, pink, and close to the horizon soon, and will polish the night shapes.

What was lost, comes back—like May—but how do we know we are not already somebody's tomorrow? Am I here and waiting, the table set and the toast warm for someone alive in a yesterday?

I was kicked out of Ma's apartment a month after she left, so I don't know if she came home again. She left me a note beginning, *Dear Reality*, and signed, *Love, Me*. The man who kicked me out of the apartment was so greedy I bet he would appraise the value of a walnut shell if an ant wanted to live there.

Is G-d a place that it should move with me in my car? Or is this ability to move a sign that it's not a place at all? The ONE experiences itself through its creation, even though it existed before and beyond that creation, I'm told. The ONE is lonely and loves voices that call to it, even when it can do nothing to help but only sympathize.

Likewise the soul informs the body of its presence but doesn't really have an effect on acts.

Stop feeling sorry for May when she's put in seclusion. At 7 a.m. she assaulted poor Sam in his wheelchair, hitting him with her fist several times on the back of the head. When the nurse came with meds to her room, she threw them back at her and became assaultive again. Was given 100 mg. of thorazine and was quiet for the rest of the night. If you feel sorry for her it's like saying that G-d has abandoned her. Imagine how that makes her feel. Just try to help her out instead.

It's all very well for you to say you don't know G-d, but what would you say if you learned that G-d doesn't know YOU?

May said, I lost my self-control. It just got away from me. Later it came out as a splash of color here, twelve smears of gray there, oak trees shot in morbid details, the hum of a cello, words overheard and a pirhouette. I think that each one now is the signature of a lost person looking for a home—not a shelter—a home like the one that was promised to us somewhere along the line.

Litter. wreckage. salvage

DAPHNE MARLATT

Below water level, behind—the dyke a road
now, back of the wharves, boats, empty sunday / spring, left with the
nets and houses left, to dry rot, must, the slow accretion of months as
horsetail heads rear out of asexual earth of abandoned gardens brambled

Steveston

your women are
invisible, your men all gone. Except for a few boats, Hey, his spring salmon
net's wet. How much you got, Ned? A bucket. Thin smile his pride will
scarcely allow. WE got—how much'd you say, Chuck? (pups at the old sea
dog) You stay away with your bucket!

Staying, straying in their individual houses women swim in long slow
gleams between blinds, day incessant with its little hooks, its schemes in-
consequential finally. They do not look at Star Camp at the company houses
broke and broken open—a litter of two by fours, old shingles, bits of ply-
wood forming / Doors torn off their hinges, glass, glass remains of what
transparent walls. Occasional boot, the wreckage of daffodils someone
planted, someone thought to haul in a bucket. . . . What matters, mattered
once has seeped away. Like fluid from a cell, except she keep her walls intact, her tidal pool the small things of her concern still swim alive alive-oh.

The salmon homing in this season, spring, the sewer outfalls upstream, oil
slick, the deadly freight of acid rain—she reads the daily list of casualties in
the ongoing war outside her door.

If "the woman is within," if that's her place as they have always said, can she
expect her walls not to be broken open suddenly: Rain, Lightning, Nuclear

Light—what attaches her to the world? Dug-up clam, dehoused, who can no longer bury her head in the sand. . . .

ii

fear of the marketplace, of going outdoors. fear of public places, crowds, of leaving home. "the phobia of every day." she trembles like a leaf. has jelly legs. her stomach is a churn, fear stirring her into separate parts: the whip of the super-ego, the cowering ego, lack of will.

imagine opening your front door and standing on the step. how strong is your fear? relax, take a deep breath. imagine walking down the path to your gate. how strong is your fear now? relax. imagine opening the gate . . .

i want to imagine being in my element, she said.

iii

Fish. paper. (value). Fish. paper. (words, work out towards . . .) an accumulation of desires unbought, nothing in this world can pay for. I want to walk down the street as if i had the right to be there, as if it were not their construction site and stoop, slipping the net of their casting eyes, slipping the net of their market price. The street belongs to the men who live "outside," whose small acts accrete (concrete) unspoken claim, a territory that cannot be trespassed except you hurry through, for loitering indicates a desire to be caught,

> or caught already, prostitute, destitute,
alcoholic, the street is where you swim for smaller fish

> Hey you! someone fishing for, Hey where yah goin?
that kick in the head recognition is, You! something other than fish, flesh, drowned in the tidal line of the unemployable left on stone planters the city removes

> Whose foot of cement is this?

I go fishing too, to bridge that gap i let my line down into the powerless depths we flounder in where the will (to capitalize on things) stands on the opposite side of the street having made this town, having marked it "No Trespassing" "No Loitering." No defenses in the smell of beer the private walls come down, lightfingered, aery as their harmonica, two young men sprawled in the heat and the young woman with them, flaunting her being there free, she thinks, for free—

Fish that escape my line in the swift and surge the street my feet keep carry-ing me adrift . . . letting my line fall into the blank, the mute, defences breached she's letting her want out there where i am, beached with their receding ebb.

iv

coping with the world outside. she copes with this and that all day long inside. a successful applicant must be able to cope. she doesn't contend or strive—her struggle is within.

i can't take the bus is the same as i won't take the bus. a failure of will. she says they are staring at her and what will she do without the right change or forgetting to get the transfer when she got on, they stared when he refused, they thought she was dumb. what attaches her to the world? is what repels: the fear of being caught, caught out, caught without—

she doesn't have the words to alter his definition of her.

v

There are no longer any real fish. only a flicker of fish—a movement,

the baiting you do, talking to me in the street, my back against the car and you playing the line, hiding behind the tease i rise to, as to the clover of your smile—

"Fish are there to be caught you know."

Will i rise? school behavior a herd of fish. just as, back then, swimming through sexual currents looking for eyes, as if they might bridge the gap, flare, romantic semaphore. gone fishing for compliments recognition is, eyes the lure. allure. not looking (out) but looking the look for certain eyes, floating around the places he swam by, i "lost" myself as they say and i did. fall into invisibility. silvered, dead. i floated up and down the school yard with the others, eyes reflecting all they saw, blind to myself, more: hoping to feel that hook when his would connect: "he looked at me!"

All action his, mine merely to be seen. passive voice. i contend with desire elicited from me, the lure, the bait: i'm worth fishing for.

(How much did he say? the boy, bragging. how much does a fisherman get per pound on spring salmon now?)

The fishy vocabularies we speak our worlds through. "the fish never says no," you say, the lure speaking. but watch that fish swim right on by. the fish is after something too. something else.

vi

imagine her in her element. not to be taken in its restrictive sense as home (is her, closed in).

in her element in other words. blurring the boundary. it's not that she wants to blur difference, to pretend that out is in, already past the gate she's past his point of view as central (hook/lure) to a real she slides free of.

free she multiplies herself in any woman paces the inside of her mind her skin half in half out of the common air she drifts along. casting a thought receives it back this we of an eye complicit in a smile she gathers fish-quick, taking the measure of their plural depth she who with every step and never once (-over) desires in the infinitive to utter (outer) her way through— litter   wreckage   salvage of pure intent.

The Arab Apocalypse

ETEL ADNAN

III

The night of the non-event. War in the vacant sky. The Phantom's absence.
Funerals. Coffin not covered with roses. Unarmed population. Long.
The yellow sun's procession from the mosque to the vacant Place. Mute taxis.
Plainclothed army. Silent hearse. Silenced music. Palestinians with no Palestine.

The night of the Great Inca did not happen. Engineless planes. Extinguished sun.
Fishermen with no fleet fish with no sea fleet with no fish sea without fishermen
Guns with faded flowers Che Guevara reduced to ashes. No shade.
The wind neither rose nor subsided. The Jews are absent. Flat tires.
The little lights are not lit. No child has died. No rain
I did not say that spring was breathing. The dead did not return.

The mosque has launched its unheeded prayer. Lost in the waves.
The street lost its stones. Brilliant asphalt. Useless roads. Dead Army.
Snuffed is the street. To shut off the gas. Refugees with no refuge no candle.
The procession hasn't been scared. Time went by.   Silent Phantom.

XIV

I advance as a white bird over your heads 　　　 With a sun in the belly

feet in the sand HOU ! HOU ! HOU ! Wind in my feet
I chose to wander STOP A yellow sun has risen on the Camp
a purple sun in Canaan's eye a green sun for Islam
a white sun on the fields of the future 　　　 a traveling shark

Oh! the sun is a shark pursuing stars in the sky's seas
I chose a tribal chief son of Andromeda and the Sun
the young king of Syria moves in the stormy instability of the skies
yellow sun blue sun tattoo in craters and wounds
They burned the chloroforms ate the antiseptics STOP They laughed
mercenary sun Arabian anti-sun BIG BLACK HOLE IN THE UNIVERSE
I climbed   the column   I climbed   the mountain
I climbed   the cloud   I climbed   the sun
And I saw: masked men execute a carnage
We have to drink blood in order to join them and wait for them in hell
O peaceful sun eternal father of Canaan's children
O Babylonian Deluge ancestor of the Arabs Wind Wind
One two three . . . messages stream from the computers
I sleep with a radio in my arms STOP I sleep at Tell Zaatar
At the door of Paradise STOP a solar bath
I see rockets among trees. Concrete catching fire
cages crumble smashing crushing merchants The cardinal points explode
Sleeps the horse innoculated with innocence under the madness of the Moon

XV

In the halls of the sun we manufactured virulent religions
We burned still-born children HOU ! HOU ! the solar goddess!
The brain is a sun STOP the sun is an eye

Each nuclear explosion blooms into a sun-brain like a flower !

Within the sun's atoms we created virulent races STOP
the sun's atoms are Moslem saints saints muezzins
We used a bistoury on each solar atom O sorrow !
the sun is an Indian snake a Sioux covered with light
Indians lead rounds in the heart of the sun STOP Vertigo!
Indians dance in their mothers' belly STOP yes ! yes!
Blinded angels are coming by the thousands carrying petroleum-spoked banners

Arabs are dancing in the dust DOUM !   the Tribe is delirious
the yellow sun children's toy in the shanty-towns is eating the sea
Each bullet is a ball planted in the brain YES !

XVII

Jupiter moves forward followed by thirteen moons STOP Ganymedes
    enamored of the sun

Beirut is a poultry yard with peacocks and the stench of poultries
Jupiter swims in a metallic solution   ◉   The discharge is incoherent

Beirut is a satellized planet domesticated by its enemy profanated by EVIL
An electric current covered with hair like a mare circulates in the universe
Beirut hides in trenches   bending its neck goes to the slaughter house

The BIG RED SPOT of Jupiter is a storm. Matter is desperate.
Beirut is eaten by civil war children listen to the roar of cannons
matter in fury turns in circles in the big void of the planets
Beirut wallows in misfortune HOU ! HOU ! HOU ! Beirut bleeds
matter circles in tornadoes on nebulae's surfaces   O Milky Way!
more blood than milk   more pus than wine ▬   ▬▬▬   ➤
Jupiter defies the sun a yellow sun makes love to Jupiter
hatred is filled with phosphorus jealousy wears a black ribbon
Jupiter revolves within the boundaries of its acid madness
Beirut turns round and round it is a weathercock of disaster
Jupiter gets away from the sun and runs back to it: it is a hunting dog
any Arab crowd is a crowd of poets. Listen to its maledictions!
incandescent planets darkly flutter in the heart of the war

geomagnetic forces dry up our regions We implore the rain
we receive solar particles We want to see We are blind

We go in hordes to praise the Lord   the solar Face is pitiless
Jupiter and the sun fight over Gilgamesh's mortal remains

XXII

I am the prophet of a useless nation   STOP   the base of my brain hurts
Smohalla Tecumtha Smohalla Tecumtha Smohalla Tecumtha Smohalla
I am a sniper with glued hair on my temples   STOP

the sun is a frozen lemon as big as Presidents' noses
Each wounded is a dead man   Beirut is a corpse presented on a silver platter

the sorcerer  sun blows into straws
Drinks lemonades in the cemetery's alleys
the sun has its phallus decorated with ribbons   STOP
I am the terrorist hidden in the hold of a cargo from Argentina
the sun is a shark faithfully following Uruguayan sailors
I am the judge sitting in every computer shouting FREEDOM IS FOR WHEN ?

the sun distributes the hours into bureaucratic drawers
The convicts drag themselves to the fountain of blood

Amidst a smell of corpses forgotten by the garbage collector sleeps the sun

while perspire the plants.

XLVIII

They sleep under wild mulberry as if they themselves were roots
the non invisible sun broils their eyes STOP They came by night
Which night?   ●   the one which outlasts the sky
let the lack of bread become a fabulous song!
the sheep share their wool and the wolf its anger
snakes come to help airplanes sting those who sleep

under the haggard gaze of black stars STOP in the smell of manure
from the banana fields the stench of despair rises in the air
there is no dialogue save between stones STOP   apples are put to sleep

pentothal is reserved for the Army   torture for the innocent
our eyes stare at the sea
refuse and crashed airplanes swim under the sun
I saw camels harnessed to the U.S.A. and going at 200 miles an hour
for one hour for one hour   ➤ ➤➤ dust has devoured all . . .
they climbed to the top of their tents to look at the future
Death wearing her ornaments arrived on her horse for a very long halt

LII

The sun has 52 vertebrae They hanged it by its neck   It has 52 vertebrae
Trinity of doom Rope for the Apocalypse   a wet and thoughtful sky
A yellow sun a blue sun a red sun   legs which number six
the sun has numbers in its food and ropes which number three
Trinity of pain I see pink roofs and restless turtle-doves
the great clouds migrate to the north   september blows into winter
They left together they went to heaven at the tip of a rope
Do you know the smell of soap that accompanied their death ? HOU
     the sun's spinal cord remains for ever suspended
Between sky and earth three Palestinians are sailing
like slow fish half earthbound half celestial they circle Mother Earth

HOU!! HOU!! HOU!! HOU!! HOU!! HOU!! HOU!!

They enter through our ears and exit through the mouth HURRAH !!!
the ropes had been thinned with soap to make torture hygienic
the executioner washed his hands not to contaminate the victims
On Damascus' Main Square three trees grew in four hours
the generals were on time the tourists at their windows
the people the people the people were saying Praised be Hell !

LVI

Sounds of laughter are back on target   Sunken suns
we find strength in carrying flowers to disemboweled corpses
the sea licks the ballast and the rails of the cosmic train
demented women stand alone under the moon's noise   ERRANCE in the basilica
bodies buried at the start of the century and momified with salt are digged out
with their legs thrown apart bodies cry the absence of their sexual parts
They will not reproduce in the other world   will not make love to laurel trees
I said that this tongue   smoking like roast-lamb   will disappear
make tomorrow's men speak in signs   collectively
They threw the Arabic language to the garbage   toads took it up
Rivers will be abundant but solitary   the mountains too
eclipses will descend on earth to eat grass   wisely

a plate and fried eggs for the prophet's assassin
from valley to valley under the subterranean sand we'll wait
Spring will refuse to come   Earth will not have seasons anymore

Main Bride Remembers Halifax

GAIL SCOTT

She's in a telephone booth in Kingston. A greystone motel like a fort or prison. And at last she's talking to the one she loves. He's on the telephone in some stone garrison, saying: "Great, let's get together. I'll call later to confirm a time." Smiling, she hangs up. Remembering all the duties of a young officer. She thinks of them in terms of clothes. Rigorously organized into red tunic and pillbox hat for gala dress; otherwise the navy tunic (albeit same pants and hat); probably jogging pants or those regulation shorts for lounging around the officers' quarters with the guys. Hair on legs lolling restlessly on beds, with socks: white; or navy if the lazy cadet has not completely changed from street wear. An officer in training (and gentleman) must be perfect. Must have the required package of condoms stashed safely in his mess kit.

She asked him once: "Don't you think all this organization kind of stifles the imagination?"

He answered, leaning his head, at the time wearing the pillbox, to one side, his lisp audible only when talking to her fondly: "Our commandant says, the more rigourous the structure, the more imagination is required to operate brilliantly within it."

She sits on the edge of the green bed in the motel room in Kingston. Amusing herself by noting these thoughts in a diary. The brown waters of Lake Ontario lap outside her window. (What's she doing in this town anyway?) Waiting for the dry little man with the hornrimmed pince-nez, a university dropout, to notify her she's received a phone call. Time goes by with greater and greater anguish. She daren't go to eat for fear of missing him. Finally it's dark. The grey day sinking into night marking a terrifying point about her personality she doesn't want to think about.

She gets up. Feeling a little guilty, stupid, she goes into the hall to try for one last telephone communication. The line cracks. Over the cracked line she asks if this is him. The voice says Jack or John Christian. It says the earlier possibility of an encounter seems to have faded. At least for tomorrow and tomorrow and tomorrow. She hasn't got the money to stay until after that. She feels the potential softness of his cheek fleeting from her grasp. There is this terrible static on the line. She tries to tell him it's just fine, in order for him not to feel pressured. At the same time trying to find out if there isn't some tiny opening in his schedule. Even if it's not the evening over drinks and dinner in a candle-lit restaurant made of stone dating from the early 1800s. She realizes it might be someone else on the line. Slowly she hangs up. And walks towards the exit.

Outside the motel front's a dusty road. Passing a little church made of very old stones. Very New England Puritan in design, with iron netting over broken stained glass windows. The road narrows in the dim grey, almost silver evening. A single raindrop making a lace pattern in the dust. She takes a step, slim, longlegged in her dark pants and leather boots. As if she's stepping towards another era. Her forgotten hunger, her fatigue still masked by nerves fed with endless cigarettes, plus the silver shadowed light (especially, the light) making her as weightless as a ghost. But she's too exhausted to make any big decisions now. Besides it's going to rain. Back on the green bedspread she stares at the nearly black water beyond her window. Taking out her diary she notes a dream:

> I'm crossing *Peggy's Cove* (near Halifax where she grew up) *in a boat. Watching the long curve of the green bay and the bluegrey waves on which the boat goes carefully up and down. Feeling worried that the boat won't get there fast enough. The high arc of its tiny bow hardly seeming to advance over the greying expanse of water in the dimming light that divides us from the shore. But at last we get there and I ask: "Where's John C.?" His family, defiant but sympathetic, say: "You missed him," from where they're sitting on a green patterned sofa against dark-blue patterned wall-paper. The mother further clashes because in a flowered housedress.*

This image troubles her. She looks between the Kingston motel curtains at the black lapping water outside her window. Sure her young officer's family had more "class." That they were members of the yacht club and had good real estate on the Northwest Arm in Halifax. That they served every different kind of alcohol in the proper kind of glass. Outside their house curled a gravel road through wooded properties in which, growing up, he pretended to be an Indian. After which the road emerged in a modest commercial district, then climbed past a graduated row of clapboard houses.

Where (although they barely met until university in Kingston) she lived, the only daughter of a sea captain father and an ordinary mother. When her father went to sea, he'd walk down the hill on the gravel road between the trees. He'd turn and wave, walk to the bottom of the street and turn and wave again. They were watching from the kitchen window. Then, her dark curls would be bent over the kitchen table, colouring, drinking chocolate. Perfect peace.

At night, between the white sheets, the windows open on the quiet street, masturbation came easily. A touch, a whoosh, and that was it: a happy adolescence. It's true, the pregnancy interrupted her, her mother's smooth domestic surface. Luckily, they were able to hide it from her father, gone to sea at the crucial moment (the last six months). He came home to find her pale, bedridden, fluish. That was all. As her mother said: "Think nothing more of it." She didn't. Until on the train going east, she saw the brother of the given-up baby's father walking down the aisle. As he held the seats for ballast, she took in his short waist, his brief, well-built legs, especially the long black hair (when everyone else wore short), typical of the men in that particular family. This filled her, briefly, with nostalgia.

Her young officer was of an entirely different type. Slightly British accent. Long-legged, big, almost feminine hips, fortunately balanced by the heavily padded shoulders of his uniforms. It was when she brought this "fiancé" home from university that her father ventured an opinion about her sexual appetite. Disgust. After he surprised them in the kitchen, kissing. Kissing, kissing: she could have literally drunk from her young officer's lips. What is the colour of an obsession? Red. But to think it could show up in a red tunic in eastend Montréal, where she found herself after his and her estrangement, was ridiculous. Québécois were known for their hate of garrisons. Yet she looked for that red jacket everywhere in bars around her flat. Which shared a common entrance with some members of a subversive anti-government group. The preoccupation showed. Her neighbours, although they liked her, quickly began to indicate suspicion of her many different lives. "Women, like cats, have nine," she answered them respectfully. For she admired their understanding of how the system makes us crazy.

"Good thing I didn't find him, too."

She suddenly thinks this, sitting bolt upright on the green bedspread of the hotel room in Kingston. Because if he'd been hanging around one of those eastend bars in Montréal, it'd have been as a plainclothes cop or undercover agent. Using his deceivingly ingratiating ways, his handsome blondness to get to all the women. So what's she doing in this town anyway? Just a convenient milkstop on the train. Besides, he wasn't what they thought. Belonging as he did to a new liberal tendency in the military. Worried about the environment, impassioned with poetry, music—like a 19th century hero. He'd only joined the navy to get to university. She now remembers: his family didn't really live on the Arm. That was another wealthier branch. His father was an alcoholic fishplant foreman somewhere on the coast. The Arm branch was headed by his uncle, Le Général Le Flô. Who used to say, sitting on the patterned sofa:

"I can't wait for the next war."

Speaking of red, maybe her young officer got turned off that day she and he were riding up to Red Lake. They were together again after a long separation. She was so happy, she sang out of tune all the way. They'd been to the yacht-club, curtesy, precisely, of Le Général Le Flô. Her in a brown dress with a drawstring at the waist. First they'd had a yacht-ride. Then sat on the upper balcony drinking gin and watching the waves gently lap the yachts anchored in the harbour. A single gull was rising in the flawless blue sky. Looking down, he saw "two girls I know from school now going to a smart New England university," on a lower deck, that is balcony. And disappeared for quite awhile. She focused on the bottom of her glass until something positive came up. His tiptoeing that morning into the room where she was sleeping at his mother's place. Blue chintz curtains blowing in the sea air. She was wearing short chintzy blue pyjamas, too. And he came tiptoeing in, his regulation condom already stuck on his hard red prick. Saying not to worry, his mother wouldn't notice.

At breakfast his mother said: "My girl, you're too conciliatory."

Outside the Kingston motel window, the lake's as black as ink. Proving what's happening to the earth depends on one's angle of perception. Same with what's happening in relationships. His and her problem likely was they could never get together for any length of time: his garrison kept moving. Halifax, Montréal, back to Kingston. Sometimes (feeling nostalgic for some of what he offered) she tried to follow him. Where she got her money was unclear, but she could still afford the trains. In fact, this whole story might be more appropriate on a train. Young officers were all over the place in those days. Post Vietnam, when men still openly dreamed of war. Their cocky voices shouting out in mess halls: LATIN AMERICA NEXT. Red and blue tunics running between garrisons, that is bases. And young women leaving Christmas balls, heading east to Montréal, west to Toronto. In railway cars put on special, with such round and steamy sides, it was thought they might, before refurbishing, have served as cattle cars. No, garrisons. The 19th century died hard in Canada. It died in 1970.*

Now it's 1975. Maybe later. What's she doing in this town anyway? She gets up from the green bedspread. Outside the motel window the black waves are lapping under dark clouds. Swollen with the night and one hundred years of industrial revolution. A few years back, they were still having real winters. She remembers returning to Montréal in one (prior to their estrangement, although she'd already, no doubt erroneously, left Kingston and only went back for visits). Anyway: still in her ball gown. It was cold and snowing. The cattle car had red velvet seats and was full of elementary school teachers striving to improve their possibilities. He stood outside in the snow. So involved with drinking from his whiskey bottle, then joking with the guys, he didn't even properly wave goodbye to her little triangular face watching through the steamy window. Her brown eyes smiled bravely at the cadet in the seat opposite who happened also to be travelling to her destination. They raised their glasses. Unfortunately, she was unable to transfer affections.

Thank God the train was moving. Her pale reflection in the window reminded her of something. Pulling out her lipstick, she changed her image from the natural look obligatory for a debutant to a cosmopolitain '40s-style woman. By simply darkening the mouth in a firm and generous stroke of red red lipstick. So that even the pink-shirred strapless evening gown she wore was transformed from demure to wordly. There she was: maybe not so marriagable. But bold, confident of her sexuality to the point of devastating. A woman who could do anything with a man because so distanced from the act she was putting on.

She smiled at the image. Suddenly remembering this persona'd been first conceived by a dusty baseball diamond back in Halifax. When the dusks in larger villages and smaller cities still gave the illusion there was space to become anything you wanted. Standing there, allegedly to watch the boys play, she was in reality sizing up the other girls. Eleanor P., whose father openly slept with women, including Eleanor's girlfriends, was overweight; Françoise M., whose father beat her mother, was beautiful but bitchy. There was *la tristesse* of Sandra M., manhandled in other ways by her old man. Compared to them, she, Adèle (a pseudonym inspired by a French poet's

---

*1970: The year of the October Crisis, when violent manifestations for a Québécois republic culminated in the kidnapping of a British trade representative and in the kidnapping and death of a Québec labour minister.

daughter) felt very fortunate in terms of family consequences: her father was mostly absent. It was up to her to ensure this situation continued. Keep a distance by putting on an act. Right there and then she determined to speak only with a deep throaty voice: a means used by courtesans in French novels. Also, they were never fixed on one affection.

The problem was a palatable way to make a living.

She gets off the bed of her motel room in Kingston. Attractive in the silver-grey television light in jeans over almost cowboy-style boots, very slim belted waist, burgundy shirt. Briefly, she leaves the room to order pizza. She eats the smallest slice, then lights a cigarette while writing in her diary. "Ce qui fait déranger une femme, ce n'est pas le sexe. Mais la bouche du père." A dried apple mouth that trembled while he bathed her. Or held some argument on politics or sea-travel at the kitchen table. She had in common with her namesake, Adèle H., that her diary, while still at home in the clapboard house in Halifax, often quoted him. At the encouragement of her mother, who had married him reluctantly. And was trying to make him feel important, "preserving certain phrases" so he wouldn't get suspicious and give up his sea trips. She, Adèle, the appointed scribe, sat down at the table, opening her notebook. Just as her father said to Victor Jean, the student working summers on his boat: "I am for both democracy and war. This is possible, since I believe in God."

"Maman, est-ce que je peux avoir mes oeufs?"

"Ecris, tu auras tes oeufs plus tard."

What makes these things come back all of a sudden? The kitchen was painted yellow. Her mother was stationed behind her big pot of tea like the Queen of Hearts. Not pleased with Adèle's fiancé, Jack or John Christian. Because the older woman'd spent years trying to pawn her daughter off on V., that boring Cancer male who finally got an engineering degree and a job in Chalk River at the Uranium Research Centre. (The river was full of neutrons.) Sitting at the kitchen table, he would try to prove scientifically to her father that a man couldn't be for democracy unless anti-royalist. (French-Canadians often felt that way). The insecurity of his presentation: always piling up the proof, opening his soul and speaking loudly, severely bothered her, contrary to her mother. "He has no secrets: he'll provide you with stability," the older woman said. Adèle preferred her "fiancé's" attitude. Admitting he knew little of politics, his fields of expertise being sports, food, love. He'd say this in his charming, slightly lisping voice, accompanied by a sideways glance through his blue eyes as his hand grasped one of her bright curls. Which he then bent over reverently.

The voice suddenly lost its lisp, had an edge of hard steel flint, that day driving up to the brick Red Lake. When he said coldly: "Stop singing. You've been out of tune all the way." In the bright sun light, the edge of flint blinded. Of course, she didn't take it passively. Always trying to turn a disadvantage, she was kissing, kissing him in the Red Lake. Pulling back the crotch of her dark bathing suit, so he would do it to her right there in the water. Forgetting (in the process of trying to improve her possibilities) to act detached. This was her fundamental error. Also, failing to consider she was neither marriagable, because always on a train. Nor suitable for an office job or teaching.

She just had to find a palatable way to make a living.

Her eyes felt that same briefly-panicky pain staring at him from the train on the dark, disappearing platform after the Christmas Ball. Until she realized it was the light of the polished steel of the cattle car windowframe that pierced them. She just had to turn from looking, her hand digging for the red red lipstick in the beaded evening bag. Boldly made up, she raised her glass again (in the game way that made everybody like her) at the cadet across the aisle. Distraught as she was, she liked this feeling of detachment. Stepping off the train, wildly attractive with excitement and with anguish, she saw her neighbours, les anarchos-écologiques, in the *Café de la Gare*. (They couldn't help noticing her). Distributing tracts calling on the workers to take forced control of public railways before the privatizing government dismantles it completely. Bertrand-de-Matane approached her, wanting something of her. But first she had to trade in her ball gown for jeans and an old army jacket in a boutique on Ste. Catherine catering to transvestites. (She refused to drop the lipstick.) "Lenin," Bertrand told her, "counselled his followers to be able to move in every level of society. Since you like travelling so much we have a job for you." Unfortunately, while waiting for the signal of departure, she still sought, with the corner of her eye, the outline of a red tunic in every bar. Even if she knew (those single-minded revolutionaries never stopped reminding her) that the military college, with its balls and formalities designed to make boys from ordinary families feel superior, was really 19th century.

If only she could get the 19th century and 20th together before the 21st arrives. These are her thoughts as she starts sitting up to go to the cigarette machine in the motel hall in Kingston. Not that time matters a thing to her. She's a woman entirely without ambition. Lying back (for just another minute) on the green bedspread, this timelessness enables her to imagine any future to fill the empty present. Example, give in to her desire to rent

a room in Halifax, where his garrison is posted. Maybe she could get to
the bottom of her obsession. Something probably led her to reject him
with a too hasty turn-of-the-hand. Looking at the motel's simulated pine-
covered walls, she thinks: if the persona with the deep attractive voice (for
this jaunt, the red, red lipstick would definitely be excluded) were to rent a
room in Halifax, where rumour has it his garrison is posted, she could re-
arouse his interest. Plus, find out why after that last Christmas Ball he never
called. Likely unreachable, due to all of those trips. Montréal and Halifax.
Sometimes back to Kingston. The train quickly became her favorite mode
of transportation. She loved the clacking, clacking. The landscape fleeting
outside the windows. The sense of expectation when the conductor says:

"Mesdames, monsieurs, nous arrivons à Montréal."

"Watch your step."

Meanwhile what to do in a motel room in Kingston? Not turn the television on because it makes her feel alienated. Light another cigarette to
mask that faint but nagging hunger? Out the window the high tower of the
Kingston penitentiary casts a moving beam of light on the black water. She
could go for a walk. Stepping forward, outlined by the silvery moon. Down
that long road with its strange light along the dark edges beyond the 19th
century buildings. Nineteenth century. There's that word again, although
it's 1975, maybe even later. Is repetition the colour of an obsession? Anyway,
this road gives her a comforting feeling of déjà-vu. Déjà-vu of what? Maybe
driving with her parents outside Halifax, before she left for the university in
Kingston adjacent to the military college. Where she saw the shiny house.
Perceiving, by looking at it, how life and death are unbelievably close. The
house was terrifyingly shiny. The roof, the dead red brick so still and shiny
in the bright green grass. Still and bright as death. Thank God (if she goes to
Halifax), her nosy mother's dead. Her father, too, who fell ill shortly after
she left home.

"M'affranchir de mon père, de sa parole, n'est pas contraire à ma conscience," she wanted to tell various people offering their condolences at his
funeral.

Probably, in Halifax, her young officer would accept to come over. Especially if she appealed to him coolly, in a letter, as a friend trying to get
reestablished in the city. (She lies back, warming to the possibility.) This
non-threatening approach should work as he's likely still suffering from
rejection because she took off so quickly from Kingston to avoid an immanent sense of failure regarding winter examinations. Albeit returning, as
she'd promised, for the Christmas Ball. She hopes, in Halifax, he'll show up

in his red tunic, having been to some dress affair first. He does look better in it than in the blue, since it draws attention from his rather large hips. He'll come in, polite, his head inclining gracefully towards the old couple: her landlords. Sitting briefly, his swagger stick across his knees. Impressing them with his manners, with his class. (She's told them they're engaged.) The old folks, who are egotistical like most old people (unwilling to accept they're empty power vessels) talk too much and refuse to leave the room. Just sit there pouring tea and trying to ask, albeit discretely, when he's coming back and when the wedding is. Before she can figure out a tactic, he suddenly jumps up, stands very straight in his military way, and says he has to leave on the pretext of some duty. She can't believe it. She hasn't been alone with him long enough even to put her pale, slightly rouged cheek against his naturally pink and white one. To hold him, kiss him (although she'd primed herself to take it easy, not to scare him).

This whole story would definitely be more appropriate on a train. She thinks of getting up to pack. Time passes on a train, unlike in waiting, waiting, in that musty-smelling room with flowered wall-paper in Halifax. Explaining to the old couple, staring honestly at them from behind her wire glasses, that her fiancé doesn't come because his commandant's bigger on duty than on giving passes to let his men leave the base. He does drop in at Christmas. Bringing her a present from his aunt, who, he says, is "worried." Yeah, thinks Adèle (unable to avoid a touch of cynicism): worried about the family reputation. As soon as the old man and woman (not wanting to be ultimately responsible for ruining a marriage: they've heard rumours) leave them alone, he whispers he needs to borrow money. To overcome a gambling shortage. She hesitates to tell him her financial situation. Outside it snows. He stays approximately 10 minutes. She follows him to the door. Wanting to put her hand out and touch his back without "pressuring" him. He turns and almost salutes without looking her in the face. A single snowdrop falling on his pink and white skin. Walking down the curved driveway, between the snowbanks, to the road. She climbs the stairs to her flowered room. And sitting on the overly-soft mattress under a heavy satin-covered comforter, she writes:

"Le mariage est une chose humiliante pour une femme."

She half sits with a start in the motel room in Kingston. Has she been dreaming? Outside the window the black water, the thin sliver of the moon's still shining through the clouds angrily. Also, the twirling spotlight on the tower of the Penitentiary. What's she doing in this town anyway? She needs to get on a train. Trains communicate from place to place. A person can travel back and forth on the train between Montréal and Halifax nearly full-time. Of course, you need some extra under-the-table money. Plus a false address in one fixed place for the welfare cheque. Not Montréal. Because her friends, the revolutionaries, caught her talking to a young officer-cadet. She tried to explain again about seeing red. That confronted with a man in full regalia she couldn't help asking the whereabouts of Jack or John Christian. But they wouldn't have it. Her buddies in the group feared she'd blown her cover. They were also getting suspicious of the trips she took that weren't for them. Now she stays at the Y des femmes when she hits the city. Hangs around the pool. Wearing sunglasses with white plastic rims to discourage broader recognition.

The chrome edges of the cigarette machine in the motel in Kingston are etched in that same terminal (end of day) light as dreams. Or as in when you wake from some heavy sleep not knowing where you are. Feeling only you must never close your eyes. Because you'll be sucked back towards that damp and smothering place you've just been dreaming of. The solution is, pretend to be somewhere else. Her empty mind drifts, a little bored, back to Halifax. Even that stuffy room at the old couple's could be stood, briefly, if daily going out for air. She could hire a calèche (they still have them there for tourists). She imagines a dusty road on the outskirts of a city. And that funny shiny house she saw driving with her parents. The same house exactly: it turns out to be the house of the aunt of her young officer. And she, Adèle, is going to pay a visit. Albeit not invited. Her pretext: she was touched by the aunt's being "worried" and giving her a present back at Christmas. It's taken weeks for her to plan just the right judicious mix of looking wonderful, but with a certain pathos in her dress. So the aunt will get the whole picture.

It could be 1870 or 1975. Maybe later. She steps out on the driveway before the shiny house. Now drawn like a magnet. (This makes her feel stupid, guilty.) The front door opens into cool airy space. The scent of apple blossoms waft through the partially opened window. While the butler gets the tea, she sits on the edge of the damask sofa. Her raised chin, strong, intelligent, lovely. Yet also devastated by the young officer's difficulty of getting off duty. She hints, as well, at having been exploited sexually. This was perhaps an error. When she goes back the next day to correct it, the butler says the aunt's travelling for a long long time to come. Backing down the driveway (now on foot—even one calèche is too much for a welfare cheque), she sees that, in the setting sun, against the gray sky, the house retains a little of its shiny quality.

In the cheap motel in Kingston, she looks in the mirror. At how the black jeans define the firm thighs and perfect crotch. If she could find a palatable way to make a living. . . . She goes out the motel room door. Takes quarters from the jeans and lays them on the chrome edge of the cigarette machine. One by one they disappear into the little slot. Around her, the place calls to mind a pool hall: green blaize rug; sparsely furnished except for a few flat surfaces disappearing in the darkness of the corners. A moose-head on the wall. She sniffs a new cigarette. Her favorite author Colette has taught her that the materiality of things is all that sometimes separates the human body from a terrible sense of nothingness. Although any sense of nothingness is better than teaching elementary school in Ottawa or Corn-wall. Slowly repeating "Dick and Jane" to sponges. Until you feel stuck. In her current way of life, each step towards the dark abyss of the future keeps the back bathed in light. Privately she thinks of this as memory's motor. Only interesting if moving in fast-forward.

She takes out matches. In this motel hall in Kingston, she could be any 25-year-old woman buying cigarettes. You see them in the cities, long (or short) hair, walking on the streets. Deciding what to do. Or looking for allu-sions. Bending shoulders, also the back, and her dark knees in black jeans and boots, she takes a high step forward. Then another, moving thus down the hall, her eye is drawn momentarily by the round numbers on the dial of the wall telephone. Maybe she should try for another (failed?) commu-nication. There must be a lot of fog between the motel and the military college.

Her hand rides absently up her stomach. Speaking of the materiality of the body, if she goes to Halifax, it will have to be reduced. Because (pursu-ing this is starting to feel good) if her young officer won't go to her when she rents a room in Halifax, like Adèle H., she will have to go to him. Yes, she'll have to be thin enough to don an officer's suit: blue tunic for some semi-dress occasion. Some occasion not requiring tickets. A gathering of the boys for an evening "mess" after an intra-mural game. The night will prob-ably be not too warm and slightly misty. Cadets are strolling on the large white verandah. She joins them, strolling up and down, too. Albeit not stepping through the French doors into the huge living room for drinks. Because, being an officer and a "gentleman," she'd have to remove her pillbox. Revealing the high-piled bun of woman's hair hidden under it.

So the verandah (the taste of victory's as satisfactory as masturbation): she strolls, dashing, euphoric, sure in this disguise she can accomplish anything. Marching up and down with a quick, nervous step. Her pink "officer's" cheek, her wellshaped lips glow in anticipation. Her hips more perfect, more suited to the tunic than ever his could be. He won't be able to help but admire her when he sees her. Expectantly, she eyes every cadet she meets. Her booted feet clacking sharply against the verandah's wooden floor. After a while, she leans against the wall, knee bent, bootsole against clapboard, an apparently leisurely pose the better to watch them passing. Such a "leisurely" pose is hard to maintain for long. She steps forward towards a group of young cadets talking. Getting up the courage to ask the youngest, nicest of them, to go inside with a message for Jack or John Christian. Except—he's there—putting out his hand to shake. She scrutinizes his face, unsure she recognizes certain traits. But he's stepping back angrily. Then leading her quickly to a misty corner of the cemetry. She tries to establish eye contact. Predictably, he's saying she's outrageous. She moves to put her hand lightly on his chest. Or almost, because to actually touch would be totally unacceptable for two young officers. The letter in her pocket cries out for communication:

Dear John: *How hard it is to write.*

Him: You have shown a serious lack of respect towards my profession, my uniform and myself.

The letter: *I can't bear how you never try to reach me. How you do nothing to confirm our love's existence. Or that it's finished.*

Him: I am beginning to realize your relationship to reality is seriously messed up.

She decides not to phone. A woman never gains by pressuring a man. Continuing down the hall to her room, it occurs to her that an obsession, if it is red, is more like waving a flag at a bull: it makes them react violently. Waving her at his family, for example. She laughs, opening the motel room door. Because later that very day he'd tiptoed to her in her chintzy blue pyjamas with his condom stuck on his stiff red prick, that aunt of his had looked at her as if she were a prostitute. She lies down on the motel bed, working up the memory. She seems to have been sitting on a dock in a bright red suit. Feeling so blissed out, she couldn't tell if she was awake or asleep. When some member of the family, probably aunty, announced the family jewels had been stolen. She said a boat had sunk and you (looking pointedly at Adèle) knew very well what was in it. Actually

(Adèle thought)—she herself had been in it. But had floated up with the spring thaw. Now she was sitting on the dock, her red suit jacket over her shoulders. A small and secret smile on her face.

She knew very well what *les bijoux de famille* meant in French.

She turns over on the motel bed in Kingston, dozily. Time to get up and pack: the train going east leaves at midnight. The problem being that with the particular dizziness caused by hunger, hours can fly by just contemplating the possibility of action. At least she hardly ate, so now can buy the ticket to get to the address of her next welfare cheque. And possibly other revenu too.

She snuggles deeper, lying on her back. Imagining herself sitting up in hopes of shaking off the dizziness in her head. Gingerly, her feet will touch the floor. Opening up the suitcase, she'll start packing various sets of clothes: short skirt and tight military-style top covered in *paillettes*. Jodpur pants and chiffon shirt. Both jockey shorts and lace undies. (Nor could anyone say the purpose of this combination of feminine and virile outfits.) For a hungry woman, the suitcase is kind of heavy. She stands up straighter. Dragging it down the gravel road, under the single bulb lighting up the motel front, towards the station. Some officer cadets are fooling round on the platform. Boarding, she hardly notices.

Sitting in her seat, it seems to her the burgundy shirt is red in the inadequate light of the coach. She adds some red lipstick. Leans back as the train wheels start clacking softly. A young officer goes down the aisle with unusually large hips for a man. She hardly sees, leaning back on the seat dreaming of a woman travelling, dressed in red. At least a red shirt or some kind of red jacket over her shoulders. A woman seen often on the train between certain stations. A woman smiling in anticipation. For in a moment the conductor will announce:

"Mesdames, monsieurs, nous arrivons à Montréal.

"Watch your step.

"Don't fall."

The Hour of Pan/Ama

NUALA ARCHER

Her hunches
hang-out

The same slit that zips the Pacific Ocean to the Atlantic unzips the connection between continents. The same canal that velcros, slashes. Both Atlantic & Pacific breezes wing their salt traces through her. For her, like rain, the setting is tropical. Water is sutured, land is unstitched. It was a horrific operation. The surgery was interminable. In 1965 she is 10 & lives where rain looms Pacific clearings. She will wave good-bye amidst the Atlantic's torrential downpour. Her good-bye-hat thrown from the ship drifts like an address card. A long-floating-fugue. She is told she is not where she is—*Place of many fishes*—Pan/amá. She is told she lives on the Isthmus, in the Canal Zone, in the U.S.A. She stares at the letters C.Z. A Crossroads. *At every stage of his career Gorgas seemed to confront the gaunt spectre of yellow fever. It was an important influence even in the love story of the doctor's life,* writes Marie Gorgas, his wife. Chagrinning clues amble toward their type face. The Chiclets she chewed climbing into clouds over Quito are a grey, uncomfortable gob in her mouth by the time the plane lands at Tocumen in 1960. Among first things in Pan/amá, she empties her mouth. Already the hibiscus, ilang-ilang & ginger have got her attention. Her ear is fluent to their accents & to the smells & sounds of Spanish. In school various possibilities are not discussed: that the canal might have been a rotten deal is a hush-hush. Also, the fear of letting go of canal control in the year 2000: another hush-hush. Galvanized by greed & a plague of power. The men who dug this particular ditch are still described in history books as geniuses. When she first hears the word *gringo,* she thinks it means *gangrene. JOSÉ, can you see, by the dawn's starry,*

starry? It is Olga who confirms the truth that she knows in her own bones. Her hunches hang-out. Some afternoons Olga says, ¡BASTA! & walks away from the moping mops and grackling kitchen. Twice, when the rest of the world disappeared to church, she spent a siesta with Olga in a hammock swinging beneath the green house built on stilts. She waits until after midnight. Then the house is quiet. Green & white tethered paths of light from the beacon at Albrook Air Force Base strip the palms and bougainvillea of their darkness. Night is striped: green & white, green & white, green & white. Blinkety-Blink. Blinkety-Blink. For a split-second a sloth hanging onto the Maytag's plumbing is transformed into an albino, then a glowing green-back. Blinkety-blank. Blinkety-blank. Our eyes catch & hold when we hear Olga's room referred to as "the maid's room" or "*cuarto de la criada.*" I knock lightly. The door's unlocked. *What is made I unmade,* says Olga, laughing in perfectly broken English when she wants to.

Basking in the afterglow of the unmade room

The wildness of domes in Samarcand. The blue domes of Meshed & Isfahan. These curves, too, arc easily like violets between the crannies of the moment's quiet. I undo my braids. With Olga the dance of conversation is an aura of hues. Caring that isn't leather-cured. Many tongues & lambent tree whimsy. Humorous iguanas. The ache is part of breathing. We take our chances. Olga removes her nail-polish. She's promised to braid my hair. I peel an orange for her. Her armpits are always wet. Pan/amá's a great place to learn about sweat. Even first thing in the morning Olga's shirt is grayly half-mooned. I listen to Olga tell about her mother. *When she arrived she didn't know she was going to be put to work covering rain barrels and cleaning out gutters. Fumigating houses & dumping disinfectant down privies.* Fronds of palms clack at us softly. Even without a verandah the bay gleams opalescent as the neck of an immense pigeon. *She said it was like arriving into the heart of a plague. Everyone was dying. At breakfast she'd look around & think, who's missing. She wasn't being funny. She wanted to know. Malaria, dysentery, yellow fever, trachoma, hookworm, red tape. It was the language of her childhood. The sound of folks flumped into coffins. Everyone in Pan/amá was cracked on the subject of mosquitoes. She said she was going to watch everything. Somebody had to remember how a groove was ripped through a mountain range in order to join two oceans. No cost was too great, they said. Witness to the making* of a sadscape. Such an egg-timer's-waist-of-a-place. Such a topographical hammock between trees. *NO PAST is part & parcel of colonization, she said. Perpetuity is its green-eyed monster. The Cucaracha Slide, in cahoots with the Culebra Cut, keeps sliding.* The brutality of immigrant dreams. Seizing the American teddy bear. Tyrannical teddy bear. And the triangular white-tipped shark fins of Freddy the flintstone. But who would have expected seals covered with boils? One weekend we went to a carnival. Scanning a crowd, on the verge of recognizing a friend, a great hollow roar of rain swept down. No sound travels through such thunder. Then, as quickly, a sunlit drizzle emerged out of the lashing. In this steaming land, rain is equally all-obliterating & connecting. In a click, a curtain & a clearing, but the dribble-dribble-dribble of the now vanished recent roar lingers in our ears. The sound of rain is always the background to our hearing. We walk down side streets that narrow into squashy shades of incessant talk tattooing time into open-ended space. The rain isn't heavy now, & it makes little noise as it falls like fine oil. No window works on the train home. All surfaces are gritty. Peanut shells, orange peel, cigar butts, stippling spittle. The myth about Yanqui trains is that they're clean, fast, even. And on time. Outside our window it's all historic & dull. Muddy & unspeakably depressing. Enough to flummox anybody. The sweetest skiddoo of truth is this stink. Fed up with high school, a zone kid is talking loud about his leaving to slave away at Wal-Mart as a minimum wage servant from hell. A month later he begins another job making stone critters out of hydrastone. He makes the critters look almost real, pouring the hydrastone into molds. In six months he has full health insurance. Dental, too. And a raise & some bonus pay for making so many critters over & above the needed amount. Chewbone. Chewbone. Axle grease & cotton candy. Zombification. Lightning is doing its usual X-ray pyro-technics, teasing sculpted shrub-stuff toward a nappy doo or the really plastic look of magnetic letters on a fridge. Lightning's topiary styles are abstract & improvisational.

Scatteration's
Autobiography

Stopping. And listening to grasses growing. Scatteration opened me, howled through me. Then a great emptiness began to happen. Meaning's arrival no longer mattered. A palpable desolation blossomed the way kisses or a body brings tears. I travelled through centuries. Aquí. A key. A quay. Akee. No more than flukes, no less than

flotsam. Winds returned only the silence of scatteration. Then a great emptiness began to hap-
pen. A great emptying. Like bivalves on a storm-varnished beach. I
watched myself open. Almost imperceptibly. I saw that heart-rending
smile. I could no longer ignore what I knew. Walking like a flayed deer
through fire. We circulated way outside the thousands of miniscule
safeguards of privilege. And the canal, of its own accord, crumbled.
Green flames of Catherine wheels opened into red flowers & domes
of indigo. In the swamp of history's spittle. Her sweet weight on my
heart at night. Dreaming of a window & a stretch of land for land's
sake, I scuttled the whole notion of achievement for an archipelago
that pointed toward an unchartered sea that the waves conceal, reveal at whim. *Dozing in the depths of wakefulness, in the warmth of each other.*
Alive, living in two worlds. More like three. Amidst Panamá's weird sunrises
and sunsets. At dusk the orange floppy of fire drops precipitately
behind the verdant Cordillera—into the Atlantic Ocean. And each
warm tropical morning the same floppy rises suddenly up in the
East—out of the Pacific Ocean. Some friends are still ingrained &
sleeping. The table with the bowl of moon is breathing. Olga & I are
walking through walls. My childhood in Pan/amá didn't hit me until
I woke up elsewhere.

Pan/amá, Pan/amá   No matter which way I turn, the jungle is always
somewhere near, just behind me or to my side,
reaching, reaching. I read to her the Estrella de
Panamá, the Spanish side & the English side both.
Her warm eyes are lovely & dark. The screen
door stays open so we can watch the saffron
finch. We do nothing in a hurry. Drawers are
often stuck, roofs leak. Christmas in Panamá.
Sounds sense. The piece of ice from Boston
costs more than a long-distance call. Clouds of tiny brown and purple
butterflies tumble across the slit of sunshine from the jungle on
one side to the jungle on the other. Silent, tangled, yet remarkably
synchronized, creating a gentle breeze against our cheeks. Roots
lift knobby elbows & knees toward these brown and purple wings.
Screeches & scritches & high-singing sounds. Birds wrangle & scold.
Amber colors whistle in green-black foliage. Blinking, startled mon-

keys squeegee the corridor of sunlight with their leaving. Orchids nod. Wet moss hangs lank. Insects everywhere. An alternative to Koka Kola, the Rio Chagres overflows her own banks luxuriously. Her dark throat is a constant chuckle. We are already supposed to be dead. We continue breathing. We imagine the bragging vengeance of the West vaccinated to a residue. A desert of voices springs from the egg-timer's waist. Square edges of individual grains are ground down, uncubed. Mileage into the past & future of quiet bestows flexible forms. Like pieces of a hologram each grain unfolds facets far beyond the proportion of its size. Tentative. Our touch interrupts history's spittle. Amnesia & avoided eyes acquiesce to remembering. Turpentine truths. Earthquakes. Fires purr, flowers chatter acknowledging the colors of our kisses.

Blue Mosque

ANNE WALDMAN

to William S. Burroughs

This is many lifetimes from the capital of India speaking. I've been out of the Muslim world now 24 hours. I've just come from Gate 4 North Block Ministry of Home Affairs. All is ok on the corners of Parliament House and President House. Tawny monkeys are lining the roof walk. They seem to be laughing. Please note I'm leaving my passport No. J193934 at the Nepalese Embassy Baracamba Road overnight after some tears with the guys from Royal Nepali Airlines. They are competing with Air India for my ticket money. I am not what I seem, tourist in pink stripe shirt, gold chain, grey cloth pants, rope soles from Italy. I am not what he wants, dark Hindu works for Universal Tires and has lived in Tehran. Terror ran. He is always waiting for me on Connaught Circus. "Don't cry, Anne," he says, tapping me lightly on the shoulder, "The authorities are ok. But you must have a cool drink." I am not all's fine with work & life PS Love. I am not enabling to get me to Darjeeling today, thank you Madam. I am not Dianne Vanderlip. I am no student discount rates please. Traveler de Luxe Olympia $150 American how many rials. Where is rials? River of laws.

Please note I am not old woman birthday April 2 still a flowing river cause you cross me, D. Peter dark Hindu will not be dining with the Madam Anne tonight. Her husband is joining her. This is not the truth this is sorta truth in rupees. Woodlands Vegetarian Restaurant I attended with the authors Giorno and Brownstein October 1973 is, I am happy to report, still standing. Mr. Jain and Mrs. Colaco on Janpath Lane are receiving guests in their hotel. This prose was speaking of Capital Delhi note leaving the Muslim world this is Ascendant Leo 4 degrees speaking.

"CABLE BLUE MOSQUE"

Leaving the Muslim world I was always watching them under their cloths and some, at airport, with platform shoes shocking pink, plastic Mediterranean blue pants with red makeup. Paula with blond widow's peak of England says some woman got acid thrown in her face for baring her face. There are hints and murmurs from all quarters. Never go bare face in that bazaar. The star People personalities of the Shah and his wife and their son with their big faces plastered everywhere and through Tabriz the scent of blood. On the Mihan bus: he loves me well, he keeps me down. Where are they putting those bodies in the Biblical landscape ah weeping my Gideon. I will go down to the Caspian Sea. I will weep for the daughters of Jordan and Zion and the little Marxist children.

And before that and before that and before that and before that and before that and before that and before that. I am not what I seem leaving the western world, boarding again the Orient Express in Bulgaria green corduroy pants, green sweater, black shawl, very cold in the morning. He grabbed my tits in Tabriz. I am not what I am doing. So the coal strike has ended at last Monday March 27. There are hints and murmurs from all quarters that the major issues have not been resolved and you will notice no one is claiming a triumph, no one. Make a note: It started with the original strategic mistake (paper ripped here) for rude and (continues fragmented) the internal cha-Taft Hartley procedure successful on a dubious sense that amatory instant negotiators on the went back to work etc. But a tunate precedent has been hangin unencable and ignored energy ago extremely rap coal produc in Appalach contact the epidemics . . . . "Jimmy" OK.

OK Blue Mosque. "CABLE BLUE MOSQUE"

This is whew from the capital of India where no man is molesting me during Prohibition. I forgot my little paper at the airport, paper says that I out of all these millions can have a spirit drink. I was so hungry so thirsty leaving the Muslim world these women coming at me in their black shrouds with their eyes on me their eyes of lust for not taking the shroud off keeping the shroud on reminds me of a friend of my mother's (this is somewhere in the Thirties) who would go around naked in her fur coat and expose herself in expensive restaurants. Was thinking of the lewd men of the Muslim world and their past beauty putting eyes on me. He grabs me in Tabriz. Another on Sizdeh Bedar April 2 my birthday wrings my hand. Then another touches my thigh ever so subtly. This is the day 13 days after the new year when it's unlucky to stay inside until after sunset. My lover and I make love in the Arm Strong Hotel, collapse into separate beds until sunset, go out braving the Muslim world.

I am not what I seem. I leave him on the corner of Ferdowski near the buses to Mashhad. I get in an orange taxi with a flat tire. Then a German enters the car and says "It is yours, Madam" 150 rials away from the airport from the lover 10 kilometers to the airport. Please note I am traveling alone visa here good till August. My No. is J193934 I have no passport for 12 hours please note if you are getting this wire. OK

BLUE MOSQUE OK

And after that and after that and after that and after that and after that and after that and after that and after that there's a little man from Malaysia who takes pity on me I am very hungry I am very thirsty he is western medicine man assures me there's sure to be a "snatch" on the plane. Then he buys me a beer (my last for 2 months) and miraculously produces a sandwich from a paper bag. My hotel stationary says "Cable: Manhood". Going on in a Muslim world.

OK BLUE MOSQUE

Then 2 Armenians one born in Russia find us on Pahlavi Avenue after eating the best chicken kebob in the world and say We knew you were Christians. We saw you, we knew you were Christians. We go home collapse into separate beds. Sizdeh Bedar. I am always asking about the massacre of Tabriz and the Marxist Muslims. You will notice most of them are waving it aside. Ah yes, the German says, I think the woman or something got some of what do you call it thrown in her face in the bazaar for baring her face for showing her face for having a face. You mustn't go there without your shroud. At Hatam the best meal in town is being served separately to women in chadors and children while the men sit 2 booths away. This is Tehran worse than Chile. But 2000 Marxists murdered in Tabriz where are they buried? Please note the beautiful stretch of land, Biblical, perhaps you find it here. Weep o weep children of the desert. Please note this wires me this wires me & no drinking in India. You are noting please, however, that liquor may be purchased duty free at the borders and cigarettes from Kathmandu only $4 a box—$12 for us Indians, could you bring me some please Madam?

I have been walking in circles on Connaught Place and before that and before that and before that and before that and before that I have been walking in circles and a long waiting period when I watched the women with their little ankle strap tall highheel pumps beneath shrouds. Black satin and patent leather and tough shaped painted eyebrows lifting in a Muslim world. And the little girls with dark blue scarves like peasants and they are so old already I was wondering it all in rials. "Khaheash-mi-Konam," I want to understand please. Pardon sorry, "Bebakshid." And before that and before that and before that Cable Blue Mosque to the young men recruited for the army and the eyes of the boy on the Bosphorus whose eyes are they? You said whose eyes are they? They are a woman's eyes. Deep pools of women eyes, black and huge I am sinking into. The young boys crowd around my young friend in his black Turkish beret. You are American? French? English? Leather? Cheap bus? Hasheesh? Change money?

"CABLE BLUE MOSQUE"

Paula's a real cockney. Note she's working at Naval Academy Tehran, for 12 thousand dollars a year expects to pack it in when she's got it together to buy a house in Holland or England. There are brawny Yugoslavs on Mihan buses seeking work. Everyone to work and making money making money. It is possible. Scent of blood. I've been out of the Muslim world 30 hours now and the shrouds are haunting me. I am going to get me one of them. Pizza Cowboys is probably not the best place to eat in Tehran but Paprika's got a nice name. Receive this wire please from not what I seem: American now wearing cowboy shirt, light green corduroy pants, gold belt and Chinese slippers. I stepped outside to observe the birds at sunset 2 days after Bedar day in a hotel cable "Manhood." The birds are whirling like Sufis so excited by the bloom in the magenta bush outside my window. Tehran is one of the higher cities in the world (at Mehrabad Airport 3,931 feet above sea level and northward at Darband suburb rises to almost 6,000 feet) but I have come down whew landed in India tropical sorta leaving the Muslim world. J193934 please to return to me I am nothing without my number pass. Ah, the German says, it is ok here. I do my work and though I can't read the numbers on the meters I can understand when they are saying it.

I am in Interior Decorating. I'm handsome German man with silk cravat, wavy blond hair, but Tabriz . . . . (waves his hand). Paula: but everyone's scared shit you know they don't even know what's going on, the papers are so censored got a friend who's told what to write, you know how it is. Yeah official number was 300 massacred in Tabriz in February but it's more like 2000 (gives a laugh) . . .

Cable me rupees. Cable me instructions. Cable me Blue Mosque. Gate 4 Home Office says it takes 6 weeks for permit to Sikkim and Bhutan. The monkeys seem to be laughing. Fill out this form please and for 2 photos I go to T. Pall on Connaught and there are 6 photos now of a barefaced woman. I have black shoes. I have a black shawl getting on and off train Venice, Belgrade, Sofia, Istanbul.

We arrived at 10 am. I could see the city across the water under a pretty dusty gold haze, and the delicate minarets to Allah's heaven. Bernard Fountain was getting off first class section just as we stopped to change money in a little kiosk by the train. You are French? I asked. You have been here before? Yes, nine years ago. Where do you suggest we stay? O the area around the Blue Mosque, the pudding shops. Very good and cheap. Cheap food. We walked further to a little tourist information bureau.

Change money? Kabul? Cheap Taxi? Cheap Hotel? all around us, chorusing. Fountain is delicate with little mustache. My friend passport No. H 3035357 is not keeping his eye on striped bag from Kalimpong trip Giorno Brownstein 1973 and Fountain says But here, you must watch this. Very dangerous. You have something stealing. He says with heed to heed all men no women all around us. We go to Blue Mosque pudding shops to Gungor Hotel name meaning I never knew. Persian blue wall in room, 80 lire cheap and cheap and noisy and we are not hippies says my friend. We move next day to the Hotel Ediz 280 lire hot water for twenty minutes. We are up where we can see a bit of the Bosphorus and sky and gulls. We eat cheap pudding shop kebob and salad and beer and visit Blue Mosque but first we visit Blue Mosque. We kill Christians in my head.

Note the graceful cascade of domes and semi-domes and the six slender minarets. This is the mosque of Sultan Ahmet I. Note instead of tympanic arches to north and south there are 2 more semi-domes making a quatrefoil design. See the mihrab which indicates the kible and the mimber (it's quite tall! and observe the narrow steps!) where the iman sits. A muezzin drones at 6 o'clock. The mosque is flooded with light from its 260 windows. It is very blue. Note the iznik tiles, some of the finest with their designs of flowers. The fabulous Kosem, wife of Sultan Ahmet, is buried here. There are hints and mumurs from all quarters.

OK BLUE MOSQUE

So three days later (after Easter on the Bosphorus, not a glimpse of Easter in a Muslim world, we kill all Christians) we meet Bernard Fountain at the bus station down from the Blue Mosque. We're all waiting for the same bus from the shady men I was remembering the lewd men of the Muslim world and their past beauty eyes on me when the bus never comes. Some say she's a bit run down at the heels, but ah, Stamboul, what memories! We go eat stuffed mussels from the Bosphorus and Fountain says: "You know it's funny how I warned you to be so careful when I should have been the one. This guy comes right up to me right as I'm leaving the station and maybe I'm a little sleepy from the train all the way from Paris but right away he says you want to change money to rupees I know a really good deal with a friend of mine and since I know I'll want to stay in India a long time I'm thinking it's a good idea. He says how much and I am thinking 200 dollars I am traveling with dollars and he says you must do this: He picks up a paper bag off the street. You must put your money in a paper bag and then give it to the guy and he'll give you your bag with the rupees. He demonstrates by putting my money in the bag and slipping it into his pocket and then hands it right back to me. Now I'll go get my friend. I'll meet you in that pudding shop. I sat and waited and had a tea and he wasn't coming and I thought that's strange and I was thinking something was wrong. Then I opened the bag and there were pieces of torn paper inside. He was a fast one. Said he lived in a camper outside of town with his Austrian wife."

Note now Fountain is $200 less in Afghanistan. We said goodbye at the border when we were turned back by the scarey uniformed men strutting around in their Muslim world, lifesize photos of the Shah as ruler of the universe. "Nix Barf" meaning no snow, said the Persian driver of the Mac truck and "Turkish, phew!" And after that and after that and after that and after that a Fundamentalist points to Mt. Ararat says, "There's a big ship up there."

And my lover, too, still with the men on the buses who were always coming to squat by my side with their lewd looks. And somewhere I saw a woman smile.

OK "CABLE BLUE MOSQUE"

Many lifetimes speaking and these are the elements of the 83-ship plan from the Western world for fiscal 1979 through 1983 (note: passport expires January 17, 1983):

New surface warships. One conventionally powered carrier to be funded in fiscal 1980; one nuclear cruiser funded in fiscal 1983; seven DDG-47 destroyers; 26 FFG-7 patrol frigates. Modernization of surface warships. Two Forrestal class carriers; 10 DDG-2 destroyers. Nuclear submarines. Six Trident Missile Boats and five SSN-688 attack submarines. Amphibious ships. One LSD-41 to be funded in fiscal 1981 and a second in fiscal 1983. The Marine Corps sought more. Ant submar and port ships Twelve Tagos ocean surveill hips one oiler; seagoing tugs one able repair one converted argo. .... Trails off here ...

I have been out of the Muslim world out of the Western world out of the Christian world I have been out of the world 48 hours. Many lifetimes. I saw a woman smile. Then three pilots and Airport Control Tower Staff saw 20 Unidentified Flying Objects which were 20 times larger than a jumbo jet. Note: Pilots of domestic aircraft Mohammad Birami and Hassan Belaghi then reported seeing numbers of distant objects "flying over our heads." A second UFO report came from an Air France pilot at 40,000 which claimed that bright objects moving very fast between Shiraz and Isfahan were causing atmospheric disturbances. There are hints and murmurs from all quarters. And an unidentified flying pilot aboard his aircraft says he saw and exchanged signals with glittering bodies poised above him. When he switched on his front lights the UFO did the same using a strong type of ray which could have been an exchange or a warning. Also please remember to note that in September 1976 the pilots of two Imperial Iranian air force jet fighters contacted the Mehrabad control tower saying they saw an object half the size of the moon as seen from the earth, radiating violet, orange and white light about three times as strong as moonlight. A man held his strong field glasses on his hotel balcony and saw a UFO emitting blue and red lights. Some say the thing chased them before rejoining the mother craft and flying away many many times the speed of sound.

> put in:
> commodities
> put in new-found seas
> put in courtesy & wit
> put in groveling wit
> put in symmetry
> put in coffin cords & a bell
> put in extreme breathing
> put in a cosmic image
> put in a feminine image
> put in politics, brass-tacks level
> put in how he was in love with Turkish eyes
> put in is this machine recording
> put in like footprints of the bird on the sky
> put in lifting arms embargo
> put in when you are cherished
> put in still a little bit up in the air

"CABLE BLUE MOSQUE. CABLE INSTRUCTIONS. KEEP THE SHROUD OF THEIR PAST BEAUTY EYES ON ME. CABLE MANHOOD. CABLE RUPEES."

Note: Joachim X. German of Vancouver Canada traveling abroad a year as a self-proclaimed Evangelist said, pointing to Mt. Ararat its top shrouded in clouds, "You know, there's a big ship up there."

"CABLE INSTRUCTIONS DATA PAULA FOUNTAIN SHAH TWO CHRISTIAN ARMENIAN PERSIAN TRUCK DRIVER LOVER JOACHIM X. "JIMMY" CHINESE MEDICINE HINDU PETE GERMAN (WAVES IT ASIDE)"

The ribs of Noah's arc are covered with black pitch and locked in the snow. I follow the Bible, J. said, that is my guide book. I will go down to the Caspian Sea.

Note: Nineteen year old Reza Bazargani took a stroll in the woods near Chalus on the 13th day, birthday Sizdeh Bedar and claims to have been "whisked away." "I saw the thing emerge from the sky and stop directly above me. I was unable to move as four space beings came out of the space ship and took me inside. The next thing I remember is I woke up back on earth in the morning, not in the lush Caspian forests but near Isfahan."

Dear Control: I am not what I seem. Cable my womanhood. Cable a black shroud emitting blue and red lights. The monkeys seem to be laughing. There are hints and murmurs from all quarters. I am not what I seem Ascendant Leo 4 degrees prose speaking leaving the Muslim leaving the Western world. I am not what I seem J193934 from capital city. But "CABLE BLUE MOSQUE," delicate minarets lifting to Allah's blue heaven.

I will go down to the Caspian Sea and weep for the slaughtered of Iran. When I return to the Harem quarters the black eunuchs will bathe me.

New Delhi
April 1978

II.   Collaboration/Spectacle

from *The Wide Road*

CARLA HARRYMAN AND LYN HEJINIAN

Held in the hands, the penis is heavy or useless. One might say, also, "Although held in the hands, the dick is light or useful." We think this while reading the copy on the back of a cereal box at breakfast. The streetlights are off and the finches make themselves known. Dim-witted, we glow a little in the musty heat lingering along the insides of our arms.

Elsewhere keeps the chill off.

Our neck and shoulders are still relaxed while the newspaper says in China children riot. The finches carry a potential of an unremitting noise from elsewhere in their garrulous song into our languorous hearts and irrepressibly loose thoughts. We have been told that the rich and powerful are equally dull and uninspired. We are in the comfort of disinspiration, contained by the opening day.

> the wind is
> Mono's voice
> that big words wind

We reach our chair to rest our arms, with assymetrical breasts and our vagina far away.

Last night's dream of a vernal (green) penis might be taken as a prediction of rain and the end of winter. We don't know. Our vagina is approaching but it is still far away.

There's so much to do.

We cannot find ourselves asleep on our side, only awake there, taken from the receptive continuity of a dream—sex with someone and solicitude for a younger man—this is a dream about birdwatching—and we get out of bed, pushing up from the pillow with the right arm, the skin of our arm still impressed with the weight of our having slept, both feet on the floor—no rug just there, only wooden slats about two inches wide and decoratively mismatched. We are round.

The room is still blind.

We brush our teeth—selecting our toothbrush is automatic—it isn't property but person.

The mouth held open, the green toothbrush reading the teeth from left to right.

The activities of the Marquis de Sade either exceed or close over the boundaries of our person. We either discontinue or continue. But in every case we've been damaged by the horror.

We appeal to our daily life, which is persistently abnormal but adorable (we are slaves to it), to provide us with the authority of our anti-authority—or should we say anti-authoritative maternity?

It is still morning. From another room we hear a man zipping his pants. We see a big dog setting the pace for another woman walking it, while the sound of a police helicopter hangs overhead, supposing that some crime can be concluded.

If subliminal means meaning that's hidden, can we say surliminal to speak of meaning exposed?

In the kitchen, where the floor meets the wall, crumbs accumulate—they get greasy—we are irritated, overwrought. We can't throw anything away.

We fill the blue and white striped coffee cup with the stained interior and return to the office chair.

The bourgeois interest is alone.

Paradise is a damaged situation.

We think—we write: we eroticize our earthly situations and conditions and likewise they eroticize us.

So we've been both the subject and the object of desire and the origin and recipient of pleasure on many occasions.

But daily life is a very ambivalent agent of desire—perhaps that's what makes it so compelling as an agent of writing. The oscillation between interior and exterior of what seem to be the contents of our experiences makes our daily life simultaneously expressive of Us and of Not-us.

We are thinking about both mitigated and unmitigated sex.

> without hiding
> we are hidden
> though monuments
> explode an interior

"A word is the purest and most sensitive medium of social intercourse," we bark. Like selves equated to distant beings, our shadows exchange fists in the parking lot. A poised fist is not sexual in its potential to select a surface, but I, a word our shadows have wandered away from, unnerves a passerby.

In its own uplifting splash, the I continues its rap, intervenes with the fist, counts out, while we, diffuse and borrowed, walk into the bank building and undress a pot that houses a more permanent resident, a nicely dwarfed palm, one of many nicely dwarfed palms manicured in rows next to the rows of elevators.

The elevators slide through the interior of the building while we write a letter to Mono. Dear Mono. Command. Command. If there is no obedience there is no privacy. After signing the letter

> we are caught
> making love
> in the pot

"Are you talking to yourself as you do that?" asked the woman. She had come into the corridor near the elevator shafts with a companion, a man. We had set aside the soft palm frond with which we had engaged in almost unbearable tickling, and we were still muzzy with desire, so that, though on the one hand the arrival of this couple in the corridor might offer us a new pleasure, that of being seen, they had in fact interrupted our lovemaking. It was difficult, in any case, to turn our attention to her question enough to understand it. What is she really asking us? we asked ourselves.

"Do you engage in what Clark Coolidge calls subvocalization?" asked the man. "Like when you read a book of poetry and sort of hear the words in your head even though you aren't intentionally sounding them out?"

"Yes, do you?" asked the woman. "With something that has a story in it, too, or contains a fragment of a narrative. Like, when I'm having sex, it's like I'm having a story. I hear things like, 'She spread her legs as he softly ran his tongue across her vagina.'"

"The third person!" we exclaimed.

> the voice is blue
> her kiss shines
> this is wonderful
> and window

The differences between sound and sight are semantically inessential—at least this seems to be true of literary experience. But the third person was asking about sound and the senses in an extra-literary experience, involving the tender but erect tip of a palm frond, the tongue, the genitals, and ourselves—all of which we took to her room, where the curtains were still drawn across the window.

Sometimes we accept the enormous situation of the subject-object, wherein we exhibit (but I could say *embrace*) some of our capacities.

"For you, then," said the man, "it isn't about oblivion? There is no privacy?"

> praises
> praises
> porosity

Palaver eros. Token eros. Palaver eros. Token eros. We chant to ourselves crossing our twelve limbs with our new friend, the third person, in her room. This is private to him who can neither see nor hear us on the other side of the door but public to you who are always up to the minute on our every change of tune and crossing. We use our chant, token eros, palaver eros, token eros, palaver eros as protection from The Whimsical Male Sexual Appetite (you can find this term in our favorite whodunit, Chapter 15). The Whimsical Male Sexual Appetite, as anybody probably already knows, often manifests itself in the guise of intellectual curiosity (as in the question "there is no privacy?" posed to us earlier), which peaks quickly ("you are the most fantastic thing on earth" when we haven't even had a chance to take off our party masks and untie our shoelaces) and is quickly overcome by fatigue. The bogus intellectual curiosity is never satisfied and our answer remains secreted behind our party masks or other unserious disguises in the nether realm of privacy. Which of course would not exist if the WMSA did not conceal its true interests behind an apathetic intellectual curiosity. However, this is a mean digression. For we have ways around the WMSA and one of those ways is our little chant, which defends us well, yes yes, while also arousing our own whims to whimsical attention as we lock arms and legs in sitting squatting lying and standing positions.

"Please feel free to question us on our side of the keyhole," we say to the man on the other side of the door asking us about there being no privacy, "but first you must get through it."

> though it prods the air
> with tiny amps
> to baffle the instrument

(While we wait for him to work or slither or prod or whisper or wish his way through, let us take you on a little journey out onto the street where we pass first a girl walking like a confetti boy whirling on a skateboard in a slump with her ears plugged into the radio. And we say she is not us. While we say this a radio from a passing car says in a song, "I am glad I'm not Bob Dylan and Bob Dylan is glad he's not me." But before we can ask why, an Egyptian woman passes us in sandals. It's the dead of winter, the trees bare, the air chill, and her feet walk on invisible pillows. But how do we know she's Egyptian? It's what the Eastern European woman with the thick skin, which she prizes above all her other magnificent physical attributes, told us in the Sauna and we believed the story teller. And we say as a lumbering man passes, she is not us, or he. The more we say she is not us or he is not us the more a peculiar sensation of not belonging grows in us: of being child-less with children, of being companionless with friends, of being loveless with lovers, of our bodies flooded with desire but repulsed by all possible objects of desire. We see a girl wrap her arm around her mother and we feel sickened by biology. . . .)

Inside, where light is a distant lesson, where time is an inch of crushed clouds, where sponges select their cosmogony, where deltas spawn sage pudding, where an upheaval of leaves fumbles the senses, we dictate porosity.

> patched prose
> turns to holes

Or was it holes turning to prose?

Finally, the man surges through the keyhole—oily and bruised (but fit enough)—onto our bosom so's we can get a few inches of wisdom from the fact of his vulnerably public open palm. It, the palm, strokes our mask, swelling with story, the inventor of privacy. We tell him, if you want our mask, we get your story. "I'll give it to you in exchange for something hot to drink," he says.

> our bodies quiver
> with angelic resolve

He sipped, we removed our mask. It was the old story, the revolutionary one. In fact, at any given moment, a woman knows exactly what she wants.

But "you too," we said to the third person as the man ran his tongue around the rim of the warm cup around which he'd curled both his hands, "you too" (the man was or wasn't listening, but we couldn't be more interesting)—"you too probably remember that time in late girlhood, that period of wiggling and lethargy, when you thought that the pressure within—the swelling inside your skull—was from something you didn't know. We know that we thought then that ignorance (increasing daily, since every experience added to it) was our Freudian destiny, part of the great triad of determinisms" (the man finished his drink and put down the cup), "along with the Darwinian one that had shaped your inadvertent and obsequious cruelty while giving you a desire for men, and the Marxian one" (the man moved as if to stand up, but with all our hands we pushed him back down and held him there) "that said you'd go down in history."

"Both Darwin and Freud say you'd go down for men," the man said.

"Palaver eros," we answered. "Go to bed."

It was a Monday of voluptuous stammerings, then a Tuesday without resolve.

> a fantastic privacy often manifest
> in us it is excited

One can see that from a certain point of view, a woman when it comes to sex is always on the outside.

But do you think that's what it's like to be a cup?

To what that are we referring, to what what, to what it?

There is a languid eros within a language eros.

As we'd lain, subject to the palm frond, subject-object to an eternal scene, outside the snow—now tinted red and blue by the setting sun and the scattered streetlights—was drifting, the sidewalks had turned icy, a slush was forming on the city's little river, and we dressed to go down to the narrow park, across which we would walk to the shops. The very young Latvian was tender as we took his arm, covering our bare fingers in the wool of his heavy coat. "When I was a very small child," he said, hunching his shoulders to lift the collar of his coat higher around his neck, "so little that I couldn't reach to hold onto anything to keep from falling in the bus, it was my greatest pleasure in life to wait in the morning for a very crowded bus, and then to enter it and find a place where many large women were riding crowded together in the aisle, and squeeze myself between them, against their warm coats and bodies—and then I would slowly fall asleep."

What is it that brings these women to city parks in the cold to feed the ducks? We ourselves love to feed ducks. More and more of them coming to what we offer. Throwing the bread, in our privacy we forget everything. We can never satisfy them.

> neither willing
> nor unwilling
> no departure
> in another hour

from *Sex and Other Sacred Games*

KIM CHERNIN AND RENATE STENDHAL

Sex and Other Sacred Games is a collaborative text composed of fictional and theoretical elements. Modeled in part on Plato's dialogues between Socrates and Phaedrus on eros and beauty, Chernin and Stendhal intended their characters, Claire Heller and Alma Runau, to become a framing device for an extended discourse on female sexuality. In practice, however, the characters appropriated the text when, as Kim Chernin says, "they became interested in one another." In this case, the materials of the novel began to usurp the structure of philosophical debate. "Sexual ideas," writes Chernin, "must remain close to the body if they are to carry conviction. In this most literal sense of the word, they must be fully embodied." And yet, as Chernin cautions, it would be a mistake to read this book as pure fiction. It is a conversation—current, visceral, unfinished. It is, in essence, a sexual exchange.

The frame story is simple enough. Claire Heller (Kim Chernin) and Alma Runau (Renate Stendhal), strangers sharing a table at a Paris cafe, begin a conversation in which each woman becomes the cultural "other," a type of woman with whom they each disagree on principle. Claire Heller, an American novelist and a heterosexual, argues that sexual power is, by definition, female, the legacy of the Mother who is simultaneously the creatrix and the destroyer. The femme fatale is one incarnation of the Goddess; she masks her power in order to protect men from their own ineffectuality. Alma Runau, a lesbian feminist, states that mythic femininity is a dangerous construct. Women, she says, are only beginning to uncover their sexual power. In order to do so, they must come to terms with the Mother, whose smothering kindness overwhelms the difference and the detachment so necessary to sexual tension between women. The text charts their friendship over time through chapters written alternately by Chernin and Stendhal.

Kim Chernin:

Claire's Eighth Letter

I imagine you recognize: the practice of magic. To make crops grow, earth fertile, keep the world sap flowing. It is hard, I know, to know it as worship. We, who do not inhabit the flesh, take possession over the body, regard it as property: my hand, your skin, his lips, her belly, their sex, cannot easily understand. To worship, with the body; find sacred, not only flesh, but its behavior; to know this longing to be inhabited, seized, possessed by the goddess. To call that desire. And surrender, that awe-filled giving over to the world's necessity. Do you understand it? Perhaps you, more easily than I?

The old women, nighttime, in the walled garden. They told us: All who worship, who serve, perform the sacred sexual act, carry between hands, lips, thighs, the earth's fertility. We were all, they said, Aphrodite, and the boy. The eagle sowing its nest. The barley sprouting. The south wind gathering pollen. The snake endowing itself. The egg flowering.

There are things, impossible to tell if the other does not already understand. That is the fear. To give the best-kept secrets. What if, lying beside you on the grass, next to a garden overgrown upon itself, near a house with eyes, one reached out to trust another, and found the distance between you so large the one lying beside seemed to grow steadily beyond reach of your fingers?

What would happen, I ask, if we, too, understood sex as world necessity? Fundamental, magical act? Without which, and the hands that have made their way to your breast, the lips that open you, fingers that search out your pleasure, there would be weariness, withering, parching, dying back among things? The rose parched on its trellis, the geranium dying in the garden, swallow unmoving below the eaves.

If we, too, falling to bed, believed that from this sweat that flowers between us, the cornfield prospered? From the juice that spurts, the mouth that receives, the womb that quickens, far from us, in swamps, in deserts, what must live and be born is brought to conception?

I want to tell you. More than anything else. About this boy. His melancholy, the distance between him and others. He came to live with us, in the women's quarters, behind the sanctuary. Or perhaps, had been there already? Long before?

Mornings, I would see him, before the others had wakened, near the stone wall. Trying to turn himself to stone. Or to flower. I saw him, at midday, watching the snakes cross the compound. Trying to shed himself, learn to slither? Others spoke, called out to him, repeated his name: he was far, they might have crossed a world to reach him. Stretched out their hand, found him. Still, beyond their fingers.

I go to him; at the first touch he is aroused, wakened. Has come to life, is rooted, pinned back to us. Have I been given for this, to keep him here, preserve him? The old women, they say: Touch is the sacred.

Yes, I know: it can't be easy. We, who use sex in the vain hope to get back to the body, long for the terror, the torment of desire, imagine passion as alien intrusion. What can we make of this people? These, whose sacred forms embrace the flesh?

The story we tell; our tedious tale of forbidden desires places itself against culture. The woman who falls because of desire. Marries the carpenter, runs off with the gypsy. The man haunted by a fallen woman. The child born out of wedlock, nameless. The nobleman who murders another man's child, driven to destroy his wife's transgression. Women of the streets, the sad men who buy them.

Modern statement of the old theme. The husband's folly takes a mistress. The woman runs off to Paris. Another, tracked down by her husband. Man dies on the beach for love of a boy.

Our secrecy. The locked doors, dismal hotel rooms, ornate palaces of black-sheet pleasure. Eyes closed, lowered, shame of the flesh. The terrible streets of our transgressions. Belligerent assertions of freedom, sexual cruelty, desolate liberations.

He is young. How young? Unbearded. Since then I have imagined: this boy longed to follow the god. Be cut down in the cornfields. Escape the senses. The body not yet fully developed. Dennie, as he might have been if he'd grown older. Was it for that? To keep him alive, to make up for my brother? He throws himself down. Disappears in the grass. For now, he is slender. The hair on his arms, the sun turning it high-red, golden.

A question of touch. How to reach him. It is a matter of urgency. Perhaps, among them, none would have felt it but I? As if I, who had set out to live the life of the body, was growing finally into a body. As a child might. Drop by drop, that time, the blood-juice of pomegranate on my lips. And now, in return, owed the favor to him?

If that was sex (the slow ride into the mountains; the silence, the shadows that climbed the path before us, the heavy air beneath the tree), what was the other? In the parked car, in the streets, in the closed rooms, with the others?

What we call sex: the itch that cannot be stilled, the melancholy violence, that shame that comes after, the haunting loneliness that drops the lovers, beaches them, in their solitary plot of rock and dryness. Later, I understood what they had been trying to teach me. In the walled gardens, behind the sanctuary, the year, ripening upward, toward spring.

That first winter, learning to grow back into my senses. I was placed at the wall, sat there unmoving. Dawn, dusk, I heard the stones growing. I touched him; the boy, the man-mother of the mountains. He grew small, curled into me, made a nest of my limbs. Mornings, we wet the stones of the compound. Dripped oil, the water of almonds. The boy, close at my side, kept an eye on me. I heard the stones breathing.

The woman, she took my hand as we crossed the fields. In time, I, too, was invited. To offer my blood. I witnessed: the first shoot, the sprouting barley, the golden flax. She pointed, named them. I saw: they were I.

Since then, I have wondered. The obsessions that drive us, our lust: is it for this? To fall back into our hands, grow back out of the grass, be turned to earth and planted? Violent, we call that desire. Because we cannot make fruit grow from our passion? My breasts, they turned green. Oozed, split open. He sucked, his lips groping their way back to me, tasting of fig.

So what, you say?

I sense it. The way you stand up from the bench in the garden. Throw down the pages you are reading. Grow furious, take a few steps toward the gate, as if you imagine it would still be possible to go after me, call me back, sit me down opposite you in a café somewhere, make me listen.

When a man goes to bed with a woman, you say: does he allow her to lay him . . . in a bed of leaves? Suppose even: our culture built on the loss, the denial, the hidden quest for this mystery. Does that bring her to life? Restore her? He has jumped out from behind the wall. Has spread her beneath him. His hands on her throat. Does it matter, you ask, if he looks for the body's magical potency, its sacredness?

Shall we argue again? Shall I, in turn, grow wild, impatient? Get to my feet, crumple the paper, toss it aside?

The uses and abuses of theory. Isn't that what we wished to explore, examine? An exchange of letters, we said: laying back skin to reach the essential, the hidden.

And why is it I cannot tell what I know? The meaning, for instance, of this traffic. Between the men's quarters and the women's? Haven't you wondered?

In time, the timelessness ebbing, my senses clearing, I saw: the old question of gender. This careful division we make, at all costs preserve. They had undone it; bearded the women, given breasts to the men. The boy, living among us, must have been taught. To take the role of mother, assume its activity, assertion. To make use of his sex: to feed, to nurture.

Each time, entering me, the mountains our cradle, night folded on us: it was he who was woman. I, the child. So that in time I learned. That is what men seek in the sexual act. It is the role of mother they wish to assume, to master.

We look closer: the active and passive. The rules of gender. We place them in nature, insist the roles are there in our genes. Could it be: the two genders, they are always only mother and child?

The man: he who initiates. He determines the act. What does that mean? He takes her. In his arms. Sweeps her, off her feet. Carries her, to the bed.

Does, what mothers are always doing?

The question of gender: do I mean, it is hiding the old story of mother and child?

The old questions. We lift them, hold them before our eyes, turn them a new way, see them differently. A missing plane, neglected facet. The way gender hides truth; how sexual role disguises the real meaning of sexual desire; the way we have made instinct of lost memory, have attributed to the urgency of the flesh our unwept sorrows. The man, driven. To take woman. Longs, secretly, to play mother, to feed her?

You protest. Take up a pencil, mark the page.

Among us, you say: the woman, she who gives herself. She hands herself over to his need, takes care, lets him take pleasure, make use of her body. Surely, you say: that is what it means to be mother?

So, we dispute. As we have done, from first meeting. Will do, I am certain, the next time we meet.

You, are you unable to imagine the mother's assertion? You, too, must have known it. Fed when you were not hungry, filled when your mouth had not yet opened, broken into by that transgression, her uninvited crossing of boundary. Made one with her, when you wished to be one with yourself. Held captive. Delivered up to her rhythm. Overpowered by her need to fondle, to touch, to hold, to join. The fear of her thrust; that horror you cannot recall. The dread, primal: the breast penetrating, forcing entry, colonizing, possessing.

Have you imagined phallic, what was once, originally, the breast's power of intrusion? Have you imagined it all as fear, of him? Fear of man, the active gender, he who thrusts, you say: breaks into, enters?

The mother you imagine: helpless, subdued, subordinate being. The father you create: the phallic bully. Have you given to him her transgressive power?

And therefore you cannot imagine the man's longing to feed you, in the sexual act. And therefore, cannot conceive: the man-mother, who feeds.

The time came, it was inevitable; I was sent to live with the men. Was dressed in their clothes: the short robes, heavy sandals. Was taught to wrestle, to hunt, dance, run wild: up into the mountains, after the wild goats, leaping from the rocks, tumbling down through grass meadows.

The old men, at night they sat by our bed. They told how the world had been made. Delivered up out of the one who had made herself. From rain and from dust. And she was alone, lonely; from her thighs, she made mountains; from her wetness, desiring herself, made seas. Trees grew from her tresses. When she sang, when she danced, when she walked, lonely in her nakedness: she spit on the earth. There were birds; the serpent biting its tail, the egg conceiving itself.

They told: their dread of that one who had made others. Her magnificence. The size of her, larger even than the world she made. Can you imagine?

I, in time, began to remember. Memory, they said, was the meaning of flesh. In time, I began to recall. They called that the body.

Claire's Ninth Letter

It began with the senses. The itch of palms, longing to touch her. The ache of lips to enclose her. The way flesh crawls. The dread: to be crushed, annihilated by her. To drown, in the outpouring of her. Burst with her fullness, discharged into me. To be torn, broken. By her entry.

The old man, he who had once played the god, held me against him. He, who had known and endured her, knew how to become her. To soften his splendor, temper the power of his overpowering, fill, feed, enfold, fondle.

In the walled gardens, behind the sanctuary. Was that their mystery?

I, who have never been able to sleep. Wake, climb from the bed. Read, write letters. Tell myself stories. It was so, in the shack near the alley. On the long road, parched with desire. The old man: wets my lips. Closes my eyes.

His touch. Can I describe it? Fingers breathing. The way skin weeps, tells its story. The infant terror, waking in darkness. He is there, his hand, on my head. I remember Geoffrey, the skin erupted. Dennie, the shack in the garden. Stories, how they never managed to fill, feed, enfold, fondle. He is there, his touch carries fragrance. Wind enters, through the tall grass, moves through the window.

Do I mean: remembering the mother . . . he had no need to inflict her?

I admit: I had not seen it before.

Man: driven to inflict on woman what he has endured from the mother? His fear of her size, her overpowering, her breaking into. What he calls sex, the urge that drives him to take a woman: impelled by this need? To make her suffer what he has suffered, and cannot allow himself to recall?

I admit: I had not seen it before.

And therefore, he cannot: soothe, gentle, caress. Soften the distance between them. Cannot remember this oldest way to restore union, gently placing part of his body in hers. Is that what they had to teach, in the walled gardens, a mile from the sea?

I, too, I have wondered; then, since then, still now, writing to you.

Then, I did what I was instructed to do. There came a time, difficult to locate in time, when I met the boy again on the mountains. This time, children together, growing older. We were sent out to herd goats, slept in the mountain pastures, covered ourselves with skins. Fed ourselves with souring milk left to curdle in an earthenware bowl, beneath juniper bushes.

As if, the two of us, we had to do it all over again. Go back to that time, we call it innocence: before loss of the body, its easy knowledge of pleasure.

The nights, cold; mornings we woke covered in dew. I had the impression: he, who had been chosen, had played the god, had known the mother, had missed a step, couldn't go forward. Had been intended to take the place of the man. The old one who touched, told stories, sat by the bed, guided the others.

With me, he was learning, all over again. To play. Race after the goats, dragging me with him. We bathed in the rivers, charging up through falling water. As if the sacred rites, they depended on this. Each of us, learning to play the roles of the sexual act, to be mother or child, woman or man, must begin again with the senses.

What was wrong with the boy?

I had the impression: he yearned to live apart from his body. More extreme than others, had drifted farther away. Could not tell with his body the god's story of willing surrender, in service to nature. Was unable to enter the life of the mountains.

Night, he slips through my fingers; adrift in darkness, he is digging stars. Looks down at me, from frozen absence. I tie the goatskin around us. Afraid he will die of cold. Be washed down rivers. Never return in his boat of bark.

It is again, the shack near the alley? Two children, skin weeping, unable to tell, unable to sleep. It is again the boy I married?

There came a time, inevitable, when I was sent back to the women. Then, for a time, lost track of the boy. Perhaps, with other boys, he kept to his games in the mountains. Learning to dig himself back into kinship. With goats and rain, the ripening of cheese, the fermenting of berries. Had I failed to learn what they expected? Must now be given to somebody else to be taught?

An old woman, impossible to guess at her age. Stooped, withered, stiff, toothless. She had her tasks: watering sage, the dense, green unflowering basil, picking flowers. Mornings, she sweeps the courtyard, gathers branches, burns them along paths outside the compound. I work with her.

What the boy had taught: to name the carob, the holm oak, suck the pomegranate, useless here. The old woman, her method was different.

In time, I had the impression: she was special to them. One among many. Understood, from her stillness, watching the fires, she had a story. Must have been young once; taken a boy between thighs, the drums beating, flutes wailing. There was something about her. Slowly imparted. Perhaps, in her youth, this role, this enactment of goddess, of mother, had been repeated? One year following another? The boy, always another. The woman, always the same?

With her, I was boy-child. Ran out to fetch and carry: the almond water, the oil. Tended the doves, bathed, fed them. Late evenings: the beating of wings over the compound. She looks up, fixes them with her gaze, raises a finger. The others fly off, into the mountains. The white birds return.

She smells of old stone; tastes of flint. Her breast bone-hard, it is barren ground. This oldest fear: the mother runs dry, is exhausted. Can I endure her? She lies down at my side. Will she survive?

Have I spoken of cold? How she is not there in her flesh. Has gone underground, is covered in ice. How my body retreats from itself, cannot touch, grope, feel, reach her. How it abandons itself, grows vacant.

She touches my forehead. I know for the first time, fully. The way skin builds a shell for itself, scabs over. To keep her out. The body's retreat behind sinew. To deny her. The bulging of muscular will. To fight off the wish of her.

She wants me to touch her. The longing of cold to be melted. I touch. Far off, the arousal of waters. She is young again; black hair oiled, curled over her shoulders. My lips at her. The small green drives upward, under my breath. I feel the weight of her hands on my back. My youth enters, makes its way through her, drives sap.

She branches, bends over. I sense: we have reached the secret, the mystery's core. The woman's burden, never spoken: he, who casts seed, will never know birth. Can I describe it, her pity? What else can it be called? This sorrow that melts her. He cannot breed; he, who makes fertile, cannot carry it through. He plants, he cannot conceive. She gathers him up, puts him against her. To console. This grief, unfairness of nature. For her, that is the sexual act. To lavish, to give. To chart his way back to her. So that he, who cannot be woman, becomes one with her. Becomes her.

How time lives in her hands. Is extended into my arms: opens out. From egg, creating itself; from seed, planting itself; from wind, carrying; from pollen, transporting. She weeps; rubs her tears into my skin. The rains have come; from the mountains, the boys and the girls dressed like boys return with the goats. Carrying the smallest. In the villages, the old women and the girls and the boys dressed like them set out the barrels. Rain falls from the eaves, the nights are long, day passes quickly, the years turn in on themselves, bite their tail. The cycle roves through, begins again, is repeated.

One day she speaks: the year, turning; the rain, the sprouting of sun, its lengthening shadow, ebb and flow of the moon: these, she says, woman. And man, her child, serves.

The boy. Returning from his mother's village, fingers purple, he has been gathering berries. I see the awe in his gaze, he has caught sight of me, striding the path toward him. My long white robe spreads through the dust. The braid tightens across my breast. I am barefoot; mine is the earth, to tread with deliberate footstep.

I touch him; he endures it. Falls back into his body, grows out through his skin. He wants me to touch him again. What is sacred is called down out of the distance, lodges itself between my hand, his fingers, entangled with us.

For the first time, he knows: this is the fate of that boy, the god. He, who wished to roam a perpetual childhood. At play in his mountains with the boys. He must return; lay aside spear, bloodlust, give up the flight from knowledge. Must endure awe, envy, the dread of her power, she is life, cannot be held, hunted, can never be killed. And he will die; cannot evade it.

Not even by making the wish for death his. Must live, owes her his seed. That is his meaning.

I touch, we turn to dust. Age in one another's arms. I bury him. I have saved him from death; his seed will go on. He hides in my lap. Worshiping, he will grow old. Yes, take his place with the others. Grow into the old man, tell the story. The promise of this, uncertain, moves into his eyes.

Kneeling, his touch carries this knowledge. So light, it can scarcely be felt: it intends to give pleasure. Mother and child are laid to rest, divested. The old skin has been shed. We return over the great sea, to breed in the marshes. Snow runs down into flowering shrub. We are sunlight, playing over the stones of the courtyard, dissolving into them.

Yes, I know, I see: what, before writing to you, I had not seen. Among us, the sexual act cannot reach this power of magical play. Because women pretend. Hide their sexual power. Hand themselves over to him. To make him believe. In his power: over the body, against nature, over woman, against the mother. Because they pity him, the barren one, the hunter. And do not allow themselves to know their pity.

That was the time. The beginning again, of time. I saw, as for the first time: linden trees, the long march of them down into the village. The flowering fields, the dense sea of them. Swallows. Skimming, pitched upward, soaring in sharp flight to fall, to flit again over green fields.

We gathered, were gathered: the linden blossom, for tea. He takes to flight. Stings me away from white flower, protective leaf. Our arms full, we creep back into the village. The ox returns, turns dust to gold, the treading begins, my feet stamp juice from him.

Lizards hide in the stone walls. Children, carrying baskets; they kick pears in the orchard. I have the impression: I will not see this for long.

He says: I am goddess of the cornfield. He wants to gather me in. He says: my hair is yellow, it grows over my fields.

Trumpeting of cranes. I am bowed, the plum drags me with ripeness. In his armpit, cicadas beating. Grain yellow on the threshing floor. We are harvested. The corn is laid up to be shelled. He thrusts thyme between my lips, prolongs me. The heat, great. He must be laid to rest near the fountain. Babble, pass by overhead, rise out of the corn to cry at nightfall.

It is too hot for the larks.

The old women, they told us: all who worship, who serve, perform the sacred sexual act, carry between hands, lips, thighs, the earth's fertility. And we were all, they said, Aphrodite, and the boy.

We heard them, from the walled gardens, behind the sanctuary. While we played. Procession to the river. White robes, robes of saffron, water splashed from tortoise shell. We knew, from among the women, from among the men: two would be chosen.

Claire's Tenth Letter

Was it madness? A flight to the past? To escape the past? I would say, rather: It was a return. For one, who had lost the meaning in things. It was meaning.

Fundamental, a bedrock. From which, somehow, in time, I was returned to time.

What is memory? A few stones, picked out of the river. Reassembled in a garden. You can make a wall of it, a skeleton, a bench, stone table.

What is sex? All of it, maybe.

What eyes say, before speech. The world of the body, its memories. First sensation: the way it fell. Into her arms. That is the way it will fall: in love, from a steep place, down a river, over a waterfall.

What is sex?

In childhood, the body learning, to grow into itself. Later, the child older, the need to keep the body. Hold it back from the exile. To which the others wish to subject it.

It is, younger brother curled up in a shack, listening. Impossible stories. Girl, making it, rite of passage, in parked car off Hollywood Boulevard. A way to learn. All that the body has forgotten. Learning it back, insisting. Marking the stages of progress, the stations. Leaving home, the taco stand on the highway. The train moves off, crosses the world. The appetite: to know, take it in, all that it offers, what it is, the risk, the unknown, the taste of its fruit. And what is forbidden: the body's ghettos, the wrong side of the track, its impoverishments. To enter, restore them.

A blackjack table. Stolen car. Stealing back what has been stolen. Setting out again. Crossing the seas. Unlearning the laws, the prohibitions. Terrible streets of transgression: the cult of sensation. Haunted by this: something is lost, missing, cannot be reached, connected.

Man, the other. The longing for him. Surely he knows, has preserved what we have cast out? The disillusion. Nobody knows. None of us. The boy fishing, the sun on the river, footsteps on the marble stairs. Can he be taught what others have forgotten?

The rage of forgetting. The frustration: we kiss, hard; we embrace, violently; we leap out, we attack, we tear open, we force entrance. And still cannot touch, reach, contact. Always, it eludes us. The body, swallowing its secrets; pleasures hidden, memories at bay.

And then there is one: more vulnerable than others, seems freer, will do anything, does not swagger. Remembers childhood, might be brother. His skin has erupted, he must be touched. To him then: open the doors, the hidden desires. Go further, admit fear with a stranger. At a masked ball, risk loss. Unleash sensation.

What is sex?

Disillusionment with the body? That too? Desert of sensual pleasures, night of the flesh, its aridity. The way you cannot go on, have reached, it seems, the end station. The train stops: the last risk, it seems, taken.

Meaning dries up; the body withers, scorns touch, grows barren. Someone is in mourning, they say. Perhaps the goddess of grain. Her daughter has been stolen, gone underground. It is an old story. Or maybe the boy she loved has been killed by a boar.

What is sex?

Above all, it seems, a question of touch. The way touch remembers, has preserved childhood. The way the body knows, has never forgotten. The fear of falling. The dread of being small. And her magnificence. The stories flesh tells: rocked back out of urgency in earth mother's arms. Touch: a question of memory. The ultimate risk, the train's return to the first station.

If you go back, there; the walled gardens. Stay a while and then come back again: the secret treasure you smuggle through. But of course you know by now: that is the body.

Vulnerable as dew, infinitely fragile, scarcely yours. It must be offered, at first tentatively. If you are lucky, she is one who remembers tenderness, calls it the old way. Perhaps she straps you to her body. Naked, a single skin encloses you. The beginning again. She wears you on her hip, slung on her back, goes about her tasks. When you are hungry you suck. She does not let you cry. Part of her, she senses your body before you do. Your legs kick. This means: soon you will wet, discharge, relieve tension. She takes you down from her back. Your fingers tighten. You are back in her arms. You watch, from your perch: the way she digs yams, plaits a basket, plucks berries, frees an iron gate from its rust. Then slowly. Detaching the small from the large, stumble out, they are your legs that totter. Her arms, there when you fall, you fall back into her. This body that will become your body. Apart from her, never too far. One day she places you near the door of the hut. When you are ready you walk. Away from her. Turn back. She is there. You reach out. You touch her.

It is your first sexual act.

Have you noticed? It is almost three years. Since we met. More than four months since I left you. Did not write my name on a stone wall. It takes time to remember.

Tomorrow, I shall drop these letters in the mail. Imagine them arriving, somewhere. In Paris, are you there? Sent on perhaps by the concierge. Following you across Europe. Meeting up with you, finally.

As for me: I shall go home. I mean: the city where the wooden shack stood. Next to the alley. The first time since I left. Returning, briefly. Then north. The road she took. Setting out into the world in search of the body. Ironic, or perhaps even: sentimental journey? Does it matter?

A city, near the sea. A house in the hills, it looks down over water. I bought it, when? On a whim, suddenly. Driving up into the hills to visit a friend. Before we parted, Geoffrey and I; before the masked ball, the walled gardens. Before I met you again in your little court. You see: I am trying. To give an order, coherence, sequence. Perhaps you already know?

What is sex? Our original question. The reason, to begin with, these letters were written. Now, they will have been sent, all of them. Finally.

Do I mean: whatever has to do with the body? Its need for the other, earliest knowledge. It will dry up, wither, without her. Sex: this groping, from one stone solitude to another. Do I mean: this confession? Taken up, tasted afresh, in the arms of one who can be trusted? Enough, anyway.

An act, the most hazardous, let us say, of recollection? Mutual memory of childhood?

And therefore: a step forward. Less than a promise. But worth the risk. A possibility.

And above all, in case you have not understood: An invitation.

Renate Stendhal:

Part Five   ALMA RUNAU: A LETTER, A CONDITION
Scene: A café
Time: Not quite three years after the first meeting

10 o'clock

I decided to slaughter my last pomegranate. It had been lying around since Xmas. Hard like a walnut. I used a screwdriver to get the seeds out. Do you like this *hommage à toi*?

I remember our conversation, something you said struck me as true: "Falling asleep at mother's breast." I didn't want to admit it but that's precisely what happened, sexually speaking, in each of my relationships with women. There was an exhilarating sense of oneness, belonging, sacred marriage, yes. But at the same time, with our ideal of sameness, we kept each other from our otherness. We grew into each other, slipped under each other's skin. We knew each other by heart, sensed our moods already outside the door. We made the other into ourselves.

But it's the dilemma, isn't it, of every relationship? (Is this why you never enter a relationship?) If there's no "other" anymore, desire dies. Wanting to encounter the stranger—wanting to keep everything familiar. The contradictory needs between which passion falters! We try to get around the conflict by keeping both needs apart: sleepy domestic security, fatal attraction to the stranger.

Your stranger. The one who has to be changed with every desire, every season. Who is chosen once a year. I would like to find the "familiar stranger," the one I can learn to love and fall in love with again and again.

If lovers would allow each other to change, find their own direction, their unique path. . . . Wouldn't the encounter with difference keep reproducing the stranger one longs to encounter? Then, maybe one would realize that the desired stranger is also a desired part of oneself. An unknown possibility one longs to become. A possibility one longs to learn from the other.

In my experience, the risk was avoided. The risk of change, estrangement, loss. My relationships became a cradle. A place where we could heal our wounds from being women. A place where we protected ourselves and each other from our difference. We were outsiders, separated from the rest of the world by our love for women. Difference, roles, anything that could separate us from each other, had to stay out. We protected each other like mothers protect their children from the world. From too much adventure, challenge, unequalness, competition. In short, from life. And thus from our truth.

Sex, I suppose, in such a cradle, can come to be felt as part of the danger of life. How can one be totally naked and open if there's a need for protection from some truth? From the memory of men in our bodies. . . . From the compulsion of gender. Shielding ourselves from the conventional notions of sex (domination, passive surrender, giving up self), we came close to eliminating sex altogether.

These sexual fears, you say, are not about men? They are about the mother lurking behind them? Behind all of us? No matter the gender—

what sex enacts is always the drama between mother and child. It does ring a bell. I can't deny it's a tempting thought that my rage against men has been a coverup for a much earlier, hidden rage.

It's true. Being the helpless doll of an all-powerful mother must mean being fed on the best as well as worst of life. The mother is every/body's wonder and terror. Every/body's initiation into the frightening ambivalence of being. (Isn't it ironic that you, the "bad girl" with the "bad mother," can allow yourself to know this? You obviously don't have to protect her, or your memory of her.)

Nevertheless, there's something you don't seem to know. Women are in a particular situation, loving other women. Womanloving brings the mother-memory as close as can be, "for better or for worse." (Reason enough to stick to men?) There are memories of a sweetness without any equal in the world. The beauty, lushness, the sensuous softness of a woman's body is without any equal in the world. But the memory of having been over- and underfed, possessed and abandoned, overwhelmed and rejected by this same body, source of life, of love—indeed also invokes an unequaled fear.

No wonder you avoided it. No wonder I did, too. The dogma of tenderness meant calling up the safe, nurturing m/other. All-encompassing, presexual sensuality rather than sex.

Most of the time my lover and I felt so closely bonded, already quasi inside each other, it was quicksand to enter and be even closer, more intimate. We had already given too much. How could we give even more of a self we didn't possess?

(Have you ever been close enough to anybody to feel this mother-*angst*? To be swallowed alive? S/mothered?)

Like any "married" couple, we would make love from time to time. With the body ease of our familiarity, we were likely to be satisfied. Or should I say, pacified? But in the sweet nest of our bodies the longing to recognize the stranger, be the stranger, to conquer, seduce, surrender, had gone to sleep.

It bothered me as a feminist to still find myself and my lovers in the same old shoe, "Sex is male, love and intimacy are female." I wanted sex. I began to wonder if I, if women, even feminists, had something to learn from men?

It bothers me, Claire, that you are still wearing that shoe. You leave out love and intimacy, you worship impersonal sex. I hit upon the right question three years ago when I asked if you were a female impersonator. You are.

I told you about Solveig and my sexual quest. I don't think I mentioned my frustrations with my "male" training. Isn't it funny that we each went into sexual training? You went for the sacred, I for the most profane. One thing in common: sex with strangers, right? Coming each from the opposite end—how are we ever going to meet in the middle?

March 5, afternoon

Not at "our" café. At the Coupole this time. It's such a strong wind I couldn't have made it farther on my bike. Here the *crème* is *minable*, as you might know. They never use fresh milk. But I'm sheltered from the draft in the soft banquettes with their high plush backs. Farther down, Truffaut actor Jean-Pierre Léaud cowers in another banquette in his eternal trench coat. The usual old ladies in furs, pearls, and heavy makeup are hanging out, chatting and flirting with the waiters, preparing to go up to the 5 o'clock *thé dansant* with their young gigolos. It's a place where nobody cares how long you hang out. My traditional bad-weather café.

I want to finish my letter. I read yours again. I want to come back once more to our favorite topic, the stranger. The mysterious lover, the irresistible *étrangère*. The one met at a bus stop, on a boat before sunrise, in a house near the harbor at a *bal masqué*. Passion incarnate.

I must have been practicing for that New Year's night. Cultivating my detachedness: my control.

What is passion?

Distance. To yearn, dream, pine. The delicious torture of putting off a rendezvous for the sake of waiting, resistance, pleasure postponed. The rising expectation: feverish anticipation, desire whipped up to an unbearable peak. And finally *Erlösung*, finally release, in a rage of body thirst. Violent greed for fulfillment, another sweet torture, so short, alas, always already possessed by the need to tear myself away in order to let desire slowly rise again . . .

Sounds familiar? No kidding. What a great *mise en scène*. Two beings forever apart, with the momentary illusion of being together. A longing not for satisfaction in fact but for longing. Provoked sensation. Why?

For the past three years this kind of passion has been my drug. An ecstasy of cultivated pain, a sickness in love with itself. It has nothing to do with love. It's not even concerned with the "beloved." The lover has to fit my game, fit into the costume I hold out for her.

It works as long as the other stays remote, unreal, always a step out of reach. An apparition, a sexual mirage. A fantasy-body that lies between me and my lover's naked flesh. As soon as there is closeness, intimate knowledge, a real face with its ugliness, a real person with her otherness, the game is over. Once I look behind the mask, remove the blindfold, once I am recognized beneath my costume, I fear the consequences. The gap opens between my love illusion and the truth, between my act and who I really am. The stranger's irresponsible daring is lost. A shyness sneaks in, a fear to show too much of myself, to give it away, to give in, to be taken.

A terror falls. To lose control over my need, to depend on the giver of pleasure. To become a slave to pleasure. The terror of wanting a fulfillment that goes on forever, never stops, leaves me incapable of tearing myself away. Leaves me addicted to a bliss that is not of my making.

(The reason I left the room at the *bal*? The reason you didn't hold me back? The reason you left before I got back? Did I dare to come back?)

I keep running. Everyone does. To the safe distance, the costume, the ritual, the sacred symbolism, the unfamiliar stranger in the night.

(Do you want to know the true meaning of the New Year's story? The two women were so hidden by roles they couldn't possibly recognize each other.)

When I started watching myself acting, acting out passion, I found that I intensified all my other feelings in the same "passionate" way. Do you remember how I loved the swifts? Their screams were my screams for my lover, their vertiginous plunges were the vertigo of my desire for her. Their beauty wasn't enough by itself, it had to be heightened. My feeling of love wasn't ever enough by itself. Without the ache, the intensifying drug of pain—what was I able to feel?

"Without pain, no pleasure," as folks say.

Why not?

"Patisseries, croissants, chocolats . . ."

The lady with the red uniform and weary face is pushing her cake wagon through the rows of tables. No request. She doesn't expect any. I secretly bite into the croissant I bought at the bakery across the street. I'm an expert at hiding food in my lap. In "our" café, I know how to choose the tables that can't be surveilled by the *patronne*. "*Une petite tarte, Mademoiselle? Un p'tit cognac?*" She has trained the waiters not to be content with a simple order of coffee. It's *pousse au crime*, a shove into the lap of crime.

Outside, wherever one looks, advertising pushes one into the lap of sex.

Ready-made s/excitements, to be easily consumed. A bus drives by, showing Mr. Muscle holding a newborn baby against his naked torso. The photo
cuts below the belt; the zipper doesn't quite close. One hand supports the
baby's head, amazingly tender. The other, gripping the baby's ass, seems to
suggest that even the tiniest body calls for rape. Across the street a movie
poster exposes the full, naked breast of a man in bed; the woman next to
him has her breasts fully covered. In the neighbor poster a man yields to a
woman who comes up behind him and peels the jumpsuit from his upper
body. Her face beams with loving authority. His is in agony, taking pleasure.

Are they ahead of our time, as your letter would suggest? Or is it that
feminism has repudiated women's attributes—babies, breasts, surrender—
and already men are taking them over, making them theirs? Turning them
into men's sexual attractions? Coming attractions?

I wonder if it's not the same arrested state of affairs. Now a woman possessing. A domina. The roles exchanged, the same old roles. Always the
illusion that some kind of authority, violence has to come in, has to be
embraced in order to overcome one's resistances. To be forced, to force
oneself into the pleasure one can't take.

The illusion of passion has the same function: creating the aloof, un-
attainable other. Distance, resistance then have to be torn away in a storm
that leaves you no thought of failure, no feeling of frailty—just sweeps you
off your feet into, finally, ease.

Always illusion of ease. In the advertisements, the fantasies, the temple
vision, the childish wish for the dream-lover, the prince(ss) charming
with X-ray eyes who recognizes you without a word. Guesses all your secret
desires, has the perfect authority to plunge your abandoned self into the
seventh heaven. (The lover I, in the New Year's story, pretended to be?)

It doesn't work. Not for me. Not anymore. To me it all looks like a mad
search, doomed, even if you call sex art or the sacred. Paradise lost. An obsession. A greed that doesn't care about the taste of food, the pleasure of
eating. Mere need to fill a void. A desperate drive to forget for a moment
how separate one is from it all. From oneself, the other, the universe.

It sounds absurd to me to ask the body for "art," or even the "sacred,"
for high and subtle sensation, if heart and mind have nothing to do with it.
Who are those others, your lovers, those boys? Long legs, pimples, erupted
skin is what I learned about them. Nothing about their hearts and minds.
The emotional poverty, the anonymity of what you call sex!

Yes, you're right, I am dead-scared of the elemental power of sex. Everyone is. Women and men force their difference upon each other to avoid

the dangers of elemental love. The nearness of goddess and child. You do, too. With another woman, however, the dangers might be unavoidable. That's what you might be able to learn with a woman. Not in the role of a boy-child. As a woman yourself.

Four Pairs

CAMILLE NORTON AND LOU ROBINSON

Trouble open

Trouble, open, I'll take anything you've got. I was an actress in the leftist theater, I slept with Grotowski, when I did *Mother Courage* strangers from the
suburbs wept over my losses. Children will begin dying all around you. What
will you give me? Give me your dirty, your guilty money. Resist me and I'll
send you seven years' misfortune. A mottling sky is a signal of depression,
when the lilacs bud in March it means extinction. The North Sea is the filthi-
est sea in the world. If you don't believe me, consider the Scots, who turn
their eyes away from Aberdeen in shame. Trouble, open, the earth moves
beneath your co-op houses, crash go the widow walks above the attic apart-
ments. A conductor mourns three killed during rush hour in a Philadelphia
subway. Yesterday does not stop. When I felt the outrages of history, my
body shook and shook. I was a monster of compassion. George Bush earns
high marks from Blacks and women. You have the option of ignoring the
truth until that moment when the dead begin inserting messages inside your
dreams. You must be brave. When I saw my own dear Kattrin felled by the
soldier's bullet I forgot she was an actress from Brooklyn. I wept for all my
children but afterwards I realized I had to eat. You must let go. De Klerk
says that if Blacks do not desist there will be no negotiation. Do not desist.
Tonight and tomorrow someone will tap a message into your hand. You can
be certain it is for you.

trouble open. a small strip still open looses its heat to gulls. gulls in trouble.
minus two degrees. seeking in a blinder way, one white male haunts corri-
dors. trouble shining. now the thing is make a list. I have a list, he says, saliva
glints, you're on it. its circular he's at the outer edge. st. teresa's swollen
vision of the universe. she says a gum will swell or an eye for a day then

its over. deep sorrow coming finds a pocket for warning, fills it, sending its agitated waves to point the brain in the direction of trouble then opens and runs. stuff she calls it as opposed to prophecy or paranoia, trouble or lies. merely reading. lately you see loss, mourn, absence, vacant spectral placed beside woman. he swallows his gum. he takes as his hero montreal. he carries himself around in that febrile man-shape, little projections, so poignantly unformed, those sloping hips, so unequal to living, opening. no one wants to enfold it anymore, become putrid. white beans grown in a closet reach long unformed limbs toward no future seeded shape, growing longer whiter dumber in the dark. or isometric. trouble open vein or fire. the earth bit her, she said, rocked by the quake refused to eat anymore inside the trailer. took her food, keys, leash to the square of earth even though it bit. he said trouble open, counting himself among it.

And we did

What do you know about sin? Your soul's a spotless milk bottle, mine's filled in, inky black like a vial of hell. *Libera me, Domine,* I'm goin' to Purgatory. Full of terror am I and I fear the trial. *Agnus Dei, qui tollis peccata mundi,* I was a girl drunk on my own reflection in the plate-glass window. This is my body and dream's a prayer. It's always his name in the inner ear, a trochaic music, Jesus, a pop and a sizzle. I must not want, I must not want. Anyone but you, baby. I studied the faces of the girls around me for signs of abdication. For the flight of bodies disintegrating in the hard light of March. The panicking auras of shame. This is what I saw and when I saw it I fell out of love with the world. We were told to deny, and we did. To grow as vigilant as soldiers at the border of the body. And we did. Her name was Ignatius after a first century martyr, she taught me that pain has absolute status. Like Love. Like Sin. You don't believe me because you gave your heart to Jesus in a revival tent the summer you were twelve. First came the testimony, then you were saved—everyone reeled night after night, stung crazy by the voices of the Southern preachers. It was the singing you were after. You were unto him like a little child while I sat inside the silence in the vestry light with the wound between my legs and the sin of the mind. Beginning even then to doubt the beauty of his face. *In paradisum deducant angeli.* May the angels receive thee in Paradise.

and we did. making up nothing. but what we did and how it writes. in the gap caused by tundras between speech and comprehension. why aren't

you talking as the car drove us east. or I can't talk because you can't follow as I fall asleep back to the midwest. always two unparallel actions are
noted. eery, mysterious intersecting barely touching strangulating charcoal
loops like the man who drew blind on the subway carefully observing the
no back contact rule. we did look at holes in the ground, ancient, october, invisible snake lined rituals pits now haunted by people on retreat
who renovate puritan houses and paint their doors pewter blue. the distance between orchestrated mood and colonizers with no atmosphere of
their own. playing music from the balcony, fingers attached to instruments
below by strings. I did gaze on a face slowly unlining itself, on the blue
green plaid folds of an open robe in that wrenching october light. cop-
per leaves falling on a swamp. donkey skronking in the voice of both our
fathers. how did we do that? so far out on a tarry night so far from home
from the comfort of the indoor ring, ceiling rosy with dust, heat rising
from horses all the colors of red. solid night before me could be the back
of a truck no lights. unfamiliar german singer on the radio, going to you.
making up nothing. making up everything secondary. I make everything
up. often am left dangling in the poised and eager paragraph. dangerous
doubling movement, to film behind the eye while living. a dream again
where someone is kissing me but I'm looking at a screen two giant heads,
kissing. can't take my eyes away. to look at the face nearby. and a voice
says that's not love. but which? take my eyes. to have refused to represent,
would that have made it sacred? they make laws against. to get the essence
inside the actions moments then it slips. you're with her when she jumps
or you're transported to another universe devoid of grace, you cease to live
you write. and we did, love, she says. but sometimes said no that's not it.

I know a lot of things I can't express

This afternoon between the Greeks and the moderns, I saw you in bed
with another woman and imagined killing myself in the back room with a
saber sword. Rage, I thought. And then: *The Greeks.* I know a lot of things
I can't express because it's already been done so well by them. One's feelings about one's parents, for example—Orestes has already carried these
to an extreme. And Oedipus—there's a kind of existential embarrassment
just thinking about it. The way it came off in spite of everything. That moment on the Theban Road when he killed his father because his father was
a bad driver. I think of all those afternoons in the back of the sedan, lurching through the stops, my father's grizzled head blocking my view. I think

of the Theban Road. It's considered a successful therapy when you admit you've always wanted to kick your father in the shins. *How do you feel now?* says the analyst. *Better,* you say. Oh, to express it. Something monumental, Byzantine. Radical disembowelment, castration, exile, all of it, the unsung death in the grove of Eumenides among a hostile chorus. But you never say that, do you? Then they might call you a radical separatist. A terrorist. From hell. It's better not to express it. Better, they say, to stick to the local scene, life as you have known it, that afternoon on the Schuykill Expressway when he almost killed you changing lanes during rush hour. The way he said: *Don't expect to learn how to drive in my car. I'm the only one who gets to drive my car. Do you hear me?*

I know a lot of things I can't express. two refrigerators. I have no refrigerator no clothes. I have to start over. whole plains are rubble with only here and there an upright refrigerator. I know a lot of things I can't express. that there will come a time I'll have to break away. a spiteful whisper spoils things in advance. when she was nine she said "the most important thing is a person's job, right?" a refrigerator, on its side. you think of yourself as part of society but then something like a hurricane and you know you are alone. have to start over. I saw a turquoise frigidaire lying down with antlers on top, door open on a moving scene. to dream of a refrigerator means you will harm an innocent by your greed. no, I answered, it's being kind. she looked at me with pity, her work cut out for her. three years later at twelve, still struggling valiantly, she said "look, tell yourself you can do anything. I say son of a bitch son of a bitch to myself to keep my rhythm." I knew someone someday would break it. last night a deer came and spoke at the foot of the stairs, what stairs I heard you say and then I lost her words. It spoke of the kind of food it wanted, it looked up the dark green walls imploring and familiar. it knew me, it showed this naked hunger nowhere else. what should I feed it, what did it say? the best I can always, never enough, never can find the right shape for the words. I know a lot of things I can't express.

Tous ce que j'écris

Leave me alone for an hour and I'll invent a fiction of abandonment. I want to fill up the page with the bunched purple clusters of early lilacs. And let the daughters of uneducated women dance. It is easier to talk about writing than to write about talking. We have done with tyranny. I was anxious about narrative that begins and ends in the present tense—I said, "We're giving

up our memories so that people we don't much respect will feel at ease."
You said, "When I write in the present it is because I am feeling everything
pressed close to the skin." And their mothers will laugh from their graves.
Your mother disliked music—she said it hurt the brain. Everything hurt her,
including all forms of laughter. My mother, on the other hand, listened to
music and wept at the kitchen table, her face in her hands. She taught me
that wordlessness induces tears. Tell me again what you mean. The other
night, hurrying through the rain to find coffee for your migraine, I decided I
had no concept for this kind of love, love that outlasts the pitch of sex and
the two year cycle of serial romance. We inherited programs for pain, now
we must supply the pleasure. Is this pleasure? Tous ce que j'écris, c'est une
histoire nouvelle. This is a test. They have given us little we can use. We have
to make it up without stopping to think if it will last. Light up the windows of
the new house, copine, let them blaze. Otherwise we will write nothing but
revenge tragedy. Nothing but elegy.

tous ce que j'écris. everything I write is for you. I used to think I was
napoleon's mare. the heart of the whole insane operation. know now I am
napoleon. as well as the sweet chocolate shadow eager to place your two
sharp perfect forefeet precisely there. everyone will wonder who. I intend
exactly who I write, after I see it lying down. écris de la mare. journal et
notes sans date. as napoleon I whipped her with an ironweed stick, the
flower still attached reverberating lavender tip. my sister, I mean, not the
mare. to make her ride the mare I mean, or else we stood to lose you. our
father didn't see the point. I like to go about the world reading placards
napoleon slept here and think, I did? then so did you. did we dream about
this page? were you stabled safe and dry below deep and warm, while your
brother lowered from pulleys into catherine the great? the last violent encounter woke me bleeding alone. napoleon had ridden me too hard. or I
had thought I was the great lying waiting to be lowered into. holding your
superior image never fails to get me there. a tear or infection darkens a line
to rootbeer down your smoky arab cheek. a mon arrivé ici, tous ce que
j'écrivais had come to pass. I've made a special machine of the bones of
napoleon's mare with which to write. a pen, suspended, moves across a
piece of tympan sheet on top of a little stool to the rhythm of the candles
melt. it's important to remove all human touch. the tympan sheet is the
skin across my chest as you write me of your willingness. everyday I write
you hard into the ground.

Reading and Writing Between the Lines

DAPHNE MARLATT AND BETSY WARLAND

Collaboration is a specious term for the writing you and i do together . . . here, even here, hovering between third person and second person pronoun, to choose second with its intimacy seems to me indicative of how i write with and to you. you my co-writer and co-reader, the one up close i address as you and you others i cannot foresee but imagine 'you' reading in for. and then there's the you in me, the you's you address in me, writing too. not the same so much as reciprocal, moving back and forth between our sameness and differences.

in our doubleness, no, our plurality as we read (for) and write (to) you, all the you's in each other reading and writing too—a polylogue, such bends and twists—you see how this writing rivers out to various mouths immediately?

which is why i find it difficult to use the word collaboration with its military censure, its damning in the patriot's eyes (the Father appears here with his defining gaze, his language of the law). collaboration

implies that who we are collaborating with holds all the power. the lines are drawn. but perhaps it's the very subversion implicit in collaboration that i might see in our favour were we to move between the lines. when i see us as working together reciprocally, then what i see us working at is this subversion of the definitive. running on together (how I love prose),

reciprocal in this, that the holes we make in such a definite body leak meaning we splash each other with, not so much working as playing in all this super-fluity, wetting ourselves with delight even, whetting our tongues, a mutual stimulation we aid and abet (entice) in each other.

'let me slip into something more comfortable'

                                        she glides across the
room
lābi, to glide, to slip

(*labile; lābilis:*
labia; labialis)
                    la la la
'my labyl mynde . . .'
lābilis, labour, belabour, collaborate, elaborate

'The Hebrews named their letters, some guttural . . . others dental . . .
and so they call others, labial, that is letter of the lips'

slip of the tongue
                    'the lability of innocence'

labium
'any of the four folds of tissue of the female external genitalia'
four corners of the earth
four gates of Eden
                    labia majora (the 'greater lips')
                    la la la   ˏ
                        and
                    labia minora
                    (the 'lesser lips')
not two mouths but three!
slipping one over on polarity

                            slippage in the text
you & me *collābi*, (*to slip together*)
labialization!
slip(ing)page(es)
like notes in class

o labilism o letter of the lips
o *grafting* of our slips
labile lovers
'prone to undergo displacement in position or change in nature,
form, chemical composition; unstable'

giving the one authoritative version the slip
graft, graphium, graphein, to write

slippery lines

thought is collaboration

or thought is reading one another's min(e)ds, stumbling onto unexpected
gaps, holes, wait, explosive devices—this is not enemy territory we're
speaking of or in, though each entry can be for the other a dark side of the
moon, its sudden craters, its dry seas or season . . .

mooning (we wander aimlessly) or spooning (with a lure, but whose?) slippery words this slippery body we tongue between us comes between us in
the ways a word can sound 'slippage' you said
      slipping in the age it takes the mind
         to turn around its mooring words that bind
you gave me the slip suggesting you'd slip into something more comfortable

negligible and large, in which we are complicit and inter-ested together
to be in this body at sea with one another in the slippage of meaning this
loss of motion forward is fear, wait, being taken off in a different direction
altogether . . .

collaboration then as power play where we breaks down into you and i and
i'm tired of defining these feints of desire, us desiring yes this third body
we go chasing after and jealousy moves in, hey what are you really after?

so let's talk about the dark side as it rises dimly behind the lit rooms of
our intentions variously engaged. let's talk about the ground rules, how i
can revise me but not you though i sometimes try. how we find the mean
in our understanding of what we're individually after. even if it lies in two
different directions? what happens to our writing when *together* to be in a
body breaks down?

not simply a working together there are challenges backings up required
words we graft from each other's texts that can't be later edited out

'where are you going with this?'
'you didn't go deep enough'

rewrites re you re me losing the rhythm instinctive steps & turns (no box/
waltz here) writing 'in the dark, i saw you . . .' the tension necessary following & leading s)witching unpredictably the doubt—

'you've written it all; there's nothing left for me to say'
'you gave me the slip'

the elation sparking the provoking each other beyond our endings
our meanings

'i didn't know that was in there until now'

playing with each other's logic like a dream dark side of the moon right
brain conversation the erotic zones of a word we're both attracted to stroke
arousing our enigmatic ménage à trois one nearly always on the outside edge
of two a living on it sharpening our semantic shifts slips yā, for the *zeal* of a
language intimate (*intimāre, to put in, publish, from intimus, inmost deepest*) we risk
jealousy the fear of losing our voice and the afterglow of finding we haven't

and what about the talking we do that underlies or underlines (between
the lines) what gets written on the page (what isn't there, the dark side off
the record as the waltz winds down)—are we dancing in the dark? as if the
page were a lit room read from outside while we go on doubling behind
the scene, the you of the page i subvert in the unwritten you i walk our
streets with, night, passing the lit rooms of story i saw 'you' of your page
subvert in me biography or writing with our lives the tension necessary
between what gets said and what gets written or left (out in the dark with
other readers-in who are also us party to the parts we play in the game,
apart and not) 'you put your whole self in' but what is yourself, your voice?
as our heads slide through semantic shifts that are not ours as language
never is

the talking we do that underlies	of the written here we affirm our
the underwriting assessing the	spiralling dominoing wandering
risks the mutual responsibilities	she-speech in the talking we do
of each other's *liabilities, leig-,*	between the sheets between the

reply in this game of double *soli-taire, sole, sel,* room two lit two dark and sometimes 'two sil-houettes on the shade' the embodiment the doubling of the chance of language the cards up our sleeves power play of our idiosyncratic synapses game of chance exposing the writer's sleight of hand which tricks the reader into believing in a voice in the wilderness singularly inspired here we acknowledge that all writing is collaboration here we question the delineation between the collectivity of con-versation and the individual's ownership

lines between the writing that intertwines it's all in the cards each deck a voice distinct to its own tones its rhythms its own feel its quirky selectivity (the mind only taking in 10% of stim-ulation at any given moment) the card's meaning particular to the relationship of the others the *sequence, sekw-,* intrinsic to math, music, literature, making love while i'm *shuffling, possibly (but quite doubtfully)* O.E. *scop, poet* dealing you a double deck but card sharps are liable to whet their tongues on each other's slipperiness then call for a redeal

the card you are in this full house dancing us room to room as the music shifts—and yes, who's leading who? you and me and language makes three, no baby she, *la langue.* she'll shift the rhythm on you, bend your sense, slam you into difference while you're still stumbling over your intent, trying to keep your word/s from running away with sense . . .

to keep (y)our word. eroticizing collaboration we've moved from treason into trust. a difficult season, my co-labial writer writing me in we while we are three and you is reading away with us—

who?

you and you (not we) in me and all of us reading, which is what we do when left holding the floor, watching you soar with the words' turning and turning their sense and sensing their turns i'm dancing with you in the dark learning to trust that

are you trying to avoid the auto-biographical? what is 'self' writ-ing here? when you leave space for your readers who may not read you in the same way the autobiographical becomes com-munal even communographic in its contextual and narrative

sense of direction learning to
read you in to where i want to go
although the commotion in
words the connotations you
bring are different we share the
floor the ground floor meaning
dances on . . .

(Carol Gilligan) women's way of
thinking—and collaborating?

whirling out to include . . .

at the bathroom sink
'so, do you think it's a good collaboration?'

'yes. do you?'

'yes . . . i don't know what others will think of it—'

i continue to brush my teeth thinking about the word *euphemism*
eu-, good + *phēmē, speech*   u-feminisms
all our yous (u/s) and all the others'

the words & sayings we're taught as children
so as to avoid embarassing adults
for u it was 'fooze'
for me 'results'
the onomatopoeia the practicality
these substitutions more explicit, subjective

gift of the ghabh-,
cohabit

'rhythmic synchrony'
a sociolinguistic microanalyst documenting the unique rhythmic patterns
of familial conversation has found the crescendos, pauses, stressed syllables, and cutlery punctuation on plates to reveal a score which is replayed
and replayed (no matter what the narrative)

are u keeping score?

'auditory touch'

lovers not only share a rhythm
but a 'sustained mirror synchrony' of movements

yes
we do write to each other's u/s
but it is out of the blue
or black
depending upon the time of day
or mood

a gift is not the received
o the unruliness of our selective minds
we read each other's entries so differently

or do we always write out of black & blue:
the in-juries of our individuality, in-, + dīviduus, divisible

u-feminisms a strategy against u-thanasia
all our u/s essential (impossible to play without a full deck)

we shuffle
cut
and play into the source of our u-phoria

when we interwrite
we call each other's u-phonies out of the dark out of the blue out of the
glare of white

Rewire // Speak in Disagreement

ABIGAIL CHILD AND SALLY SILVERS

[Sally Silvers speaks in the indented text that follows; text that is not indented is Abigail Childs.]

1. Almost Necessary But Not Sufficient Criteria Particular to Women for Production of Modern Art
> *We defeated the lack of expectation.*

Enter the social, conditioning, context . . . OK, OK.
> Perhaps we should use the word girl in every sense of woman in this essay—would that drive the point in a way similar to your suggesting a she when the he was always written. When writing about girls and modernism we have to talk about oppression . . . and find the rambattering tiresome.
>
> Women have been traditionally involved in issues of the body in art—arts of presence—theater, dance, voice. This is partly economics (body is cheaper than paper and pen even), but also women's bodies seem definitional—as presence, as objects. Our bodies are expected information. Women tend to see themselves relating to and as bodies instead of to and as history.
>
> Men with their tangible symbol/organ/phallus are challenged to compete to locate their desire in the (unattainable) power of the world. Women are more ambiguous in locating an identity, a location in relation to the world (in addition to being appropriated in men's sense of the territory available for them).

I disagree here with your analysis, where you talk about "women lacking a lack symbol." I think phallus just never had, has any power, real power to explain anything regarding women.

Power again. How we live in a world of male language and the need to redefine this: their terms.
> But what I mean is that women not being trained in the unattainable desire

for power/authority have a chance at a clearly distinct kind of maneuver-
ability—which to me is one of the essences of modernism—maneuvering,
recreating the subject using the materials of our mediums. Modernism as
getting legs instead of power.

To put down their reigns (reins): defeat prior constitutionality.

*To give our readers an idea of what P. Charles gazes at in the royal bedroom every night,
the Examiner placed Di's face over the body of a fashion model exhibiting the lines of sexy
lingerie.*

Genital identification. *Even the maids aren't black.* Historically women have
been bound to bonds of relation. Conditioned to condition. Women are
like nature which is what modernism bases its conquest on. *Women were
domestic goods so didn't sell or were sold and had earlier obsolescence.* They enter the
economics but not the politics. Survival based not on knowledge, information, self-sufficiency but on finding a mediator and not going public. *Reflex
survivors.*

*Demonstration photos inevitably show a young Japanese woman, a tentative smile on her
face, with the robot's 7' 5" arm coiled around her.*

Possession of the token of power = has a man.

Domestic speech—what is used in the home in the nuclear family—is ir-
relevant in the American version where father/husband supports wife/
mother, kitchen, kids—the division then of experience is so separate—the
wife/mother homefront limited to children's speech, consumer advertisement, pubescent addictions and advocacy of prevailing (and duplicating)
role models from a limited closed spectrum—how is an exchange of experience to be realized?

Women's lack exists—is this endless elaboration of perverted social realities, social psychologies, social behavior dysfunction. Feminine, the adjective, and equally masculine, the adjective, partake of the restricting cultural
values, *define your restraints, shape the lacks.*

The gender argument is fucked—making dogma out of social conditioning.

It's just a speech defect because women are forced to accommodate men.
Dichotomous thought is antagonistic to the future, locked into the past.

~~It's not~~ nurturer = ~~earth~~
~~mechanizer = destroyer~~

No female essence—intuition the small change of the patriarchy. We have
to guard against feminizing the irrational, women's prelinguistic association with nature. *No primal liberty between the meshes of the social body.* As you
say, destroy the dichotomies which structure and wash the patriarchy and

insure our position in relation to and formed by power. At the same time defeat coherent subjectivity on which capitalism, idealism is based—point up multiple contradictions which are clearly delineated and not unspoken, silent, taped shut. Constant strategies.

Which means there is something to *do*, rather than apologize and explain endlessly the state of things—both male and female have the political/aesthetic job to fracture the social conditions we in this present exist in—for life as well as gender reasons.

Articulate the differences with a fig. New realities into new speech. Speak in disagreement, enter the discourse.

Unless the woman sees her role as humanizing—emotionalizing the forces, personalizing—and then we're cooked and women leave modernism altogether.

Perhaps they have to become more improperly bred in the fear of desire. Obviously women know too much to try to join the club.

Oh dear little brushes. You can buy a kit and decorate your loved ones. You can buy a kit and go into business. Tattoo—the contact sport of the 80s. Darwin Was Wrong—across their young men's chests.

Obsolete mothers play a role in our lives.

The logo for his museum the design of a heart beating the single word "mother." (= the most popular tattoo ever created. Defensive signaling of a dying ethos.)

Went up there to prove their manhood, saying: be an essayist. Be focused. Exclude trivia.

Bull on the above rationalized clarity of expression.

A good thought is a series of resonances.

The English makes its propositions apparently verifiable.

A road to power in quick thinking.

A seduction to think office-ties-master-electronics.

While knowledge is another kind of power and is genderless. This our entry.

Yet when you say fuck clarity of expression/focus, I disagree. "Oh what a pretty cute thing, so enigmatic, so easy to ignore." It fits too easily into the basis of existing repression. Our entry is knowledge but if it is to be 'genderless,' it can't reinforce stereotypes of the dark, mysterious internal = female expression. Our thoughts will contribute through multi-valenced force; with a vision, a uniqueness that has clarity as an intention. How else are we to have a dialogue and learn from each other as women. Let's go beyond the role model method; beyond just another woman on the list.

I'm not talking of hiding behind veils of obfuscation. I'm suggesting rather that the 'call to order' is played against us, played against our mediums. That the traditional limits of the form define in a prohibitive way the boundaries of the possible. And the thrust of extension, of criticism which I choose to see as part of the work can be blunted by an obeisant clarity. My work is clear to me. Is as complicated as it appears because it wanted more complicated clarities to keep going. I don't want a work I could see in my mind's eye at the start from the front. I wouldn't make such a work, not need to, no need for. I'm against a *solved* work. Not a triumph of failure. But a material (unmartial) term of manifold contradictions, construction, stand (fall) (the body metaphor doesn't hold)—complete parts. Non-hierarchical.

I'm looking for an unsolved work that satisfies. You want to be as clear as possible. But not some predestined clarity.

What you didn't understand in my text wasn't where I thought you wouldn't. Accepting the authority of their definition is playing their game.

> Can figure out the project of undoing the damage. Not rewarding ourselves for not fucking up the world when we've been fucked instead.

Yet still. The terms of the indictment: who's inventing whom? The question of power and not the question of "why not enough women."

2. Every Bite Is a Revolution of the Material

> *We got to it before it had time to finish.*

Modernism for me is not minimal. Is rather inclusive, something of the Futurists' action momentum, naturally fractured as movies are (machines are/'organic' cells are/attention is/'component'), and the unity humans regularly seek (habit) would be by now outside a system—shakes the habituated, no form/force/system of givens encompassing truth enough.

> Instead a charge, a fracturing on all levels of our consciousness, finally getting legs instead of power. Modernism for me is definitely not orderly (as you say minimal). Even surrealism, cubism present the unconscious as surplus code, as orderly explosion or worshipful progress of the imagination. Expressionism was messy, chaotic, but too attached to the existential self. (Our) modernism is realism in the sense that it recognizes the complexities, the identities of things, of material (the components, the cell), but it doesn't make organic relationships between these things. It also interprets the things themselves as relations.

It makes sense to me that the modern insistence on discourse, the text, emerges now as a substance that doesn't try to remember, doesn't represent, is not dream, is itself and actualizes that.

Modernism could be a platform for women perhaps, a stance outside the patriarchy. Gertrude Stein for instance is much more modern than Joyce or Pound; her work less hierarchical, less harkening back to king-catholic-aristocracies. Levi-Strauss speaks to this sense of an evolving aesthetic that reflects its contextual worldview when he analyzes painting as a movement in the definition of the Sublime. I.e.: early 19th century extols the romantic, waterfalls, nature just as the machine age is about to encroach; the impressionists create suburban painting—their vision applied to parks, bounded fields, yards; the cubists celebrate the machine while the surrealists look to the imagination as post-war reality crowds in on their vision. And though Levi-Strauss does not name it, he suggests a future SuperReality to compensate a world grown increasingly potentless—which I interpret as the point of entry for photography and film. So that the Sublime in our time has become the unreal, is defined as illusion. The photo is the modern world. And for the artist living within this paradox, the Sublime registers not as representation but as the frame, the medium itself. The natural so banished in vectors of economic-atom-pressure that the Beautiful is what is not simply not-natural (i.e., machine) but what takes its force in being forcefully Unnatural (i.e., reflection/photoreality). With the added irony that these means seem even more convincing an 'illustration' of the real.

> History—a fiction we overthrow.

> Modernism not as a cure but as a finding of the go button. To open out options, as a stance, not just in opposition but to make something new, "to willfully not remember" the way things are; to not have to exist in relationship always to authority, to make a new position. As a building of desire, not limited to symbols of lack; not being stuck with an overdetermined symbol.

> Pop song: "Slave to my dick."

I'd maintain that part of our modernism is this unceasing attempt to maintain a realism—of the disparate committed opposition to the "Setup"—the totality and totalization of life as lived in the corporate image, corporate entertainment, corporate work, postures that dominate our society. The script packages life, makes brackets out of what I experience IN FACT as vortices. I don't want to follow this stricture/sequence. Each blink of my eye disproves—

> No totalities based on the mode of the natural organism. Give me fallacies any day. How can you believe in the model organism and believe in change? The corporeal surface as the location for new organs—Artaud—the organless body.

The body is the material and its deformations, errors, fallacies are what is of interest. And you—we—eat because every bite is a revolution of the material. What's so great about cinema is it takes the body and alters it, beyond the natural. Vertov's machine eye relevant here: that we learn to see differently, the tool changing our vision. "How" has altered the landscape, reorganizes the organic, distributes new information (language).
Extending the matrix of what constitutes the image.

Internal organs create responsibilities and minds of their own creation. Active complexities. Analysis, not synthesis.

The ideas are a struggle of contraries always in movement. Whereas dance, the organic unity, the "released" body, implies a single identity, a paradigm of the body. The body is already seen too much as property. To try to make it more "mine" is cowardly, miserly. I'm not writing owners' manuals.

Modernism seems an attempt at timelessness or everything at the same time, eliminating hierarchies in the form. In your films, in my choreography, there is an immediate reading of juxtaposed meaning and no need to connect the elements—it is intelligible each moment and not through the passage of time. Each moment rises done.

Your films strive for that instant in painting when you can see the whole divulged in each instant. So as in Shklovsky—the process of perception becomes an aesthetic end in itself. In Brakhage for instance, this perception becomes like a fetish whereas for you it seems more defamiliarized because of the way you cut sound, rhythm, point of view. I could see *Ornamentals* as pure fetish however. Film is always in danger of that moment of seduction; *Ornamentals* a seduction through specialization of its elements perhaps. Well, I'm not a puritan. I can stand seduction even though it's art. *Is This What You Were Born For?* cracks the subject—enter the social albeit in modernist dress—the emperor (empress) is naked and dead. The subject becomes an activating process.

Dripping sweat. Yet, to understand is to be struck.

Modernism—no resolution possible.

Operative: the image of Science. The dream landscape of the century. Science a code word for modernism. The arena of an ideology and the arena in which conflicting ideologies are and will be fought.

You could define modernism in relation to 20th-century science and its precepts:

critical stance : investigative reasoning
reflexive : relativity
disorder : entropy

> boundaries of the field : the new/also ideas of torus,
>   pushed to their limits   matrix, field, etc.

Knowledge now a sum of uncertainties. Entropy abolishes the monuments.

> More chaos—anarchy—means politically more open to discussion.

Acceptance of decay, confusion, unresolved states = events shaped to your singular vision.

One needs a point of view—can that be one of chaos?

> My vision of modernism is not from the theoretical position of idealism—
> that the human, the subject, the art maker is the point of origin of meaning
> or of practice. The coherent subject is a lie. How far outside ourselves can
> we go before realizing that we don't really manipulate it.
>
> *I believe I am a unity but I am a construction.*
>
> In my work, biology takes care of itself—it is its own structure but not a
> model for construction or thought. My organism is not action, but it is
> material. It doesn't hurt to know it as in learning the chemistry of paint pig-
> ment. (When I was reading *Scientific American*'s brain issue, I could get high.)
> I don't like thinking of the body as something that can be finally 'known'
> with correct and more correct manipulations, releasing of the final ten-
> sions. Tensions are interesting as sites of power formations. That is one
> reason I'm interested in untrained dancers. Technical or released trained
> movers have only habituated their bodies to an ideal, be it distorted (ballet)
> or natural (release and some modern dance). Habituated means thoughts,
> tools, no longer can respond in an exploratory, investigative mode. End of
> interest.

For me the rejected or everyday demagnified gesture is used in your work to construct a choreography of parts. And what touches the viewer is where the inarticulate, the error or tension find concrete manifestation and are recognized.

Speak here on the relation between form and content: not that they are identical. More like content is the air around the structure, what the structure breathes. Content has a smell which sounds the structure (the synaesthesia essentially a reflection of relations, not dichotomies).

Simple schematics don't work in these definitions. Perhaps typologies emerge with the division of labor, and are false in light of post-Newtonian physics: that classic modernism is a response to 19th-century mechanization and must change to deal with the development of the electronic/information era.

> I'm jealous of your time machine: film. Although I write compositions,

they are realized completely in vanishing. This is my body—doing time.
Your machine possesses it.
Whereas for me dance has the advantage of utilizing the material of the
body—the internal structure (in all of us) externalized, plus the facility/
ability to improvise—changing contexts. If film possesses time, your body
processes it (though I would maintain that is what film does as well—
no illusion out-of-hand). In your work, you have access to all (social and
historic) movement immediately and are not dependent on the laborious
technical recording procedure of film.

> Film sets new standards for time that are hard for movement, writing and
> sound not to lag behind. The speed of visibility.

The seduction of Machine. The metaphor progresses—triumph, battle, defeat (i.e., defeat of nature) and as well projects the analogue of the Body:
muscle power, gigantic 'bones of steel.' The age of electronics gets rid of the
need for muscle—is subatomic—electronics the model and means. Maybe
you could say the age of information *uses* nature as its model. At the least,
it rids us of the muscle analogy and thereby the relative value of muscle
strength and thereby divisive measures of male/female strength.

> The information age gets rid of muscle applied to task but not the training
> of the body, the desires that are structured through the pores—these appli-
> cations must not go unchallenged. Training of the senses (film), the body
> (movement), these are not outmoded unless you think society's meaning is
> only a translation of the forces of labor as constructed by science. But what
> about ideology—the source of what gets developed. What meanings get
> developed in the future—these realms are for politics and art, not just as re-
> active mechanisms to science. Art and politics are formative, an advancing
> of thought.

Yes, but there is an interrelation here between art and politics and science
and ideology—not cause and effect.

> *We all do social work, all of the time.*
> I believe we (our modernism) are incorporating the context and content of
> the social in the materialistic integrity of our mediums.

Shaking a paper bag, be it dance, film, writing—the creating of interior
space, exterior space, the bag itself = the tradition of the field, the membrane that defines. The membrane (could anyone write a critical statement now not using scientific terminology?)—a tautology of the reflexive
necessity.

from *Black Holes, Black Stockings*

JANE MILLER AND OLGA BROUMAS

The very perfume Kienholtz must have used in his environments on the 1950s—the slow music, the polyurethane men at the bar, or servicemen in the waiting room of a house of prostitution, memorabilia about Eisenhower—all on a brown and red carpet of roses. Your mother's letters at your bedside table, unopened, overpower the wilting cherry reds. She follows you to Europe with her drawl and plaint. I practice the flute, cascading cheerful melodies with low notes on the end. The Festival, the tinsel, the flash of light in the eyes of the well known and us, driven into the event by your departure. That day we heard of the terrorism and shootings and were sorry we had believed you were going for a rest. Not that you would be involved, but that once there would find consort among those wronged. We surfaced among costumes on the promenade, the faces of the hotels marking a period of history when architecture was sculpture: colonnade and white facings below black ivory domes, crystal high in the dining rooms' omphalos. We drank Samboca under the celebrated sky, blacker and more riddled for your absence. It was your drink, and we sipped to the hard coffee bean, split like a nipple; we were surprised—very few people had heard of it, although it is not uncommon.

Her first few times had been in parents' cars and even with a few parents, but mostly with boys a few years older—and better than their fathers. Girls talked about her and imitated her speech without knowing it. Teachers put her in front or in back of the room depending on their openness to sport, for she understood clearly the despondency of a high school education and of its educators and played upon their broken fields; or, rather, behind them—where the tall hedges met the low wall. Intimate with self-knowledge, she knew what to like and what was all right to like and liked confusing the two. And she liked two at once—though it would be years before boys became man enough to see themselves in other men. She was healthy because she was careful because, free of guilt, she often chose the hand over the heart, specifically, over the pants, clean, quick. When the police pulled up with their hard rubber flashlights banging the window, her clothes were in evidence on her instead of against her. Animal, vegetable, mineral: the sun is probably shining over her now in a convertible. She would tell a lot of women where to get off; some knew what she meant.

Like a cousin who fell from a horse, the weather changed suddenly, thrown into mistral. One of you went away, the other inside herself, from whose window a face shone, but shaded. I walked many hours each day without pleasure, like jogging, because the exercise was good for someone I might want to be later. The morning jasmine, dogs, kids skating too fast or falling, materialized slowly like dampness from stone rained on in the night. By four in the afternoon, perhaps, a clear thought; or a stone from the morning walk remembered like a hard decision, its cold beauty there on the strewn path. Too many birds, singing. From the other side of the valley a tractor engine, heard when I concentrated. A tight muscle, petals heated in the suddenly too hot sun drooping, behind a sealed window a slammed door—windwheel, will o'wind. Giving in—to the thousand dizzying steps you might take in a different direction; and you other, taking them into your room and mounting them in a narrowing perspective away—I bury a cry in the jowls of the wind.

A cry comes out and is the changing exterior, particles without apparent cause in threes who vanish without a trace. Here and there and where, moebius space. Who heard suck, who sucked? In the heaven of intuition, a network of pearls where one reflects, where one reflects all others, transient appearances are made. They are made without choice and catch in the netting below or fall through but as through space without gravity, the famous and unexplored falling-not-down. How long they hold there or are absolute elsewhere changes in timeless pandemonium. No one notices probably; probably notices no one. The sea in the distance is now pulling the stars, in the distance at any time and at will, awry as sparkles on the water. What matter! The perfect thing for you here. World polite as it collides, as it surprises. Assume the simplicity of the lattice: in our alternative or became *and*. And how! How can two of anything communicate so quickly, carried from one place to another like a light-wave for all it seems instantaneous. I seem to see. Therefore under the blue lights rests a girl with a fan and her dress tied under her breasts. She is large, filling half a large chair, looking ahead at herself discreet. Impossible to imagine her not there. The intoxication of the mind is the matter with the body. Colors are outlines with special effect unforeseeable—scarves, capes, nightgowns willing the wind to arrive, imported curtains to part. And one evening half asleep like a drug also arrives, late, making signs like a crazy person, a violin by itself. So the poppies out of the stone are drawn, curious, to love as to fresh air, waving, aware, complimentary, waking the sun.

The hundreds of leaves inside our dreams also quiver, they quiver, believe it. Like a range of mountains, out of hearing they are earth visited. Bay-leafed, the hands we hold. And on them the maps crossing from right to left, beginning to end. Bodies sequestered into souls. When they are laments we hear them as if they are immersed in water, blurred with tears. And as blessings, if at all. No doubt where I walked as a child, razing the air. If we dare, if we are the cage we painted with an open door, one of the many like a touch of dust in sun accidentally fells the outline with its colored chalk. Little tokens of myth, dream. On a stalk the water lily, on its spring the mushroom, such clamorings on the white pillow! Pass by. Because atop midnight like a scaffolding already we change our mind not sad together, interminably between, flower and fruit. The hexagram which forms RAIN in the sky falls as rain to sweeten the salt water. There we go swimming out in it at the ends of the polished fingers pointing at us, gradually merging into wave. Of the slender towers, gorges, beehives, hermitages, tumbling ranges, waterfields, the sea stradles the globe, more moon than earth, vicarious. One passes with a loaf of bread on her shoulder wrest from the burden of the sea, its great salt lips that search for mountain streams by squatting at the shore or throwing themselves like a discord upon it, familiar but elusive, one of the different women who invite you home as though there were such a place, as though such women find you. They do not become destiny. With their song of the sea, with their timepieces, their waterpipes, they are the hours of the day, the hours born in the alley, the hands taking the glass off the lamp and lighting it. The garlic and peppers hang from the

ceiling. The honey and lemon, great nocturnal watches, gold pieces in the
other life, whenever you wish. Not much different from advancing you will
speak simply, one word in front of the unspoken.

She swam out in her see-through suit after I told her this story: he used to
fish floating the flies and metallic pictures of worms, or real worms which
he tied rather than pierced to the end of the line. He never used hooks. The
nylon lay lightly on the water; he thought it was like a mating game because
the lures were the same color as the trout, silver-blue, and sometimes with
feathers, which he preferred because they were more buoyant. He bought
the lightest nylon, the most delicate lures, so that there is the sharp image
of him slowly pulling in the line as if pulling in the horizon, with the fish
following once in a great while the long way to him submerged to the hip
in his rubber boots, green like the lake algae. The algae were different in
the higher elevations, oily and thin, and a kind of person was called to that
place who would like to see through the water—the rest of them caught
and ate their fish. Fish with fans iridescent and, unfortunately, irresistible.
Sublime drop, as from mountain to sea, where she rolled her one-piece
down after the fashion, shoring up all her hair with two pins, among the
wealthy and not.

O restless one, who climbs to the top rung in the rain and slips on the
last dowel, searching the far hills for morning in its yellow slicker; or, on
the way home at the dinner hour, late autumn mulch smell in a gust with
evening-roast, you take the wrong turn suddenly into a thicket; the stray
dog there, his snap, and the eyes on a tree trunk with coarse brows; a creak;
a cry, yours—covered with a quilt in your sleep like moon by fog—wres-
tling the hammer of the woodpecker out of its parody of your heart; and in
a sweat throwing the cover off now, freezing the cat on the sill by dilating
its gold eye with the one of yours whose door snaps mistakenly open on
its crusted hinge. Sleep shapes the pillow of the weary and infirm, of the
one woken by rain, and of the others in thought and in love, turning. A rise
of late moon chafing the sky slips between earth and a few stars, perhaps
the one you were dreaming of or, through a closed lid, projecting from;
therefore the disc must be rolled away with an arm as if across a dark sheet.
Inertia squares itself, yogic, and breaks you almost into consciousness to

budge it, falls into the perimeter of the circle and tumbles in its moon finally away from you. Heavily the magma of earth's core shifts, throwing a few warm coals into your hands; and then, because you have sunk so far, rested, believed, you reach the fires kept burning. And burn your craft there, waking.

Women who fly on separate planes to meet in strange cities, poppies with their black follicled centers, chicken eggs with a little blood on the shell like a stain on a sheet, the stain soaked through and left on the bedpad unwashed, print housedresses washed and, in the wind, torn at the hem; pneumatic alliances: the plane too low, a drinking glass pitched off a table, uncracked, but with its blow to the head, unmarked, bleeding inside a drop; bird coo, too regular, parrot trained to the French national anthem, bumblebee, its lion markings burned black, stabbing the window and otherwise horrible fly. Brain dust, spindletops blown in the air, brow furrowed with electric violin practice, seeds planted too close in a furrow, tomorrow, because of a dream; giving orders; taking orders; the wearing of black, the wearing of mirrored glasses; dust; haze; ants on a naked woman, lipstick on a man; with a penknife, manipulation of a developing Polaroid; periodic rinsing through the night of the menstrual sponge; the days and the nights sulphuric between golden and leafy, between the sun and the moon: discharge, between flights in an airport: dizziness; black, yellow, red; yolk, ink; the beautiful striations after the sun sets invisible, as without love.

September of mother small and of animal, autumn of wood smoke. I was twenty-five, I had bought a cabin in the north in the tight hills. Maple and pine, and beyond, pine and oak, and behind, birch. I heard a sound in the woods as if it stopped for me, dog or bear, and when I woke, when I walked, I deferred. Waiting, feared, afraid, found nothing and knew the loneliness which is nothing, and started into recognition: a deer. And then the shot out of season, someone else's loneliness pinched into repercussion, the will demanding of the soul-off-guard and seizing its game. I ran into the deeper woods, the giving up getting over you, a liberty I had taken into the forest and gutted.

Sparklers from the July sky crease through the organdy and in autumn you burn again when the owner of the *bacal* at the corner raises your woolen skirt. The moment illumines a path through the crates of vegetables and fruit in the partial sunlight, the sacks of chestnut and raisin, to the window behind the counter where the sewing things lie on the sill, to pick a thread from the colored boxes that matches the fabric in your hand. You gasp, you exclaim, he withdraws, you buy the thread and mostly forget it until the year when, at home, you flush as a woman with what was thrust on you then, desire electromagnetic and adult, the massing of an arousal you couldn't possibly stop alone and yet, in the gravitational field of the village with its bakers and families of streets, did, which confused you. You do more yoga. You make yourself by posture and breath relax and lapse, taking from each what can rouse in you now a force to equal it easily, to come to discard it.

The greens grass, outburst toward the sky, the fig tree dances with Matisse as he cut himself out before dying in the shape of its leaf and the gorgona shape, curly-haired half-mermaid, half-weightless bird smaller and more precocious than the dove: *rossignol, hirondelle, mésange*; and somewhere the expensive alizarin streak a masquerade, *maquillage*, rouge on the body.

I alter nothing for her; that is how change sweeps me. Imagine the momentum of sea, how at the shore the pressure is realized in the slightest touch. Where there are pines and sea together I arrive in the present. The sea, the scar it makes each time it cuts the sand. Three smooth stones, their musical bodies in my hand. Turning, I turn them over. If we think, we aren't in motion. I stand and walk across the red tile and open the window by the center clasp. Each side goes out from me into the room. The rocker, the red lampshade, the two flutes and photographs of events, the French lilacs stolen. Their hair is ruffled, they've just gotten out of bed. I am the bird that flies out when they part. Each side goes out from me into the room, red hair, brown, the chiseled chins, sun and moon. When one is out I forget, I go into that one until the details are so great I recognize them in myself and can't remember where I am. April the almond tree, April the waterfall, April the first of summer, for summer then is a surprise. They wear each other's clothes, the red sweater that once was a guide, the white sweater and white shirt, white so different from white. Young, younger, youngest. The path to the olive grove, the grove, the black olives. Each of their mothers arrives, one takes her away and one takes her away. I have the time to myself, watermark where minerals once slept; jays tumble into dry rushes from the air. If I might complete a gesture on the flute, nothing can equal the radiant human element. Returning is a message. She invites me into her room. At last I'm alone.

The gods are never the same but remain the same body or rather the sign for it, hearts like pears like beacons. It was only a bird! skirting the salty bands of sea air. You flew. The small good-byes thank you but only because they are following. The large and the best, the ones who must duck to enter, the peaceful black squares asleep on their funny white circles, they will never stop you with surprise. You have an idea in four colors—on the indigo blue sea with a yellow ribbon around it, a fishing boat with red oars floating on the waves a spiral fishnet orange like hot coals. The smell permeates the whole memory, tickles and clucks and crackles as it comes in the small window, past and able to hurry you toward the beach with good humor. There you are, ever since childhood, that warmer country. As legend says nothing, you pick up the sounds and feel. Turn, the curly hairs waving in the south wind. Turn, the whistling. The plums falling on the fallen blossoms. Freshly whitewashed, the bases of the plane trees, minutes going by. And the flowers in the sand like spirits that close in daylight. Very rested, very smooth, all on the glassy surface patiently. Matter as instinct like eyes gleaming. Equally rare, this massless grace, beautiful white cloud I feel as a child in the blue sky, are the last made yesterday. They aren't personal, nor is one stone on top of the other a temple. The first days there are as one drunk, the vertigo of palaces and villas. The ravine in front inspires a sacrifice, but. Nerves ringing. No background. Riders flung. Eyelids lowered. Waves flash, being chosen. Not thinking, reverberating as eating and retiring for the night. A line is drawn like a tributary and in a circle a garland where, at the tops of trees, milk cools slowly in a footbath waiting for a guest. The symmetry of half-closed eyes along the line of bird flight, and the flags so sure of their movement. The mountain ranges fade that all day lowered bushels of light on prickly trails. I remember when the splendid mouth separates from land and sky, water again as I go out to meet the paired eyes of the fishingboat lights. Gleaming in their heads, sexual, tilt the whirlpool irises, off-centered dahlias, flowering scents confused at the hypotenuse of honeysuckle and mint. Making icons

in their saffron and purple robes, in their monasteries, the flowers intend
and imply. Beauty abandons the traversed latitudes—seven thousand and
seven pagodas the work of people. When the faithful want to pray, when
the prayer alights, it is dawn. And, extricable like yellow ochre from earth,
when desire spills out of synch it finds you absent-mindedly spinning a
globe, the bazaars, the exterior lives. Tin the boxes. Gold the rings. Nails,
clocks, tobaccos, hashish in its powdered form, dust and cobble in theirs,
green kohl, carved scarabs, silk, fringe, garlic, eggplant, chickens, leather,
cooked meat, yoghurt, flatbreads, camels, mules, cows, sheep, dogs, par-
rots, canaries, chess games, old books, candelabra, paperweights, sandals,
slippershoes, prayer rugs. Embedded, wedded, the stall to the hangings.
Before the snakes are brought out, the northwest you see how they will be.
Called to, you and I. Isn't the other dazzling? I stood in the high sun looking
down. In a shallow bowl lemon light pulled in the wind like a boat onto
shore. No other pelago than this when nostalgia seeks a vessel. Tenden-
cies to exist, details expressed, unusual features of the world like the spiral,
place next to large public events private ones. Without thinking the meeting took place, prescient; as long as the well-known took to cross, longer
was the anticipation, ethos large and in front of me aristocratic. All that I
knew imagining went beyond. Churches and baths—churches out of sand
and baths when the sea floods in. Beautiful arches like bodies in love and
veins of darker sand leading to the water, labyrinthian, hold like cathedral
light whatever I say after the fact: energetic mountains beauty tires of; therefore the miracle of the tide accepted. The hymns and the prayers fire, the
rhymes air, they are cheering. Breath of god and with two unspeakables!

Four kinds of song, at least—sweet, insistent, erratic, shrill; and hare tra-
versing the thorn bushes that would berry. Butterflies paired, almost clapping to their flutter; and the rustle of olive, pine and fig. So the porch
overhanging the valley signaled the hours with its players. Time rounded
into a sun who appeared to stand still, then flattened to the horizon, became measured and horizontal again like Euclid's geometry, explainable.
Matter, at a perfect temperature, a certain mood, dematerializes before us,
takes on more than its qualities and irrecognizable, we say it disappears.
Love, calling itself into being. Or the dancing bear at the end of a pin—
happy relative molecule. A haze of heat, an idea, a chance meeting, color.
Made of mutually exclusive vibrations each with its unknown, its irrecon-
cilable heartbeat, insect-whir. We traveled here and arrived after. We play a

duet and don't hear it, hear it differently, hear it later, heard it somewhere before. The heat, the song fills us, therefore we say we are hungry, and we uproot the lettuce at dusk. "Lettuce," "dusk"—they mean something and are funny, a sort of a song.

She left the party saying I should drop over, which I heard an hour later. It was on my way home, barely, but because of the road I took, exactly. The light was off, which should have been enough, except a candle shook a circle onto one wall. I said I was sorry to stop by so late, and indeed was; we drank and I watched her drink, pouring that slow Southern voice. She took the stem with two long fingertips and thumb, twirled it like a cliché, and laughed. She held the glass and our laugh and our few hours up to the light and we saw them and tumbled them darkly about the room. She pulled and I buried my face in her so I wouldn't hear or heard other, through the tall grass and moonlight I made of her hair and eyes. I was there because I separated my eroticism from love; in love, sometimes I was erotic, through a chink where I flew out of time; but where I didn't belong there was never time, and I hoisted myself onto its smooth back, broke and disappeared and recollected myself, and left. I stood on the night porch with my shoes off, feeling the cool painted boards, golden under the rural street lamp. Night tossed back its head and a star fell, slowly and then suddenly into the far fields, like a look someone gives, anonymous, and touching in a distant fecund place. The car was a cool animal in a night I didn't have to look directly at nor speak to but who understood I was grateful to be passing through and, through, home and, home, that he was asleep, whom I almost desired.

It's a precise preference, the panorama divulging its inner trigrams duration and grace, unequal and absolute. Adding silica to these minerals obtains a *cristal* free of molecular angularity, known to the Chinese as exhaustion-of-the-masculine, such its clarity their book of wisdom places it at its close, torture and eros before completion.

She whispered *anemones* naming the flowers the boy had brought, a minor scene against the erotic masterpiece of the girl and her older lover Brando. We walked in in time for and accentuating the suddenness of their first intimacy in an unfurnished apartment. Driving home, after the movie, people we passed almost knew what they were doing in the back. The sunroof was open on the powdery sky and the narcissus from Tangiers smelled differently on each. One wore it like a light laugh surprising the air, the other like a vapor. I drove carefully exercising my hearing—I loved to hear first and see later and later still to touch. Taste, the darling of life, lay on her rosy couch on the other side of arrival, where we would fall as into a great beginning elsewhere, after acceleration, after light and sound. First it was like talc and then oily. I let myself take in from the back a finger, and there the darkness of all our colors lacing the room quickly magnetized in one spot like absence focused upon and enlarged—light, lightly. I was disappeared into an impersonal moment where the casual is sacrosanct; that anemone, for example, into which I was driven and from whose center I was pulled, into time, rested, ready to sleep.

Thirty mirrors ranged round its periphery, each tilted slightly from the next. The images cast by the mirror-drum as it revolves pass over three apertures so arranged that each gesture explores one-third of each image. Behind these apertures are three photoelectric cells, connected to the necessary amplifying equipment. At the receiving station the currents enter three neon tubes. The light from them is focused by means of a lens upon a revolving drum, similar to that at the transmitting station, the light being thus reflected upon a translucent screen. Two black and white goats running into their full three-dimensional image where the high rock meets the low-hanging limbs, a view of the opposite hills. What a few days of transparency would do. You keep pulling fibers out, distracted by birds. Fish-shaped flowers and bird-shaped leaves. Blessed again, wrong again, even measure, that relaxed vocal style, the gender of deities. Polyphony appears feminine. Slowly and seriously the petals falling down, a little schoolgirl madness in their trampled gowns. Slips. Gnats, wasps, calla lilies, a woman drawing her lover on the grass. The grass! Spring risks. The lover making the gigantic trust with and without knowing. Everything else is fantasy, peace sans form. Anger, resentment, bitterness, rage, displays of temper profile when you play.

from *Life, After All*

SUZANNE JACOB *Translated by* SUSANNA FINNELL

"You say *perambulator*. You do not say *baby buggy*."
—Jachar

"You do not say *cover*. You say *blanket*."
—Jachar

I had to think quickly. I saved the old black baby buggy. I threw newspapers into it, old newspapers and newspapers that were stuck to the curbs of the streets. When I saw it coming, I knew I wouldn't have much time. It all went through my head very quickly. You had to think fast. Know what was important. Without having to decide I held on to nothing. When it came right down to it, the decision came all by itself, I held on to it tight, I left.

The baby buggy was out there, I pushed it, I dragged it. Or was it the baby buggy that pushed, pulled, and dragged, I don't know, never knew, don't remember. Often you can't tell whether the ends of your fingers are where things begin, or if the things themselves are the beginnings of your fingers. There are fewer things here now. Now, things are simpler. There is only the little old baby buggy and inside that, newspapers, and inside them the weather reports and new news; I always knew that news is continually new, and didn't really need confirmation. Why bother, I equate it with the weather report. I alternate good weather with bad weather, creating a balance.

So, here we are. The fault engulfed it all. All this time we had lived on top like owners. The edge is a lot farther back now. There are some who went back with it, they started over again. As for me, I left.

It's a pretty solid one. Even though the wheels appear to be fine and delicate, they should last. It pulls me along. We take turns pulling, it's the best solution, since it wasn't possible to know anymore who pulled, who pushed. I didn't know if I should be grateful, if it was right that it was always the buggy that worked and never me, or always me and never it. I mark an X so that we don't get mixed up. I put an X in the margins of the paper, so that I can keep track of the turns. I make a cross with the nail of my left thumb, the one that is the longest of my ten nails. I keep it sharper than the others; it helps me to know who worked the evening before, who will work tomorrow and who is working at the moment. In my daydreams, I could very well make predictions, in order to know who would be working ninety-three days from tomorrow, or in going the other way, who worked ninety-three days ago counting from yesterday. This way there is a built-in future in this story.

We're all alone. We settled in far from the edge, and took it from there.

In the paper dated March thirteenth, it says Stravinsky's widow burned her love letters for personal reasons. Did she foresee the receding of the edges? Either she must have been swallowed up, or she left, at her age, and she did not have to think yes or no was she going to take these letters, since according to the paper they had been burned. As for myself, the letters quickly crossed my mind because it was necessary to hurry and not being used to catastrophes, it was strange to have to hurry so. But no, not the letters. The buggy only. It's all black. Its roof is torn. The newspapers are inside. Everyone really takes a turn here, we agree on this without formalities because there are fewer people than before. Before we needed contracts if we agreed to take turns and raise our hands. Here I don't raise my hand anymore, the right one naturally, never, no need anymore.

I was all dressed because I had been sleeping with my clothes on for a long time. Still, at another time I used to sleep naked. At that time there was another skin. You used them to cover up, and with time, we needed to make a collective agreement because we didn't know anymore who was covering whom and who got warmed up. And because certain skins were cold-blooded, the purchase of thermometers helped to make the agreements fair according to the temperature of the skins, and so everyone could sleep in peace. Often we suffered from insomnia despite the clarity of the law, so I started to wear a sweater, then I kept on my panties; after that I kept on my big wool plaid shirt with the blue squares. After that, I kept on my red flannel skirt, and the other skin, each one having its own, could continue sleeping naked. We didn't really pay attention any longer to the laws of the night ritual.

As I said, I was already dressed and left very quickly without taking the time to consider if I should alert the skin that slept without insomnia. I think that that skin was swallowed up, I have no news. News doesn't exist anymore where I am and where we go, both of us, me and my buggy, we have only old news to digest and that turns out to be eternal. The news from before, we feed on from time to time and we don't miss news from after since it's eternal.

But what we missed in the beginning was tobacco. It was lucky that in the beginning and even still today we reeked of it. I would never wash the buggy with its torn hood or me and my shirt. We pretend to smoke by smelling the parts that reek the most, it's a good way to save. So much for what's missing, the craving comes in the evening with the ringing of the vespers and with the taste of red wine; it's crazy but it's in the memory banks and they can go off at the most unexpected times. You can't second-guess your memory. Almost without reason, it unwinds itself anyway. You stick your nose into the shirt and fall asleep like this, the shirt then becomes a sleeping pill. So you are careful never to wash it, it would be a total disaster, like the disaster of the edges receding, rather total.

I got rid of the brown stone. Back then I kept it in the big pocket of my flannel skirt. It would make me dream, and then it would wake me up if necessary. I imagine that I wouldn't be needing it anymore except to stimulate certain memories. The only thing left for it to do was to wake me up in the night from an uncomfortable position. I could have thrown it into my buggy, but what's the use. If you agree that everything must have a use, then everything must take its turn when its turn comes up. Looks like repetition, but not because we're settling in. We are settling in far from the edge. And took it from there.

Chances of going around in circles are great. We should mark the bark. That would give rise to the problem of traces. Do we want or do we not want to leave traces. Before, the question was what sort of traces. As a result of the different marks, there were jobs created at the Ministry of Traces. The skins discussed the marks and when it was applicable, declared them "traces." Signposts were put up at certain marks that had been declared traces, and you didn't bother with others to avoid administrative hassles.

Not everyone could be a troublemaker, after all. It took hundreds of years in the offices. Luckily I was not assigned to the offices nor did the offices summon me. Just once, I was assigned to the subject of which I have already spoken, the skins and who would make whom warm. You had to go into an office, by that time I had been sleeping in my skirt for a long time, but still I had to be summoned. No, we decided to take the risk of going in circles rather than leaving marks that might possibly serve as traces for a newcomer. There is only the same old news and raw roots are edible. Of course we thought of cooking our roots, but we remembered that fires leave traces, marks, circles, indentations, wounds on wood, and so, no, no fires, only raw food, it's important if you want to eat.

It must be said that we have used a lot of our newspapers since our run for life. First, we gave up the top of the pages, all the tops. Now our news have no more dates, it's the dates on news that make them so immortal. So much was used up already, but it was necessary because they were needed. Really. My bodily functions continue as before, a little less, considering the rarity now of the old feast days, but still I want to continue to wipe myself as if nothing has happened, the little drops, and the little hole, so that it continues to stay pink, I keep to that because of pride, and also, I continue to menstruate but my skirt is red so even if I spotted, because of economic considerations, it would hardly be noticeable. Difficult to get rid of all old habits, or new ones.

Because we needed to sacrifice parts of the newspapers, there are no more dates, as I said, or names, or information as to where they came from. In any case, we're not good with names, or dates, or places; I remember March thirteenth because of Stravinsky's widow, it struck me simply because of the word "love," to burn love letters; I think this is timely news for widows, and that's the reason why it struck me.

No monkeys in sight. But lasting existence through us, black buggy and me, red skirt and blue shirt with big empty pockets loose on my breast, monkeys seen and loved long ago on the edges; impossible to get rid of the images from those times, impossible to erase the images of big monkeys with flowering hemorrhoids even after all these days, all these nights, of examining and deciphering the roots.

I have someone to talk to. I remember that this used to be a problem on the edge; skins tried to find someone to talk to, it was called despair, nothing eternal, just historical. Me too, I often looked for addresses, the ones I had never seemed enough, it was a real problem, especially on hot nights. The other skin said that at least I could take off my constant skirt despite my resolutions. There must have been some connection. But even when entertaining the idea of a relationship, I did not like to go against my resolutions. It was one of the ways of distinguishing myself for myself, without egotism or anything. It's perhaps this character streak that allowed me to escape looking like an old black buggy.

I have been worried ever since this morning. I feel that we are being followed. I don't know exactly what I saw that triggered this intuition. With me intuition always comes from something that I notice without being conscious that I noticed it. It's been awhile since I have worried, because the roots take up all my time, I no longer remember how to wrinkle my forehead to worry productively. I remember everything had to be efficient, it was of foremost importance before the edges fell in on us and their receding or their advancing, you never know.

You say perambulator, you don't say baby buggy. Never heard this statement again since my departure. Resolution: never name a root. Enough to know whether they're edible or not, that's plenty. No christening is called for. There is no need to debate on the subject of pram or buggy. Good riddance.

It's a pretty solid one. It has a fine suspension. We rest in natural trenches. Before, there was absolutely no agreement on how to determine what was natural and what was not. Since the catastrophe an agreement came about, easily. I have a natural aptitude for getting along with myself and this simplifies discussions. That was one of the reasons why I was summoned to the office. It took me awhile. Days and nights followed each other, like now, but with time, back then, they became heaps, whereas now, there are no more heaps even in their succession. And I took no stance concerning what was natural. I looked. I thought about it. The most difficult was vinyl. Vinyl posed a special problem because it did not have pores. I slept once with a skin without pores. Lying down, it's not comfortable when you have to resort to a microscope to find the pores at night. It continued to trouble me even afterwards, long afterwards, this absence of pores on the photos left behind by that skin.

Heaps of cigarette butts, too, and all sorts of pots in the bottom of cupboards, earthenware pots, glass pots, porcelain pots, terra cotta pots, pots without necks, with necks and all, it stays in your head long afterwards, but it doesn't bring up the question any longer of what is natural like it did before, each time I opened the door. How we got there, was the question. In front of any pile, the question was how we got there. Heaps, how did these heaps of things get there? All these variations on heaps and the wind had nothing to do with it, even though we don't really know if the wind had nothing to do with it, it is like my memory of the big monkeys, even if we are farther away now, very far, I am afraid that we are very near, considering the possibility of going in circles and that before there were also skins determined not to go around in circles, at least in the imagination of the river population.

That's resolved now. Everything is natural, with or without, the concern is simply not in the pores. It's the question that's not natural. It was just that you often got bored on the edge and that you knew how to invent things without wind, without grain, without sperm, without heart or anything, neither tail nor head, you often called it pleasure, or somewhere else metaphysics, depending on the different vocabularies from one heap to the next. Different vocabularies come from heaps, that's all. Now, it's all so much clearer and buggy and me, we get by pretty well with edible roots.

Perhaps the feeling of being followed comes from a dream. I thought I saw a bird. Were we still asleep in a trench, buggy, sleeping on the side, with the wind making the two wheels spin as if there was something to be milled? Did I sleep? It's difficult to admit to a bird, with everything being cut, except for the roots. Not a dove, it would all begin again, I don't want it to be a dove. Invariably there would be someone waving a white flag, and then, it's possible, if I saw a bird, that we would be followed by a skin waving a white flag, or if he was by himself, without a flag, he would be animated with his white hand as a replacement for the flag. For me, no, never again a white hand or a dove or an olive branch, all that was the same shitty vocabulary, and we took it from there.

Some sky is still left. A sliver. A bit of a cover. A bit of blue. All around it is the void, the nothing. It did seduce me when I saw that we were going to live like that, with just a sliver of the sky and everything else all black. Because of the cover it made for us and that travelled overhead with us, I was stuck, like that, like in a trance. It took some time. I stayed there for a long time not quite believing it and I said to buggy that I was on a sit-down strike, despite the fact that we were far from the heaps because of the catastrophe and all, and despite the fact that we left everything behind to be swallowed up in the fall of the edges.

Astonished. No recall of order and efficiency. No need to keep track of the input and output of participation. No shitty masses. Astonished, this cover and nothing else, roots and bark. Buggy. Red skirt is holding up pretty well, and the shirt and the empty pockets loose on my two breasts. Newspapers for news. A little more and you would have too much. As it is, this absence of belonging to a heap, this sensation blew me away. I keep thinking about it, experiencing it, I recall the smell of lavender; but here, it's better still, it's above and beyond everything.

Dreamt about the label of Chablis-Moreau. It still is sticking to the top of my neck. Pleasure: the sky lost its horizons. Horizons, before, eternal subject, created aims, ideals because of the symbols implied in the contact with nature. No more horizon. Just a cover big enough for the eye, without going overboard; before the sky was always going too far, you could never take it in all in one look. It created impressions of solitude and it created nearly all of philosophy, always trying to take in the sky in one go; this problem filled libraries to the roof. With the edges swallowed up, we go without news, the skirt is holding up, we go barefoot, we get scabby, it's OK.

Nothing new in terms of news, easy to forget them with time. Generally, news isn't sticky, that's what makes it so eternal. Only Stravinsky's widow makes me think; her story was really temporal in the sense that it continuously stuck to my skin, starting up thoughts from there. Had to sacrifice several entire pages. They had been rotting in the bottom of buggy and started to include buggy in their decomposition. I didn't think that old newspapers could rot like that by themselves; I found out. Oiled our wheels with earwax, it was all there was. Will see how it holds up and whether this will fix the slight squeak.

Found a new root. Pink. Careful. I'm making some tests. It's pink inside and outside, milky, flexible like licorice. There are no rats here to use in experiments. It smells. Reminds me of the smell of one of the skins from before on the edges. Neither salty nor peppery. Sea-like without salt. Often it was vice without the versa. Often, it was versa without the vice. When vice and versa came together, I tried again to go naked at night. But in the end, I abstained and my skirt stayed on again. The suspicion that I carry around on the subject of the pink root poisons I think the motion and the luminous blue of the cover above.

Today, the thought of flying on the edge keeps me entertained. It is perhaps the smell of the root that triggers the memory of highs. Put the root into the buggy to see if the thought of ecstasy would leave me, it's difficult, I would prefer it would not. Especially the thought of this one single time, in a city on edge and a night in July, two skins, one on the right, one on the left, almost not touching the sidewalk, desire, ecstasy and hair and the hot night, staying up, that was it, especially not going to bed, because going to bed would be to renounce the balance of the high, a rose in the mouth and a bunch of greens yanked from the gardens of a big hotel. I won't forget the balance was kept; I don't know what was saved, but balance just for balance was a rare pleasure, in its time, in the flights on the edge. After that, dawns which most people never saw unless reflected from a subway window, under the bark.

Other advantage: I deal straight. No exile or waiting room. No leftovers, nothing to recycle or to fix in formaldehyde. You don't have to make yourself understood. There is only buggy that pulls me, and me pulling buggy when it's my turn. I am in charge of the roots, I find this fair because it's impossible to do otherwise.

For music, I have words. It's soothing. Today I played Ribambella. It's OK. I change music as needed, but sometimes before going to sleep, I play something that I particularly like; there are two or three that I like best, I can say I like Ribambella very much; then, it's Tattoo, which is full of the best of sensations. Tattoo, before or when I suffer a bit because of the scabs, is best.

I am followed. I told buggy that and I said to buggy that I should carry it because wheels leave marks on bark despite the fact that we had decided not to leave marks because of the traces. I am forced to change my decision, which is not difficult, seeing that there isn't a single skin around who could reproach me for the change of heart like before on the edges where it was not seen in a good light, disapproved of, yes, to change a decision, whatever one says and despite the analyses. So, buggy on my back to avoid markings.

Painful scabs on the knees because I often am down on my knees to search for roots. It's OK. No use for this back, this surface that sometimes should come and take the place of the skin of the feet or of the knees, but it's fixed and alone back there. That's it, it's my back, that's what's following me. Discovered that yesterday evening when I slept on it and when intuition stopped. I should have thought of it; never sleeping on your back makes you forget it and it becomes another part altogether.

Days, nights, roots. Still not made a decision about the pink root in the buggy that I see each time I take an old newspaper to get up to date with news. I am happy though to be the only one to experience a new thing about which no one around me speaks, seeing that I am alone. It makes me laugh. A laugh that is absolutely mine that flutters around in my mouth like tiny black flies on the bananas from before. Am I obsessed by the pink root. My mistrust is not asleep. Going over the old story again of the skin's erection. Skins did not like to be surprised in the state of a hard-on, there was a need for conditions, the time and place had to be right, so that skins felt OK morally, otherwise, you didn't live right. Once in a while a shaking of a bus started it, and the skins perspired a little. I liked that. Never understood why not. Why not let the tongue go towards the mouth towards the tongue and everywhere on other skins since you did not risk to turn in circles on the edges considering the paid controllers. But it was the question of honour that was important and it won against the sublime.

The pink root makes me more and more uncomfortable. Option: get rid of it, let's not talk about it anymore. If you find another one like it, just pretend not to see it and you will be OK. It's not shaped like a thorn, even though, little by little, in my head it's taking on the shape of a thorn, well, well.

I was walking with buggy on my back even though we are not being followed, buggy got used to it and likes it and this way my back can serve and not live any longer behind me completely apart, so, I was walking with buggy, when one of its wheels fell off. No use to tell stories or to invent cataplasms or stories of knots made with wheels, no, not here, we are without news. Except the news which really are eternal here, they stick less and less, difficult to make them come even to the retina. Fog.

Good riddance, good-bye and all, to the pink root today. Thrown behind my back. Asked my back to watch over it as long as it could feel it lying in the distance. That's the end of the pink threat story.

With only three wheels, buggy is almost always on my back. I don't know if I could tell its age now. Mine has no use here whereas before it had purchase power attached to it. The cover is still luminous. Blue. Stretch of sky too big before, now I would like the form to undo itself, but it's fixed, enraptured.

My hair is falling out. I had to go back to make sure that no tufts of hair had left markings. No. It's recent, from today. The cover cleared and there was hair on the bark. I compared the loose hair to the ones on top. Same colour. It's my hair. My root diet is perhaps not balanced.

Turn the back to the light, try to change the room without packing all my luggage, for example, get close to the music without towing in the tobacco, the wine and the ashtrays, that is the advantage here. Come to think that my skirt is a soft bone that started to grow from the waist.

I played Tattoo last night, full moon in the cover above. Tears welled up in my eyes. Enough to water the lemon tree also swallowed up in the receding of the edges no doubt. I lifted up my skirt. I slept with my head on my knees. This morning my eyelids stuck together a bit. Short impression that I could not take in all the cover in one go. Memory of crazy women from before on the edges. Finally, in the end, they were parked in heaps. That way the confusion that risked to bring us closer to chaos, that risked to wake the fear of big monkeys so far but maybe so close, was avoided.

Here, the question to go forth and multiply is resolved, good riddance. No need here to contemplate obstacles to feel unified. The son of Abraham may well go on to devour his heritage.

Today, little taste on the tongue. Felt my breasts under my blue loose shirt, no bad bumps and it's still there, the same happiness at the two ends. Broke the nail on my left thumb.

Gave up on crosses in the margins. Let go of a traceable future or past. Buggy definitively anchored on my back. Knees scabby. Inevitable four-legged position.

. . .

There is life, after all. I thought as much. Others are no doubt fishing from where we are absent.

A Motive for Mayhem

ABIGAIL CHILD

She's looking out of the picture. The bars across her face hold her in the picture and hold her from us.

The next is a negative. There's a pause in her lifted left shoulder. She's about to say something and he's listening, but his attention is in the other direction. There's another person in this room. We can't see them.

Now it's later and we're up closer. There's a sense of action in the angle of her head, her sharp chin. Her collar is rolled which both covers and seduces.

He's twirling something. Behind him are two maids. That's the second thing you notice. Imperial twins against a backdrop of altar. The altar is this stage, the curtain: the space of strangeness. The dots on the curtain and the patterns of the cans (stacked) mime the whirling flags he circles. The maids wear aprons, are ikons of discomfort. The magician needs aprons on bodies behind him to underline his possession: these are his maids (not apprentices). The maid on the left is relaxed. She won't go "on" until later. The second bends forward to see what is happening. The two women are the background to his repeating circling. In the background, they are the repeating figure.

Here is another. She is on her knees between chair and umbrella. The field is interior. The body is waiting. She looks up, seductive and luscious. She's arrogant. Her breast is big. It's a perfect volcano. In an encased waist, glitter to point with just a hint of fat pout.

The light makes her dangerous.

194

The onslaught of someone else. A big back in front of us. A dead body. A big cop cap. These are the business dead. You can tell by the brims of their suits and their posture. One's got his hand in his pocket. The women are screaming.

The light makes them desperate.

Significantly earlier, pictures are taken. It's poses happening. It's a stage, a stage against a wall in the outdoor. We identify with the one being kissed and as well, with the camera. We are both subject and object. We're the movement between the subject and object. We become the subject and we can also become the object. We can tell. NO. This picture is about us as subject. But we have not yet been forced to see that the subject might become the object. This is because there are no eyes looking at us.

In the next picture, everything changes. The flesh has been used. The brow is tense and along the nose is a wary ennui (a weary abrasion). He is looking out from under. Everything is covered. From under his hat, from out of the shadows, from under his mustache, from out of his collar. His ears are flat. Their color is silvered. The skin is lived. Like a tree, he's been there. His hat could be a priest's hat, but you know it is not. It's a worker's hat. The lips are firm. The frame is tight. The person is deep inside himself. He is close up, he is on the surface, but there remain his unassimilated parts.

It's the surface and the unassimilated parts that give us a grasp of the world. They provide the stage for our imagination and what the author can do with absolutely ordinary people.

This is not really comfortable. It does not climax. Everything is off-balance. The wall is tilted, the hair hangs weirdly, the leg's not at ease. One eye looks out, one looks off. Nothing has connection. On second look: though their bodies are entwined, his hand on her leg, her arms around his neck, they are falling off each other in perpetual stasis.

This is just the beginning. This moment says stop but is not going to make it.

I'm moving faster. There's a sense of humor with all this action and nothing happening. There are also holes on the wall. They tell everything.

Here is an other. She is reflection. She is texture and seduction and she's lying under the light. She's the point of focus. And yes, she's unclothed. She's holding a drink, inviting you in. She's holding a drink and the bit of cloth draped across her loin looks like water, a waterfall. Her breasts hang down. There's all this darkness. She is so *actually* distant. She just moved in with my action. But really, she is so distant. She's more like the door. She's double-handled. It's a double-handled door. It's a door which leads you on. There's a light under this door, luring you in, up to the window: her stage. This is the stage of the still life. We try to move away our eyes, but the folds, all the imperfections, the shadows force, focus us back onto the figure. You attend. She waits. You look. She eludes you. You wait.

You pick up the original. This is the hubris of definition. You fall. This maneuver introduces clarity. You foreground the exception and the threshold, deflect the mean, redefine the motive, reread the need for causality. In the largest sense this means we shape our causes, we expect them and then reshape them.

I BEGIN MY PICTURES UNDER THE EFFECT OF SHOCK. IN A PICTURE, IT SHOULD BE POSSIBLE TO DISCOVER NEW THINGS EVERY TIME YOU SEE IT. FOR ME A PICTURE SHOULD BE LIKE SPARKS. A MODELLED FORM IS LESS STRIKING THAN ONE WHICH IS NOT. MODELLING PREVENTS SHOCK AND LIMITS MOVEMENT TO THE VISUAL DEPTH. WITHOUT MODELLING, DEPTH IS LIMITLESS. MOVEMENT CAN STRETCH TO INFINITY.

OUR AGE IS DISTINGUISHED BY ITS DISTORTIONS. OUR VISIONS ARE FULFILLMENTS OF OUR NEEDS.

I had long conceived of a film composed only of reaction shots in which all causality was erased. The isolation and dramatization of emotions through the isolation (camera) and dramatization (editing) of gesture. What would be left would be the resonant voluptuous suggestions of history and the human face.

Some of my love for found materials must in part lie with this sense: of the value of the half-formed, the incomplete. An artist who seeks a classic unit, a formed whole, a balanced vision or harmonious work is looking for a different landscape. My topography demands negative capability.

As clear as I can see it. Rough and expansive, wet and dry, angles irritation cogs smooth-running fondnesses mixed, not anything, but everything and silence. Held together by the wires of its exhilaration. Raining art out of cross-purpose. Living off tension, squirming to earth, reexposing shock and the mind at its metaphorical limit. The mind itself is a network of channels. The mind is shocked and flooded. There are no borders in the mind.

A BACKBRACE OF PILEUPS. ALL OUR NEEDS ARE PERJURED.

This manipulation tries to hide itself, so the spectator sees only the arranged reality. Explosive force is attractive as a means to escape the arrangement. It arranges its escape. It deforms the attraction. This form reordered rereads the audience. The audience knows the language, recognizes its disorder and denotations. Is not really comfortable. What is two is one and one also. What is separate is lost and immanent. There's the tension and impossibility of fact. It's all surplus.

This is how generation works. The edge moves out from the center. The spaces get occupied. The not-previous becomes present, is named, to eat away the boundaries of the art. What type of sentences move through this space? The sentences are true when true spaces move through it. If there is enough of the world in the work, it is a world, and if not, you add more.

TO GET THAT ENVELOPE OF SOUND. THEY WOULD HIT THE SPOTS AND I WAS INTERESTED IN WHERE THEY WERE MOBBING. THE EXCITING DRAMA IN THE MEETING BETWEEN AMBIVALENT SHAPES. SEXUALITY EVOKED AS A LINE AGAINST WHICH THE BODY CAN MOVE.

Against sad mechanics of distribution and an economics of production held by a nostalgic politic in obeisance to the observant authority. Misappropriate this moment. Demand its emergence, blunder, unbounded. Will you to it. Exterior anomaly equals organic splice. This is not comfortable.

THE MEAT OF ANY IMAGE IS THE SUGGESTIVE MATERIAL THAT CIRCLES THE EDGE OF THE BODY RUNNING ON A TANGENT TO IT.

Surname Viet Given Name Nam

TRINH T. MINH-HA

Note: Women speak from five places in this excerpt from a film script: voices over, Vietnamese sung folk poetry (followed by the English translation), interviewees' voices in English, interviews conducted in Vietnamese (translated into English), and quoted texts read on screen. These diverse voices are represented by either roman or italic type. Sung poetry and quoted texts are indented.

Do you translate by eye or by ear?

Translation seeks faithfulness and accuracy and ends up always betraying either the letter of the text, its spirit, or its aesthetics.

> "The original text is always already an impossible translation that renders translation impossible."—Barbara Johnson

> Co chong chang duoc di dau,
> co con chang duoc dung dau mot gio.
> (With husband, she can't go anywhere,
> with children, she can't even have peace for one hour.)

> Co con phai kho vi con,
> co chong phai ganh giang-son nha chong.
> (With children, she would have to endure hardship,
> with husband, she would have to bear her husband's patrimony.)

The exiled: "But if I don't have roots, why have my roots made me suffer so?"

Running mute among other survivors, your heartbeats echoing with each footstep, you were led by an American officer to a large, deadly silent auditorium where suddenly upon opening the door, you found yourself in the company of thousands of voiceless presences—a soundless, densely packed mass of people awaiting their turns to be lifted off the ground.

In certain cases, the only way to enlighten one's surrounding was to burn oneself to death.

You ask me to write about what I remember most from my stay at the refugee camp in Guam. I shall never forget the day when we left. I was suffering from excruciating stomach pains and was getting ready to go and see the doctor, when an American officer showed up to tell us we had to leave in five minutes. As you knew, since father chose not to leave at that time, we were four women then, mother and daughters. Upon our arrival at the airport with our meager bundles of cloths, we were struck by the sight of people carrying suitcases of all sizes. Mother, who had had experience in fleeing war on foot, was convinced that not only we had to reduce our belongings to the minimal, but also, that the clothes we wore and carried be dark colored so as not to draw any attention to ourselves as women. The Americans were brash and coarse and they were yelling at us as if we were a bunch of cattle or pigs. At Guam, a limited number of tents and of folding beds were thrown at the flock. People panicked and everybody was shouting and crying. As the law of the jungle dictated, only the most physically brutal and aggressive succeeded to lay hand on these things; we could not compete with the men. We waited until nighttime before additional beds and tents were brought in. None of us could really sleep for weeks, especially mother whose anguish in sharing a tent with others came not from the fear of theft, but from that of rape.

Most unbearable were the public washing and toilet facilities enclosed in some crudely assembled wooden structures. The latter were mere holes dug in the ground in which overspilling excrements could never be evacuated fast enough and could be smelled from miles and miles away. I was so obsessed by this that even today when I go to national parks, it is a real ordeal for me to be forced to use their restroom facilities; however distant the memory, I can hardly bear the sight and smell of these wooden cabins.

Lan and Sue, day; transcribed from conversation:

Lan: sitting here thinking about my mom. I can't believe how much change she went through since we came here. . . . She went through so much transition from one culture to another, and, like, remember those spandex pants you bought me, with the snakeskin patterns? New Year's Eve I brought them home and put them on and I didn't have a matching sweater so I asked her if she had a black or grey sweater. She said, "Here," and gave me this sweater and I was going to sneak out the door so she wouldn't see me but no, she comes out: "Let me see those pants—."

Sue: I can't believe it—.

Lan: I thought she was going to be scandalized, like, they're too tight. She said, "Oh, I can't believe how much that matches!" She took a look at me and said, "You know if you'd worn those a couple of months ago you'd have looked overweight, but you've lost just enough weight so you look good. I like that design."

Sue (laughing): That's insane!

Lan: When I was looking in her closet for the sweater she had these leopard-skin pattern silky shirts, something I could wear. I couldn't believe it— Mom's going wild. . . . But that's just one of the things. I see so much gradual change in her, her values.

Sue: Well, you helped her a lot.

Lan: It's not so much help—I put her through a lot!

Sue: Remember when you first moved out of the house after high school— that was a big drag for you.

Lan: Yeah . . . dramatic.

> I am like a jackfruit on the tree.
> To taste you must plug me quick, while fresh:
> the skin rough, the pulp thick, yes,
> but, oh, I warn you against touching—
> the rich juice will gush and stain your hands.
> —Ho Xuan Huong

Che la che lay,
con gai bay nghe: / ngoi le la mot,/ dua cot la hai,/ an khoai la ba,/ an qua la bon,/ tron viec la nam,/ hay nam la sau,/ hay an do chau la bay.
(The seven deadly sins of a girl: one, sitting everywhere; two, leaning on pillars; three, eating sweet potatoes; four, eating treats; five, fleeing work; six, lying down too often; seven, wolfing her nephew's sweets.)

Dear Minh-ha, Since the publication of the book, I felt like having lost a part of myself. It is very difficult for a Vietnamese woman to write about Vietnamese women. At least in France where, in spite of the Mouvement de Liberation de la Femme, maternalism remains the cornerstone of the dominant ideology. To have everything as it should be, I should have accepted a preface by Simone de Beauvoir . . . as my publisher had wished.

—Mai Thu Van

A million of Vietnamese dispersed around the globe.
It will take more than one generation for the wounds to heal.

Of course, the image can neither prove what it says nor why it is worth saying it, the impotence of proofs, the impossibility of a single truth in witnessing, remembering, recording, rereading.

As I was about to leave her, she reached for a magazine and asked me whether I have heard or read about the refugees, especially the mountain peoples, who had passed away in their sleep without any evidence of heart attack or any other recognizable disease. "The reporters described this as one of those mysterious, inscrutable oriental phenomena, but I think they died of acute sadness." *Buon thoi ruot*, sad to the extent that one's bowels rot, as we commonly say.

from the Miss Vietnam 1988 Pageant: Candidate H———P——— , *please tell us what characteristics of Vietnamese culture we should preserve in American society?*
I think that, as far as women are concerned, we should preserve our Vietnamese heritage and the four virtues Cong Dung Ngon Hanh.

Phan gai tu duc ven tuyen,
cong, dung, ngon, hanh, giu gin chang sai.
(Every young woman must fully practice and scrupulously conform to four virtues: be skillful in her work, modest in her behavior, soft-spoken in her language, faultless in her principles.)

Tai gia tong phu,
xuat gia tong phu,
phu tu tong tu.
(Daughter, she obeys her father,
wife, she obeys her husband,
widow, she obeys her son.)

Theo luan ly tam cuong ngu thuong
dan ba khi nao cung phai tuy thuoc dan ong

khi con nho thi phai theo cha
khi lay chong thi phai theo chong
khi chong chet thi phai theo con
suot doi la ke vi thanh nhan
phai dua vao mot nguoi dan ong lam chu chot
chu khong bao gio duoc doc lap.
(According to the moral of the three deferments and five human virtues,
women must always depend on men,
child, she must follow her father,
married, she must follow her husband,
widowed, she must follow her son,
all her life she remains a minor
depending on a man as on a central axle
and can never be self-governing.)

Kim in her office and at the substation—voice off and sync voice are heard simultaneously and are translated from Vietnamese: *In Vietnam, when I quit school, I got married and had a child. I stayed home and didn't have an outside job. But when I came to the U.S., the sponsoring church members found a few small jobs for me. For example I babysat for a month, after that I taught French at a grade school for three or four months. Then I helped in a retirement home for half a year before I applied to work for an electric company. From 1976 until now I have been doing electrical drafting for a hydro-electric power station. I am the only woman in this job.*

Kim, sync: *At first I was very hesitant when you asked me to participate, but then I thought: why would I refuse, when I am a Vietnamese woman myself, and the role in the film speaks the truth of the Vietnamese women still in Vietnam as well as of those emigrated to the U.S.? Especially since this film, unlike the commercial films is not about love stories featuring some Hollywood stars, so I didn't think there was anything excessive in my accepting to be on film. I have also read about you and your films, and am proud of your being a Vietnamese woman filmmaker.*

Kim, voice off: *My son's friend who is very fond of the Vietnamese told me "You should take that role so as to speak up the repression of your mother and sisters in Vietnam." So, because I care about Vietnamese women in general, I want to get involved in this film. I still have many friends in Vietnam. Compared with Cat Tien (my role) their condition is much worse. Some of them who were highly placed*

in the past are now selling treats on the street,
or trying small enterprises to survive with their
children.

Generally, every girl or woman in Vietnam
I asked my husband who saw nothing wrong
must practice the four virtues. She must
and encouraged me to do my best to contribute
know how to sew, cook, speak and behave.
to our native country. Otherwise I would be too
Obviously, she is subject to the three
shy to appear on TV, not to mention film!
submissions vis-à-vis her parents,
her husband, although not always vis-à-vis her son.

Kim, sync: *A friend of mine opened her eyes wide when she heard I was going to be on film: "You've never been an actress, how can you fake it?" Another friend of my husband teased me, "they know you can act, so they have selected the right person. Who knows, maybe you'll act so well that the Americans will notice you and you'll be a Hollywood star in the future?"*
Voice off: *I keep on thinking despite our emigrating to the U.S., if our surname is Viet, our given name ought to be Nam—Vietnam. For the Vietnamese woman, the family closest to her is her husband's; as for our native country, we all love it, young and old. We will always keep our last name Viet and first name Nam. Even when the women marry foreigners here, they are still Vietnamese, so I think your film title is very suggestive . . . very meaningful.*

One thing the man said he learned to let go of while in prison, is identity: this singular naming of a person, a race, a culture, a nation.

Vietnamese adjusting to their new lives: mastering elevators and escalators, learning wrist-watch-type punctuality, taming vending machines, distinguishing dog's canned foods from human canned foods, and understanding that it was not permissible to wander the streets, the hotels or anywhere outside in pyjamas.

Yen, translated from Vietnamese: *When I accepted to help in this film, it was because its subject, as you told me, concerned Vietnamese women. Since I have always praised their ability to sacrifice and to endure, I thought this was an opportunity to speak out, although I was going through a lot of pressure and difficulties at the time. Once I worked on my part, I wanted to give my best because I don't think it is an individual matter but one that concerns* a whole community. An actress or a singer is looked down upon in traditional society. People used to say that in a respectful family, the woman cannot be involved in cinema or singing; they have many derogatory terms to qualify such a woman. But more recently, with the West's influence, cinema is considered an art and most actresses would like to play the role of a beautiful woman, so my friends were all taken aback when they heard I was acting the role of a 60 year old woman.

Yen, sync: Everyday I go to work before 8 a.m. and come home around 7 p.m. Then, I hurry to cook for my husband and son. Only after that am I able to rehearse my part for this film. Once the rehearsal is completed I can eat dinner and get my son and myself ready for school and work the next day.

Yen, voice off: I have been in the States for sixteen years. I've been working for an electronics company for almost ten years in chemical processing. The number of Vietnamese engineers working for technical companies grows larger everyday. Eight or nine years ago there were only three or four engineers, but since then many who came in 1975 have graduated, and there are now about three hundred or four hundred Vietnamese engineers at my company, but only two of us are women. . . . When I started working there, I encountered lots of difficulty, first, because I am Asian, second because I am a woman. I do have to overcome these two difficulties. The Americans have always looked down on Vietnam as a second-class country. Now we Vietnamese are entering professional careers and are competing with them. So although they do not really show it, you can feel that they don't accept the fact that there are more and more Asians with Ph.D.s working in the company, especially in Research where Asians form the majority because a Ph.D. is required.

Yen, sync: Concerning my younger brother's wedding, it is in our family tradition that I, the eldest sister, be responsible for it since my father is no longer with us and my mother is advanced in age. That's why I was very divided during the filming week.

What did your Vietnamese friends think when they heard you're going to be on film?

Their reaction is very different from my reasons for accepting. They all laugh and tease me, saying that I'll become a movie star and will earn enough money so I can quit my job in the future.

Traditionally, the Vietnamese woman who gets married must endure many hardships. She almost never lives for herself. When she lives with her family, all decisions are made by her father. When she marries, she must obey her husband's family. All decisions belong to the husband and his family.

Surname Viet, given name Nam. I think when a man asks a woman whether she is married or not, by such a question perhaps she is expected to wed a Vietnamese man and to keep the Vietnamese traditions. Perhaps she expects her husband to have patriotic feelings towards his country. Every woman would want her husband to be a hero for the people.

On TV and in newspapers, the tendency most often is to side with the North; only in a few cases the siding is with the South. But I have never come across a film or an analysis that is truthful, that stands in the middle and looks at both North and South with unbiased eyes. This is very sad, because I just want to see all the good points we need to keep, and the faults we need to change in ourselves so that we can build a new Vietnamese society. As for the foreigners, of course they look at Vietnam with their own eyes. I don't even want to see films that speak only for one side or the other. I want to find a book that speaks truthfully of Vietnam because everything I read either praises or blames, but always in an absolute, black and white clearcut manner. And I don't think there is anything absolute; each side has its rights and wrongs.

War as a succession of special effects; the war became film well before it was shot. Cinema has remained a vast machine of special effects. If the war is the continuation of politics by other means, then media images are the continuation of war by other means. Immersed in the machinery, part of the special effect, no critical distance. Nothing separates the Vietnam war and the superfilms that were made and continue to be made about it. It is said that if the Americans lost the other, they have certainly won this one.

—Inspired by Jean Baudrillard

Kim: These images call for human compassion toward countries in war.

There is no winner in a war.

Yen: These are images that are emotionally moving. They can change the way you think. For example if you don't like war and you see images of mothers holding their child in their arms to flee from war you'll be moved and stirred to do something to help. These images are very painful. What is often brought up is the mother's love for her child. In war the mother always protects her child's safety.

Lan and Sue, fireplace; transcribed from conversation:

Lan: Here in Berkeley it's not so bad—you have so many Orientals that people recognize the difference between Oriental cultures like Japanese, Chinese, Korean, Vietnamese. I don't know how many times I've run into people that, like, first of all they pretend like they're interested enough to ask you, "Are you Chinese or Japanese?" "No, Vietnamese." Then they have the nerve to say, "Oh, same difference." I find that really insulting.

Sue: I would too. It's ridiculous.

Lan: I wasn't so aware of it until recently, when you told me that story of—what was it?—the bus. . . . How it works both ways. What happened?

Sue: Oh yes. It was really funny. I was living in Taiwan and I got on the bus—the only white American—and this guy spots me from across the bus. Of course it's jammed packed and everybody's in each others' armpits and we're holding on for dear life because they're maniac drivers, and he starts making his way back. He wanted to get a little English lesson, which is fine—you like speaking English to people when they want to learn. But it happens twenty-four hours a day, so you're constantly speaking English.

Lan: That gets on your nerves.

Sue: By that time I felt pretty comfortable with Chinese. So he comes up and starts asking me questions. I told him in Chinese that I wasn't American, that I was French. And he was like, "So what, you're European, you speak everything, right?" So I said, "no, I only speak French not English." He said, "That's impossible, you're all European." So finally he said okay and he just started speaking French.

[laughter]

Lan: Oh actually I'm German.

Sue: Oh, that was embarrassing. I just had to be snobbish.

Lan: So that's why I like this place. When I first came to visit you, I'm walking between you and Julie, you both have blonde hair and blue eyes. Julie's speaking Japanese, you're speaking Chinese, here I am, "Hi, Pennsylvania," speaking English! It was a nice change of role.

For years we learnt about "our ancestors, the Gauls," we learnt that "French Indochina" was situated in Asia under a hot and humid climate.

Grafting several languages, cultures and realities onto a single body. The problem of translation, after all, is a problem of reading and of identity.

Van-Lang, Nam-Viet, Hoang Viet, Dai-Viet, An-Nam (Bac Ky—Le Tonkin; Trung Ky—An Nam; Nam Ky—La Cochinchine), French Indochina, Viet-Nam ('Nam)

"Vietnam" (American accent)—*they also call it 'Nam.*

Reeducation camps, rehabilitation camps, concentration camps, annihilation camps. All the distinctive features of a civilization are laid bare. The slogans continue to read: "Work liberates," "Rehabilitation through work." Here, work is a process whereby the worker no longer takes power, "for work has ceased to be his way of living and has become his way of dying" (Maurice Blanchot). Work and death are equivalents.

"In Guam, I recognized a general," she said. "He [had] been one of the richest men in Vietnam. . . . One morning in the camp, a mob of women came up to him. They took off their . . . wooden shoes and began beating him about the head, screaming: 'Because of you, my son, my brother, my husband was left behind.'"
—Wendy Willer Larsen and Tran Thi Nga

"The world is like a butterfly," wrote a Japanese poet of the seventeenth century.

A woman discloses the content of a letter her father recently wrote in prison in Vietnam. A poet, looking desperately fragile in a photo in his long silver hair, he did not write to complain about his politically condemned status, but only to weep over his eldest daughter's death on the very birthday of Buddha. Forty days after she died, he wrote, she came back in the form of a golden butterfly, encircling him insistently for an entire day.

Cong Dung Ngon Hanh. What are these four virtues persistently required of women? First, Cong: you'll have to be able, competent and skillful—in cooking, sewing, managing the household budget, caring for the husband, educating the children—all this to save the husband's face. Second, Dung: you'll have to maintain a gracious, compliant and cheerful appearance—first of all for the husband. Third, Ngon: you'll have to speak properly and softly and never raise your voice—particularly in front of the husband or his relatives. Then fourth, Hanh: you'll have to know where your place is; respect those older than you and yield to those younger or weaker than you—moreover, be faithful and sacrifice for the husband.

The boat is either a dream or a nightmare. Or rather, both. A no place, "a place without a place, that exists by itself [and] is closed on itself, and at the same time is given over to the infinity of the sea." For Western civilization the boat has not only been the great instrument of economic development, going from port to port as far as the colonies in search of treasures and slaves, but it has also been a reserve of the imagination. It is said that "in civilizations without boats, dreams dry up, espionage takes the place of adventure, and the police take the place of pirates" (Michel Foucault).

> Than em nhu tam lua dao
> phat pho giua cho biet vao tay ai?
> Em ngoi canh truc, em tua canh mai,
> dong dao tay lieu, biet lay ai ban cung?
> (I am like a piece of silk
> floating in the midst of the market, knowing not into whose hands it will fall
> sitting on a reed, leaning against an apricot branch
> between the peach tree to the East and the willow to the West.
> Who shall I befriend for a lifetime?)

Hope is alive when there is a boat, even a small boat. From shore to shore small crafts are rejected and sent back to the sea. The policy of castaways has created a special class of refugees, the "beach people."

Each government has its own interpretation of Kieu. Each has its peculiar way of using and appropriating women's images. Kieu has survived in hundreds of different contexts. First appreciated for its denunciation of oppressive and corrupt feudalism, it was later read as an allegory of the tragic fate of Vietnam under colonial rule. More recently, in a celebration of its two hundredth anniversary, it was highly praised by the government's male official writers for its revolutionary yearning for freedom and justice in the context of the war against American imperialism. For the Vietnamese exiled, it speaks for the exodus or silent popular movement of resistance that continues to raise problems of conscience to the international community.

La Luta Continua

NTOSAKE SHANGE

The sunlight hit Jean-René. The sepia half-moon of a mole by his right cheekbone glistened, steaming coal in a fast car gliding through the hills of Morocco. We stopped to have a very French picnic: kisses. Shadows of lips and teeth against luxurious auburn soil. The sun always slipping in and out of the bends of limbs, wine from Lisbon dancing mouth to mouth, tongues tracing patterns of clouds, scents of goats, sheep, and the last of my Opium, somewhere near Meknes. I wanted to stay in Paris I'd thought, but no. He said he'd have to have me somewhere I'd never been. I'd laughed. I woke in Casablanca to morning prayers and croissants.

If only my mother could see me now: Jean-René meticulously placing strawberries, blueberries, kiwi, grapes, melon balls, in a crescent round my vulva. Oh dear. Oh dear. Oh dear. My cat has yellow eyes. Now my pussy has lime green ones, amber pupils, slits.

Casablanca was hot, noisy, trashy, roadblocks everywhere, the war in Spanish Sahara. We retreated like Anaïs to the countryside. This Guadalupan velvet spur of a man and me, Liliane. I travel a lot. I look at men and take some home or leave the country, borders have never intimidated me. My passport is in order and I carry letters of credit, perfume, four fancy dresses, and six nightgowns. I always sleep naked alone at least once a week. I pray and say Hail Marys by some window at dusk. It's always best for me to deal with the sacred when I'm naked. For me it has something to do with humility.

I found Jean-René at the fast-food place eating souvlaki next to the Moulin Rouge. I was flirting with some Brazilians from the Folies Bergères. I'd just left Lisbon and Angola was on all our minds.

In my last paintings, before I left New York, I superimposed AK-47s over fetal transparencies under Frelimo banners. La Luta Continua was the name of the show. There was no way to stop my fingers, my arms, I was jumping up and down ladders to get the touches of blood and fresh corpses finely detailed so there'd be no doubt that the Portuguese left a country the way vampires leave blond white women: drained of life and scarred. I paint. I don't talk too much. The world overwhelms me. I can give up what I see. I see a lot. I believe in honor, color, and good sex.

Machado and Axel from the Folies were doing their best to entice me to La Plantation, an Antillean discothèque near St. Germaine des Prés. I looked Jean-René in the eyes once, and knew that would never happen. Why would I want to dance in a plantation anyway? Even in the presence of the singularly defined muscles of Latin dancers, one on either side, the man I was slowly seducing across the room just kept looking at me, knowing where I'd be going. I like that. I like a man to know what the deal is going to be in an instinctive, absolute, lyrically facile manner. I like a man with confidence. Take me from these two sweet muthafuckahs simply by looking. Do that and I'll be gone. Wherever we are going. I mean, if a man's up to that. I love double entendres, double negatives, duels. Some cocks have triggers; others are freckled or uncircumcised.

I decided I wanted some baklava. Right over there where the man with eyes was sucking me up. Imagine that, disappearing into a stranger's eyes in Paris. How would they find me? Who would know to look? I don't leave any tracks, am quick to burn bridges. My friends, well my friends, the real ones, wouldn't think twice. Liliane's, she's having dessert. They'd smile, unless no drawings arrived in say a month or two. That is my signature, after all, an image. I forget what I was wearing that night. Probably the floor-length azure crepe with lace triangles up to my hips and no back at all. I like that dress, but I'm going to dye it grise: ma robe grise. Oh, Jean-René slid his eyes into my mouth and asked me if I had plans for the evening. "Mais non, Monsieur, j'ai pensé que tu voudrais faire des arrangements." I told him my name several hours later. By then he could barely speak.

Jean-René with the black nipples that grew. Each tongue flick drawing licorice sticks tiptoeing over my teeth and tongue. Third-world delicacies. Cascades of caviar round my neck. Noire et blanche. He played the piano, when he wasn't near me. Actually he was a concert pianist. He played Bach and Stravinsky, when he wasn't near me. He sometimes played scales, but anybody can do that.

Coming down the Champs Élysées all the record stores blasted Stevie Wonder's newest release, Songs in the Key of Life. "Isn't She Lovely" chased me from corner to corner. I didn't know if I should hide near the gated windows or fly through the night like some paradisiacal bird of color: many colors. Any color, everything matches: spirit; free spirits; about to be in love a lot. Stevie Wonder pushing us closer together. Eventually, I stopped running. I walked fast. Waited by the curb. At some point he put his arm over my bare shoulder. His fingers grasped my skin so there were five imprints. A woman with three sets of fingerprints. That would drive Interpol crazy. I was already grazing the edges. I didn't leave his side till we got to where we began. Remember the hillside outside Meknes? You won't believe me, but I heard Charlie Palmieri in Paris on our way to heaven. Those fingers again. I'll have to draw it for you, okay?

Such character you'd expect from C.T.'s, Cecil Taylor's, fingers or my grandfather's, Frank, who was a master carpenter. My fingers still smack of perfumed talcum, white gloves, and honied lotions. My calluses are elusive, if ever present, closer to my heart than my wrists, which are deceitfully delicate. Veins, blue-black pulsing, rise eloquently from Jean-René's hands, small muscles throb over the white and black keyboard, eliciting the reveries of Bartók, Monk, Abrams, and Joplin. My back refused to sound anyone but Satie, Bobby Timmons, and John Hicks. This frustrates Jean-René. When he smacks my cheek with the back of his hand, only Andrew Cyrille comes to mind. The Frenchman is unnerved. The music of my body is deliberate. There's nothing I can do about how I sound. When I open my mouth, Shirley Cesaire and Jeanne Lee scramble for the skies, my tongue finds his somewhere high above the treble clef. We're pulled back, flat to the soils. Sun running us *pianissimo* while our sweat moistens the virginal African grass. Our bodies lay claim to the earth, silhouettes of lovers, smooth unbroken lines, enveloped by tall brush, quivering in the wind, as tongues would wag in whatever language were our license with each other known beyond this side of the road. Meknes.

I want to paint now. Throw Jean-René's swarthy limbs over the pillows I laced with scents of raspberry, bay leaves, cinnamon. He'll rest in soft fragrances: me and my spices. I pull out my brushes and pastels. Sequester myself on a rocky cliff before the walled village. Women wrapped in blue-black swishes of spun cotton float through the streets. The men in white and tanned robes saunter with a holy gait toward a precipice. It is dusk. I am using wine as water to moisten my paints. The air is too light for oils. Watercolors, moistened pastels alone, capture the haunting prayers of these disciples of Allah. I am allowing my fingers to float as the women do, over the cobblestones, reddened dirt paths, billows of dust following donkeys, mules, bicycles. My brush strokes unevenly. The abyss around which we assemble in honor of Allah. The evening prayers begin. The sun splits open, cries for atonement and adoration pierce the clouds, hovering weights above our heads. I feel a sharp pain in my groin, my heart is racing, I am losing my breath. I see Jean-René. His eyes are glazed over as if in a trance. I swoon. My blood has come. The forces of this sacred earth have drawn menses from my body. The sun sets. I use this last scarlet liquid to highlight the figures in my painting. Hundreds of women, floating blue-black apparitions etched *rouge*, the soil *rouge*, the brush-colored caftans of the men dragging in blood. The Jihad has simple implications. Holy War. Where is there war without blood. Blood falling to the ground. I am weak now. I leave my paints and brushes alone, slide over to Jean-René, who holds me close to him as if we'd been in danger, as if communion with God was a travesty. We can't kiss, not now. Fierce angels are everywhere, sneering and eager to mock our frailties. Mortals, flesh, driven souls, seeking wholeness with mouths, fingers, wrapping limb over limb to become one. Music issuing forth from their depths, entering one another, desperately seeking that one song, one melody of peace. The angels gather above the rushes, snide, shaking their heads, wagging their fingers through the air, lighting up the sky and calling thunderous rhythms to startle us, to insist we acknowledge our nakedness. I pull my paintings to me. The colors pour onto my skin. I am now streaked blue-black, reds, yellow, luminous blue. Jean-René grabs my hand. I hold my paintings, soaking in the downpour. Scarlet drops fall from my bosom to my toes, to the soil, blue-black smudges crowd off my own sepia tones. Lurching toward the car, I turn. Drop the paintings. Fall on my knees, bleeding. Pleading with Allah to bless me, to accept me as an instrument of the holy spirit. Jean-René whispers Hail Marys in my ears. I am digging for the scent of my god. My hands are covered with small rocks, brown mud and slivers of brush, up to my wrists where the clay has dried like bracelets. Jean-René lifts me in one movement, holding me a statue over the ruins of my art.

My hands were small fists, knotted round the earth I'd gathered. Jean-René glanced at me once. "We're going to Fez. If you want to save that dirt, there's a small box in the back. Wipe the blood from your arms and face or we'll never get a hotel room." My eyes followed the rise of his cheekbones, the arrogance of his slender nose, and the flippant curve of his lips, those finely wrought muscles in his forearm. Yes, the box, save the soil for earth paintings. Wipe the blood away. Watch Jean-René take the road, soaring, an ebony eagle, round mimosa and hibiscus and palms. Jean-René smoldering like Mont St. Pierre, but this volcano was holding the eruption for me.

The woman shedding blood and soil in the back seat of an Antillean eagle's flight to Fez.

I liked to kiss Jean-René on curves or steep downhill glides. I liked the wandering tree limbs to let their shadows enter his mouth as my tongue did. Shadows and tongue skipping and sliding over his pearl teeth and blackberry lips. Dangerous, you say? *Mais non.* You're talking to the woman who was physically searched three times at Kennedy Airport because the buzzer went off whenever I went through the screening device. I had forgotten to take my ben-wa balls out. They're no threat to international security. When they're working, the last thought on my mind is hijacking a plane. Why should I swipe an airplane when young Guadeloupean peacocks stalk about Paris and fly me to Morocco in the middle of the night. All he needs is a piano and me. I carry my own entertainment: color, wine, brushes, pencils. My ben-wa balls attracted no attention at Orly Airport. I guess they could see the contentment of my face, or smell my pleasure. I always assume people can smell how happy I am, how full of love I can be. That's how Jean-René found me in Paris at that fast-food souvlaki place. He could smell my joy, he said. I told him I heard Eric Dolphy in his eyes.

The Sofa Is Black

ANNE WALDMAN

Monsieur is here. I am reading. Reading the novel. In it a woman feigns ill is reclining on a sofa is revived but wants to die in the arms of her lover. Lover is monsieur is here. Am here reading. She says in the 18th century she wants to be caressed by the arms of death and the phallus of death. She is feigning. He, another Frenchman, the architect, wants none if it and I want none of it he says. He is monsieur the husband. He, another one who fucked her once got tired. Got tired reclined on a sofa. The war continues beneath their balconies. *Voile* is not the order of the day but volley might be. They (the countries) play war beneath their shuttered windows. He picks up the pen to write to his mistress "They play as if at war beneath my shuttered windows. . . ."

She remembers the first day her mother said Save your leg hair for shaving later you want something to look forward to. And she, another one, a nun, dropped out, became a mistress. Of any household, dust & sweep, dust & sweep. She is like to strangle herself in mirror in the tedium of dust and sweep. But is rescued by any man who is Back Door Man who is the butler in any century. Mommy, (he heard it on A.M. radio), what is a gigolo?

She is another victim that week. He writes "I worry for you."

(We scan down the street to see brief lives.)

She was a mighty matchgirl and displayed her wares in the heyday watering spots all about town. She is secretly dealing a controlled substance. I love you I love you she cries to the cop who plugs her.

& Marietta Martine is the Mata Hari who stole in a bigger time at a bigger angle and developed her lethal weaponry to be marketed in Iran, secretly in Israel. I am reading. Monsieur is here. He gets up to gather his opium paraphenalia. What is a novel? In a title? In the act of? Of what? Someone is doing something. Someone is torturing someone. Woman are being the victim of this or any other story. She is feigning to get the best of the plot. She is feigning until the denouement to show true colors. The sofa is green. No the sofa is red. No the sofa is blue. The sofa is blue. No the sofa is black. The sofa is black.

Laments

JENNY HOLZER

Note: The following texts are reproductions of the original drawings used for the inscriptions on thirteen stone sarcophagi installed at the Dia Art Foundation in New York City on March 1, 1989. The texts are the voices of ten adults, two children, and one infant.

WITH ONLY MY MIND
TO PROTECT ME
I GO INTO DAYS.
WHAT I FEAR IS
IN A BOX WITH FUR
TO MUFFLE IT.
EVERY DAY I DO NOTHING
IMPORTANT BECAUSE I AM
SCARED BLANK AND LAZY,
BUT THEN THE MEN COME.
I PUT MY MOUTH ON THEM.
I SPIT AND WRITE
WITH THE WET.
THE WET SAYS WHAT
MUST STOP AND
WHAT SHALL BEGIN.
I SPIT BECAUSE THE DEATH
SMELL IS TOO CLOSE TO ME.
THE STINK MAKES WORDS
TELL THE TRUTH ABOUT
WHO KILLS AND
WHO IS THE VICTIM.
DEATH IS THE
MODERN ISSUE.
I THINK BECAUSE
MY BRAIN DOES IT.
I WANT BAD IDEAS TO STAY
IN THE MIND TO MAKE
PLEASURE WITHOUT HARM.
A CLEAR THOUGHT MUST
COME TO STOP THE MEN
AND MAKE THE AUDIENCE
LAUGH UNTIL THEIR
INSIDES BUBBLE.

IF THE
PROCESS STARTS
I WILL
KILL THIS BABY
A GOOD WAY.
SHE CAN LIE
ON MY
FAMILIAR BELLY.
OUR BACKS WILL
BE IN LINE
AND THEN
INDISTINGUISHABLE.
I WILL TAKE
HER DOWN BEFORE
SHE FEELS THE
FEAR THAT IS
CAUSE AND
RESULT.

THE NEW DISEASE CAME.
I LEARN THAT TIME
DOES NOT HEAL.
EVERYTHING GETS
WORSE WITH DAYS.
I HAVE SPOTS
LIKE A DOG.
I COUGH AND CANNOT
TURN MY HEAD.
I CONSIDER SLEEPING
WITH PEOPLE
I DO NOT LIKE.
I NEED TO LIE
BACK TO FRONT
WITH SOMEONE
WHO ADORES ME.
I WILL THINK MORE
BEFORE I CANNOT.
I LOVE MY MIND WHEN
IT IS FUCKING THE
CRACKS OF EVENTS.
I WANT TO TELL YOU
WHAT I KNOW
IN CASE IT IS OF USE.
I WANT TO GO TO
THE FUTURE PLEASE.

THERE IS NO ONE'S
SKIN UNDER
MY FINGERNAILS.
THERE IS NO ONE
TO WATCH
MY HAIR GROW.
NO ONE LOOKS AT
ME WHEN I WALK.
PEOPLE WANT ME
TO PAY MONEY FOR
EACH THING I GET.
I HAVE EVERY KIND
OF THROUGH AND THAT
IS NO EMBARRASSMENT.
I LOOK AT MYSELF
WHEN I BATHE.
WHAT I GIVE
TO ALL THE PEOPLE
WHO DO NOT WANT
TO LIVE WITH ME
IS ARITHMETIC.
I COUNT INFANTS AND
PREDICT THEIR DAYS.
I SUBTRACT PEOPLE
KILLED FOR ONE
REASON OR ANOTHER.
I GUESS THE NEW
REASONS AND PROJECT
THEIR EFFICACY.
I DECORATE MY
NUMBERS AND
CIRCULATE THEM.

NO RECORD OF JOY
CAN BE LIKE THE
JUICE THAT JUMPS
THROUGH YOUR SKULL
WHEN YOU ARE
PERFECT IN SEX.
YOU POSITION
YOUR SPINE UNTIL
IT WAVES.
YOUR HANDS RUN
TO SPOTS
THAT FEEL
DIFFERENT.
BREATHING TELLS
THE PERSON
WHAT TO DO.
YOU TRY TO STOP
BECAUSE THAT
IS THE FUN.
THEN YOU SQUEEZE
AND BECOME
UNCONSCIOUS NEAR
WHOMEVER WHICH IS
THE DANGEROUS
THING IN
THE WORLD.
AT THE END
YOU DO NOT WANT.
YOU CARRY THIS
SENSATION TO THE
CRUEL PLACES
YOU GO.

I WAS
SICK FROM
ACTING NORMAL.
I WATCHED
REPLAYS OF
THE WAR.
WHEN NOTHING
HAPPENED I
CLOSED A ZONE
WHERE I
EXERT CONTROL.
I FORMED A
GOVERNMENT THAT
IS AS WELCOME
AS SEX.
I AM GOOD
TO PEOPLE
UNTIL THEY DO
SOMETHING STUPID.
I STOP THE
HABITUAL MISTAKES
THAT MAKE FATE.
I GIVE PEOPLE
TIME SO THEY
FEEL THEIR LIVES
MOVING OVER
THEIR SKINS.
I WANT A
LARGER ARENA.
I TEASE WITH
THE POSSIBILITY
OF MY
ABSENCE.

I GO TO SCHOOLS
TO SEE CHILDREN
RUN HARD.
I OBSERVE PEOPLE
WHEN THEY STAND
TO HAVE SEX.
I PHOTOGRAPH
PRESIDENTS.
I LOOK AT
ANIMALS IN FIRES.
I AM NOT WORRIED
WHICH IS WHAT
EVERY HUMAN BEING
HAS WANTED FROM
THE BEGINNING.
I WAS NOT
BORN LIVE.
THIS BODY GREW
BUT I DID NOT
FEEL CELLS SPLIT.
HOW I ACT
DOES NOT MATTER.
I AM WAITING FOR
EVERYONE TO DIE
BECAUSE THAT
IS THE POINT.

THE KNIFE CUT
RUNS AS LONG
AS IT WANTS.
IT IS THROUGH
MY STOMACH.
I KEEP LOOKING
AT IT.
I HAVE MORE
COLORS THAN
I WOULD
HAVE THOUGHT.
THE HOLE IS
LARGE ENOUGH
FOR MY HEAD.
THE HOLE WAS
BIG ENOUGH
FOR THEIR HANDS
TO MOVE FREELY.
THEY PUT THEIR
FINGERS IN
BECAUSE THEY
SHOULD NOT AND
BECAUSE THEY
DO NOT GET
THE CHANCE
EVERY DAY.

IT BECAME TOO HOT.
THE BLACK DIRT'S
HEAT MADE THE
AIR WRIGGLE.
NEW WEATHER
WOULD NOT ENTER.
FIRES COULD
NOT STOP.
I DID NOT SEE
MY NEIGHBOR.
I TUNNEL
FOR RELIEF.
I DIG WATER AND
PUT IT IN AN EGG.
I BREAK INTO
OTHER BURROWS
BECAUSE YOU
CANNOT ENJOY
RUNNING IN A TUBE
OF YOUR MAKING.
I SHOULD FALL
IN FREEZING WATER
TO SAVE MY PARTS.
I CANNOT GO
WHERE IT IS
COOLER BECAUSE
PEOPLE THERE
ARE AWAKE
AND ARMED.

I HAVE A
HOT HOLE
THAT WAS
PUT IN ME.
I CAN LIVE
WITH IT.
PEOPLE MADE IT
AND USE IT
TO GET
TO ME.
I CAN HURT
IT TOO BUT
USUALLY I PUT
MY THINKING
THERE FOR
EXCITEMENT.
WHEN MY MIND
IS RIGHT I
CAN SAY WHAT
NO ONE WANTS
TO HEAR.
I BRAG ABOUT
KNOWING
BETTER,
BUT THE LAST
KIND PART OF
ME RAVES
BECAUSE
I WILL NOT
BE THE ONLY
DEAD ONE.
I KEEP THE
HOLE OPEN.

I WANT TO LIVE IN
A SILVER WRAPPER.
I WILL SEE
WHOOPING ROCKS FLY.
I WILL ICE ON MY BLACK SIDE
AND STEAM ON THE OTHER
WHEN I FLOAT BY SUNS.
I WANT TO LICK FOOD
FROM THE CEILING.
I AM AFRAID TO STAY
ON THE EARTH.
FATHER HAS CARRIED ME THIS
FAR ONLY TO HAVE ME BURN
AT THE EDGE OF SPACE.
FACTS STAY IN YOUR MIND
UNTIL THEY RUIN IT.
THE TRUTH IS PEOPLE ARE
PUSHED AROUND BY TWO MEN
WHO MOVE ALL THE
BODIES ON EARTH INTO
PATTERNS THAT PLEASE THEM.
THE PATTERNS SPELL
OH NO NO NO
BUT IT DOES NO GOOD
TO WRITE SYMBOLS.
YOU HAVE TO DO THE
RIGHT ACTS WITH YOUR BODY.
I SEE SPACE AND IT
LOOKS LIKE NOTHING AND
I WANT IT AROUND ME.

[child's text]

DEATH CAME AND HE LOOKED
LIKE A RAT WITH CLAWS.
I MADE HIM GO
INTO THE WALL.
I KEEP HIM THERE WITH
THE PRESSURE OF MY MIND.
I HEAR HIM SCRATCHING
AND CLIMBING.
MY THOUGHTS FLY TO THE
WALL TO SEAL THE CRACKS
AND TO ADD PLASTER
LAYERS FOR STRENGTH.
I KEEP MY BRAIN ON SO I
DO NOT FALL INTO NOTHING
IF HIS CLAWS HURT ME.
I DO NOT WANT TO LEAVE
MY HOUSE AND THE
PEOPLE I LIKE.
I DO NOT WANT TO STOP
KNOWING ALL MY FACTS.
I DO NOT WANT MY BODY TO
TURN INTO SOMETHING ELSE.
WHEN A RAT MAKES YOU
UNCONSCIOUS YOU GO ON
A CONVEYOR BELT AND ARE
DUMPED FROM THE END.
YOU DROP IN SPACE AND
NEVER HIT BOTTOM EVEN
THOUGH YOU NEED TO
AS TIME PASSES.

[child's text]

I CAN MAKE WOMEN'S
BREASTS WEEP. I DREAM
WORDS. MY IDEAS COME
FROM MY SKIN. I WAKE
IN TERROR FROM WHAT
IS IN ME BEFORE
EXPERIENCE. I CONJURE
WHAT HAS NEVER BEEN
TO DAZZLE MYSELF.
I DO NOT WANT TO BE
LEFT TO BE EATEN.
I MOVE IN AN ENVELOPE
OF ALL SMELLS. I HOOT
WHEN MY BRAIN FILLS.
I AM NO BETTER THAN
A STUMP BUT MY
POTENTIAL FRIGHTENS.
I SHOULD BE THE FIRST
OF THE KIND WHO IS NOT
HOMICIDAL. MURDER HAS
NOT KILLED EVERYONE
BUT NOW IT MIGHT.

[infant's text]

A Barrel of Her Own Design

ELLEN ZWEIG

Note: "A Barrel of Her Own Design" is a performance piece and installation about Annie Edson Taylor, who, in 1901, was the first person to go over Niagara Falls in a barrel. First performed in July 1988 at ArtPark, Lewiston, New York, the piece includes nine performers in turn-of-the-century dress, whose movements are projected inside a silo that has been converted into a camera-obscura. An audiotape inside the silo-camera plays a poetic investigation of what happened to Annie in the few minutes that she was knocked unconscious as she went over the Falls. The piece is part of a larger series, Ex(Centric) Lady Travellers, which explores Victorian lady travelers and other women who travel alone.

I

The images kept rising to the surface of her mind.
She was riding in this strange craft,
                              a barrel of her own design.
It was all so supernatural, so pale, so still.
The images kept rising to the surface of her mind.

The images kept ringing in the surface of her mind.
She was riding on this strange map,
                              a barrel of her own design.
It was all so tense and musical, so dark, so still.
The images kept ringing in the surface of her mind.

The images kept roaring on the surface of her mind.
She was riding on this strange gap,

                     a barrel of her own design.
It was all so deep and vertical, so far, so still.
The images kept roaring on the surface of her mind.

She was on the brink, the precipice, the sound of falling water.
She was in the dark, unconsciousness, the crash of falling water.

The images came rushing out the surface of her mind.
She was flying in this strange craft,
                     a barrel of an old design.
It was all so like the cinema, no eyes so still.
The images came rushing out the surface of her mind.

The images enveloped her, the surface of her mind.
She was fearful of this strange craft,
                     a barrel of an old design.
It was all so like a chimera, no edge so still.
The images enveloped her, the surface of her mind.

The images fell out of her, the surface of her mind.
She was speaking from this strange craft,
                     a barrel of an old design.
It was all so like a waterfall, no end so still.
The images fell out of her, the surface of her mind.

She was in the deep, the cataract, the gap of falling water.
She was on the edge of consciousness, the flash of falling water.

II

All these little stories made the front page news.
She was falling in this dark trap,
                     a barrel of an old design.
It is the motion of the water which fascinates the eye.
The stage set for three forms of danger.

It is the motion of the water which fascinates the eye.
She was calling from this dark trap,

a barrel of an old design.
It had an actual opening, but not for looking out.
The stage set for three forms of danger.

It had an actual opening, but not for looking out.
She was dreaming in this dark trap,
a barrel of an old design.
It let a little water in, but not enough to drink.
The stage set for three forms of danger.

She was on the brink, the precipice, the sound of falling water.
It was a suicide, an accident, the crash of falling water.

A fluid structure arises, never resolved, never pure.
She was straining in the hard straps,
a barrel of her own design.
Time was just an element, like gold and air.
Her choice was the third form of danger.

Time was just an element, like gold and air.
She was holding to the cold facts,
a barrel of her own design.
Inside was like a reverie of eye and ear.
Her choice was the third form of danger.

Inside was like a reverie of eye and ear.
She was silent in her bright thoughts,
a barrel of her own design.
It shuddered through her consciousness and then was gone.
Her choice was the third form of danger.

She was on the brink, the precipice, the sound of falling water.
It was not suicide, not accident, the crash of falling water.

III

She heard music like a map of falling water.
He captured the whirling, tumbling foam of rushing water,
    which to some observers seemed almost audible.

He heard her voice that sounded faint inside the barrel like a map of
    falling water.
She saw a travelling Niagara, Niagara itself.

She heard music like a mirror of her memory.
He captured the effects of sunlight on water,
    which to some observers seemed almost audible.

He heard her whisperings and thoughts, inner yearnings, like a map of
    falling water.
She saw nature in her wildest, Niagara itself.

She heard music like a tremor of her poverty.
He captured objects as reflected in the water,
    which to some observers seemed almost audible.

He heard her basest dreams, for fame and fortune from a map of falling water.
She saw a three mile picture, Niagara itself.

She heard music like a murmur of this novelty.
He captured the geography of the entire region around the Falls,
    which to some observers seemed almost audible.

He heard the shouting of the crowd like a map of falling water.
She saw rapids, islands, whirlpools, caves and rocky gorges, brinks and bridges,
    houses, spray clouds, rainbows, stairways, people.

She heard music like a map of falling water.
He captured a view by the light of a huge fire,
    which to some observers seemed almost audible.

He heard she was afraid of a penniless old age like a map of falling water.
She saw an almost supernatural effect, Niagara itself.

She heard music like a murmur of this novelty.
He captured the hazy atmosphere, motionless and vague,
    which to some observers seemed almost audible.

He heard that Mrs. Taylor is well-read and a good conversationalist like a map
    of falling water.
She saw the earth's formations, Niagara itself.

She heard music like a tremor of her poverty.
He captured the history of the Falls,
    which to some observers seemed almost audible.

He heard that she has crossed the American continent from ocean to ocean
    eight times like a map of falling water.
She saw the natural order of geographical succession, Niagara itself.

She heard music like a mirror of her memory.
He captured the great wonder of nature,
    which to some observers seemed almost audible.

He heard that she died in the poorhouse almost twenty years later like a map
    of falling water.
She saw herself like a map of falling water, Niagara itself.

She heard music like a map of falling water.

IV

She is as determined as ever to make the journey.
Was it like a dream or different from a dream?

She believes she will live to tell the tale.
Did you think you were dying or close to death?

The body of a woman was recovered from the lower river yesterday.
Did you hear any noises or unusual sounds?

The two pairs of shoes she possessed were in the customary place.
Did you feel as though you were travelling or moving?

While dancing last night
Did you, at any time, feel as though you were separate from your own
    physical body?

Miss Maggie Mock
Is it roaring in your head like Niagara?
Accidentally tripped on her skirt
Did you, at any time, have a sense of approaching a boundary or limit?
And fell
Is it another superb view?
Striking the back of her head
What were your feelings and sensations?
With great force
This experience of yours, has it changed you in any way?
On the hard wood floor.

She is as determined as ever to make the journey.
Is this a panorama of the Falls?

The successful trip of the barrel and the experience of the cat have
        inspired her.
Was it difficult to put into words?

She was rescued and taken from the barrel in a more dead than alive condition.

V

So severe was the shock that she wanders in her talk.
Niagara itself means nothing.
She will tell you a story all out of order
                              and often add things that are not in the song.

So severe was the shock that she wanders in her sleep.
None of her shoes were missing.
She will show you a drawing all out of order
                              and often add things that are not in the song.

So severe was the shock that she dances on the waves,
striking her head while falling.
She will build you a barrel all out of paper
                              and often add things that are not in the song.

So severe was the shock that she thought she was the cat,
going over the Falls, the roaring.
She will send you a vision all out of paper
                                    and often add things that are not in the song.

So severe was the shock that she thought she heard a crash,
more terrible than that of thunder.
She will play you a music all out of order
                                    and often add things that are not in the song.

So severe was the shock that she heard a ghostly voice,
more terrible than that of music.
She will show you the soundwaves all out of order
                                    and often add things that are not in the song.

So severe was the shock that she saw it in a flash,
the live, pulsing scenes of a movie.
She will draw you a map all out of order
                                    and often add things that are not in the song.

So severe was the shock that it entered her mind,
the live, moving scenes of Niagara.
She will show you a life all out of order
                                    and often add things that are not in the song.

VI

In the dark room of her mind, music like cartography records the simultaneity
    of conflicting orders.
Among the tightrope walkers, the greatest of all was the Frenchman, Blondin.

In the dark room of her mind, music like cartography records the simultaneity
    of conflicting orders.
Among the barrel riders, Carlisle D. Graham made the first trip through the
    wild rapids.

In the dark room of her mind, mapping like philosophy records the
    simultaneity of conflicting orders.

Among the tightrope walkers were Farini and Leslie, McDonald and Peer,
    Dixon and Maria Spelterina.

In the dark room of her mind, water like psychology records the simultaneity
    of conflicting orders.
Among the barrel riders, Anna Edson Taylor was the first one over the Falls.

In the dark room of her mind, music like photography records the
    simultaneity of conflicting orders.
Life is full of noise and death alone is silent.
Maud Willard died shooting the rapids.

In the dark room of her mind, pictures like geometry record the simultaneity
    of conflicting orders.
Life is full of visions and death alone is blind.
Webb and Scott died swimming the rapids.

In the dark room of her mind, dying like metonymy records the simultaneity
    of conflicting orders.
I am sincere in this matter.

VII

She told of the awful journey in a rambling sort of way.
It is the motion of the water which fascinates the eye.
I first made a barrel of paper in my room.

It is the motion of the water which fascinates the eye.
Music like photography regards the simultaneity of conflicting orders.
I prepared myself as if for a trip and got into it.

Music like photography regards the simultaneity of conflicting orders.
It is very unusual for a river-wave to be silhouetted against the sky.
Mrs. Taylor changed her clothes and donned a blue skirt and blue blouse.

It is very unusual for a river-wave to be silhouetted against the sky.
The barrel was in the boat; the woman beside it.
Her choice was the third form of danger.

The barrel was in the boat; the woman beside it.
A fluid structure arises, never resolved, never pure.
The straps were adjusted; the pillows arranged.

A fluid structure arises, never resolved, never pure.
She's coming, she's coming, was the cry on the lips of the crowd.
The appeal of Niagara to the human mind is not merely the appeal of beauty.

She's coming, she's coming, was the cry on the lips of the crowd.
The images kept rising to the surface of her mind.
The barrel danced and plunged down the rapids.

The images kept rising to the surface of her mind.
It seemed to poise an instant at the brink.
This music is not innocent.

It seemed to poise an instant at the brink.
And stood up on its end and made the awful plunge.
There is so much that suggests a terrible doom.

And stood up on its end and made the awful plunge.
The great spectacle of noise is only a spectacle.
She was unable to give a clear account of the trip and seemed hysterical.

The great spectacle of noise is only a spectacle.
She seemed to be spinning around like a top and her mind began to fail.
Here we see the act of falling.

She seemed to be spinning around like a top and her mind began to fail.
I felt that all nature was being annihilated.
This music is not innocent.

I felt that all nature was being annihilated.
We are not explorers; we are not believers.
Once for a moment, I seemed to lose my senses.

We are not explorers; we are not believers.
In passing over the Falls, she admits to having lost consciousness.
Accompanied by music and commentary, unrolling the grand canvas took
an hour and a half.

In passing over the Falls, she admits to having lost consciousness.
It was now mere spectacle.
Mrs. Taylor groaned and feebly waved her right hand.

It was now mere spectacle.
What fills the mind is the roaring of the water.
It was necessary to saw a portion of the top away to get her out.

What fills the mind is actually moving.
She says she wants to make the trip without looking at the water.
We must visit many times and spend many days.

What fills the mind is awareness itself.
Though she was somewhat hysterical, her condition was not at all serious.
What we see is not what she heard.

What fills the mind is beyond thinking and beyond words.
She went to Niagara Falls, a subject difficult enough to draw from nature.
She has scaled the Alps, made dangerous swimming trips, and explored wild
    countries.

What fills the mind is a map of falling water.
In passing over the Falls, she admits to having lost consciousness.
What we see is not what she heard.

VIII

She was on the brink, the precipice, the sound of falling water.
She was in the dark, unconsciousness, the crash of falling water.
She was in the deep, the cataract, the gap of falling water.
She was on the edge of consciousness, the flash of falling water.

The images kept pouring out the surface of her mind.
She was riding on her wild talk,
                                    a barrel of her own design.
It was all so real, subliminal, so light, so still.
She saw movies like a map of falling water.

She was on the brink, the precipice, the sound of falling water.
She was in the dark, unconsciousness, the crash of falling water.
She was in the deep, the cataract, the gap of falling water.
She was on the edge of consciousness, the flash of falling water.

The images kept storming her, the surface of her mind.
She was floating on her bright thoughts,
                                        a barrel of an old design.
It was all so unconventional, sublime and still.
She saw lightning like a map of falling water.

She was on the brink, the precipice, the sound of falling water.
She was in the dark, unconsciousness, the crash of falling water.
She was in the deep, the cataract, the gap of falling water.
She was on the edge of consciousness, the flash of falling water.

The images kept rising to the surface of her mind.
She was riding in this strange craft,
                                        a barrel of her own design.
It was all so like a waterfall, no end so still.
She heard music like a map of falling water.

Acknowledgments

ETEL ADNAN: from *The Arab Apocalypse* (Post-Apollo Press, 1989). Copyright 1989 by Etel Adnan. Reprinted by permission of The Post-Apollo Press, Sausalito, California.

ANNE-MARIE ALONZO: "Love, Pain, and the Fading of the Orchids" was originally published in f(Lip), Vancouver, Canada. Copyright 1989 by Anne-Marie Alonzo. "Sables Fous des Dunes" is reprinted from *Le Livre de Ruptures* (Edition L'Hexagone, 1988). Copyright 1988 by Anne-Marie Alonzo. Reprinted by permission of Edition l'Hexagone and Anne-Marie Alonzo.

NUALA ARCHER: "The Hour of Pan/Ama" originally appeared in *Sulfur* (26, 1990). Copyright 1990 by Nuala Archer. Reprinted by permission of the author. It appears in *The Hour of Pan/Ama* (Red Dust Press, New York and Salmon Press, Ireland, 1990). Copyright 1990 by Nuala Archer.

OLGA BROUMAS AND JANE MILLER: from *Black Holes, Black Stockings* (Wesleyan University Press, 1985). Copyright 1985 by Olga Broumas and Jane Miller. Reprinted by permission of University Press of New England.

THERESA CHA: "Melpomene Tragedy" from *Dictee* (Tanam Press, 1982). Copyright 1982 by Tanam Press. Reprinted by permission of Tanam Press. *Dictee* is currently distributed by McPherson and Co.

KIM CHERNIN AND RENATE STENDHAL: from *Sex and Other Sacred Games* (Times Books, 1989). Copyright 1989 by Kim Chernin and Renate Stendhal. Reprinted by permission of Random House, Inc., New York.

ABIGAIL CHILD: "A Motive for Mayhem" from *A Motive for Mayhem* (Potes and Poets Press, 1989). Copyright 1989 by Abigail Child. Reprinted by permission of Potes and Poets Press.

ABIGAIL CHILD AND SALLY SILVERS: "Rewire//Speak in Disagreement" originally appeared in *Poetics Journal* #4 (1984). Copyright 1984 by Abigail Child and Sally Silvers. Reprinted by permission of the authors.

KATHLEEN FRASER: "this.notes.new year" and "Five Letters from one window, San Gimignano, May 1981" are reprinted from *Each Next* (The Figures, 1987). Copyright 1987 by Kathleen Fraser. Reprinted by permission of the author.

JENNY HOLZER: *Laments* has been reproduced in its entirety from the original Dia Art Foundation catalog by permission of Jenny Holzer. Jenny Holzer's biographical note has been provided by Clare Bell of the Guggenheim Museum.

FANNY HOWE: "Perfection and Derangement" first appeared in *o.blēk* (No. 4, Fall 1989, The Garlic Press). Copyright 1988 by Fanny Howe. Reprinted by permission of the author.

SUZANNE JACOB: from *Life, After All* (Press Gang Publishers, 1989). Copyright 1989 by Suzanne Jacob. Reprinted by permission of Press Gang Publishers, Vancouver, Canada.

JANET KAUFFMAN: "The Blue Door of Detroit" originally appeared in *Caliban* (No. 6, 1989). Copyright 1989 by Janet Kauffman. Reprinted by permission of the author.

DAPHNE MARLATT AND BETSY WARLAND: "Reading and Writing Between the Lines" was first published in *Tessera* (Ontario, Canada). Copyright 1988 by Daphne Marlatt and Betsy Warland. Reprinted by permission of the authors.

DÔRE MICHELUT: "About Flight" is reprinted from *Loyalty to the Hunt* (Guernica). Copyright 1986 by Dorina Michelutti and Guernica Editions. Reprinted by permission of Dôre Michelut and Guernica Editions.

Contributors

ETEL ADNAN is an Arab-American poet who writes in English and French. She was born and raised in Lebanon by an Arab Muslim father and a Greek mother. *Sitt Marie-Rose*, her novel about the civil war in Lebanon, was first published in France and then translated into five languages.

ANNE-MARIE ALONZO was born in Alexandria, Egypt, and has lived in Montreal since 1963. She has been a quadraplegic since 1966. While writing her Ph.D. thesis on Colette, she published twelve books and won Le Prix Emile-Nelligan 1985 for *Lead Blues*. She is cofounder and coeditor of the revue and the publishing house Trois.

NUALA ARCHER'S first book of poetry, *Whale on the Line*, won the Patrick Kavanagh National Poetry Award in Ireland in 1980. *Two Women, Two Shores* (1989) included poems by Nuala Archer and Medbh McGuckian. Her two manuscripts of poetry were launched in spring 1991. Archer is an associate professor in poetry at Cleveland State University; she has also taught at Yale University.

NICOLE BROSSARD lives in Montreal. A poet, novelist, and essayist, she is the author of numerous books, including (in English translation) *A book*, *Daydream Mechanics*, *French Kiss*, *The Aerial Letter*, and *Mauve Desert*. In 1965, she cofounded *La Barre du Jour*. In 1976, she codirected the film *Some American Feminists*. In 1974, and again in 1984, she was awarded the Governor General's Award for poetry, Canada's most prestigious literary prize. In 1989, she received Le Grand Prix de Poésie de la Fondation Les Forges. Her work has been translated into English, Italian, and German.

OLGA BROUMAS'S first book in English, *Beginning with O*, was the Yale Younger Poets Selection in 1977. Other books include *Soie Sauvage*, *Pastoral Jazz*, *Perpetua*, and translations of the Greek poet Odysseas Elytis, *What I Love*, and *The Little Mariner*. A recipient of Guggenheim and NEA Fellowships, she is a bodywork therapist in Provincetown, Massachusetts, and teaches at Boston University and Brandeis University.

THERESA CHA emigrated from Korea to the U.S. in 1963. In 1980 she moved to New York City and edited *Apparatus*, a collection of film theory. In 1982 she published *Dictee*, one of the most important experimental texts of the decade. In 1982 Theresa Cha was raped and murdered in New York.

KIM CHERNIN lives in Berkeley, California, where she works as a writer and psychotherapist. She is the author of both fiction and nonfiction books, including *In My Mother's House*, *The Hungry Self*, *Reinventing Eve*, *The Flame Bearers*, and *Sex and Other Sacred Games*, with Renate Stendhal.

ABIGAIL CHILD is a filmmaker and writer based in New York City. Her books include *From Solids*, *Climate/Plus*, *A Motive for Mayhem*, and *Flesh*. Her films include *Mayhem* (1987), *Mercy* (1989), and *Swamp*, a video soap opera. She is an associate professor of film at Hampshire College in Massachusetts.

JUDITH COWAN is a bilingual poet and short-story writer who teaches English literature to French-speaking students at l'Université du Quebec à Trois Rivières. She has translated selections from the works of many contemporary Quebec poets. Her work has appeared in, among others, *Liberté*, *Matrix*, *Ellipse*, and *Le Sabord*.

LOUISE DUPRÉ, literary critic and fiction writer, has contributed to various Quebècoises, English Canadian, and European journals. She has published several books of poetry, including *La Peau familière* (1983), *Chambres* (1986), and *Bonheur* (1988). She has also published an essay, "Stratégies du vertige" (1989) on the poetry of Nicole Brossard, Madeleine Gagnon, and France Théoret. She is a professor of literature at l'Université du Quebec à Montréal.

SUSANNA FINNELL received her Ph.D. in French Canadian literature from the University of British Columbia. She is on the faculty of Washington State University and lives in a grain elevator in Eastern Washington.

KATHLEEN FRASER, poet and fiction writer, founded and edited (from 1983–89) the journal HOW(ever), devoted to contemporary experiment in women's poetry. Notes Preceding Trust is her ninth volume of poems. She was founder of the American Poetry Archive and teaches writing at San Francisco State University, living every spring quarter in Rome.

CARLA HARRYMAN is the author of Animal Instincts: Selected Prose, Plays, and Essays, Vice, The Middle, Property, Under the Bridge, and Percentage. She has written a number of plays, with productions staged in the Bay Area and in New York. Since 1987, she has been collaborating with Lyn Hejinian on The Wide Road, a picaresque novel containing views of contemporary erotic life. She was born and lives in California.

LYN HEJINIAN is the coeditor, with Barrett Watten, of Poetics Journal and was for a number of years the editor and publisher of Tuumba Press. Her books include Individuals (written with Kit Robinson), My Life, Redo, The Guard, Writing as an Aid to Memory, and a collection of poems, The Cell. In Description, she has translated the work of the Soviet poet Arkadii Dragomoshchenko. She is the recipient of an NEA Translation Grant and a California Arts Council Individual Artists Grant. Hejinian was born in California and has lived there for most of her life.

TOBEY HILLER was born in Massachusetts and grew up in Ithaca, New York. She has lived in California since 1963, where she received her B.A. from the University of California at Berkeley in 1966. She received her M.A. from Antioch University. She is a certified psychodramatist and psychotherapist, married, and the mother of two children, both in college. She has recently completed a novel.

JENNY HOLZER was born in 1950 in Gallipolis, Ohio. After completing a B.F.A. degree in painting and printmaking from Ohio University in 1972, she attended the Rhode Island School of Design, where she received an M.F.A. in painting. In 1976, she moved to New York's Lower East Side, where she joined the Whitney Museum's Independent Study Program and turned to writing. Her messages have appeared on a variety of media: posters, metal plaques, t-shirts, tractor caps, and electronic signs. She has also paired L.E.D. (light-emitting-diode) signs with stone benches or sarcophagi engraved with her texts, which have taken the form of cryptic narratives. Holzer represented the United States at the 1990 Venice Biennale.

FANNY HOWE has published *The Deep North, Famous Questions, In The Middle of Nowhere, Holy Smoke, Bronte Wild, First Marriage, Forty Whacks,* and *Body and Soul,* all fiction. Among her poetry publications are *The Vineyard, Robeson Street,* and *Introduction to the World.*

SUZANNE JACOB was born and raised in Quebec. She has been acclaimed for her writing and for her dual career as a singer and composer. She has published seven books—short stories, novels, and poetry—as well as numerous scripts for radio and television. Her novel *Laura Laur* won the Governor General's Award in 1984. *Life, After All* is the first of her books to be translated into English.

JANET KAUFFMAN has published two collections of stories, *Places in the World a Woman Could Walk* (1984) and *Obscene Gestures for Women* (1989). Her novel, *Collaborators,* was published in 1986. She lives in Hudson, Michigan.

DAPHNE MARLATT is the author of a number of books of poetry and prose, including *Ana Historic* and a poetic collaboration with Betsy Warland, *Double Negative.* She has coedited several small magazines and is a founding member of the feminist editorial collective *Tessera,* which publishes a semiannual journal of new Quebècoise and English-Canadian writing. She makes her home on Salt Spring Island, British Columbia.

DÔRE MICHELUT was born in Friul, Italy, grew up in Canada, and studied at the University of Florence and the University of Toronto. She has published *Loyalty to the Hunt* (prose poetry) and *OUROBOROS: The Book That Ate Me* (a self-study in interlocking genres). She has also published a collaborative work of linked poetry, a collection of renga (an adaptation of the Japanese form) titled *Linked Alive* in English, and *Liens* in the simultaneous French edition.

JANE MILLER'S latest collection of poems is *American Odalisque.* She has also completed a book of essays on poetry, culture, and travel, *Working Time.* Among her honors are fellowships from the Guggenheim Foundation, National Endowment for the Arts, the Four Corners Book Award in Poetry, a *Los Angeles Times* Book Award nomination in poetry, and the National Poetry Series Open Competition (for *The Greater Leisures*). She is on the creative writing program staff at the University of Arizona and lives in Tucson.

TRINH T. MINH-HA is a writer, filmmaker, and composer. Her works include the books Un Art sans oeuvre, En Minuscules (poetry), Woman, Native, Other, African Spaces: Designs for Living in the Upper Volta (in collaboration with Jean-Paul Bourdier), and the films Reassemblage, Naked Spaces—Living Is Round, and Surname Viet Given Name Nam. She is an associate professor of cinema at San Francisco State University.

LOU NELSON is a freelance translator and poet living in Montreal, Quebec.

NINA CROW NEWINGTON has finished a novel, Harvest of Ghosts, and is working on a second as well as a collection of poems. She is English, lives in rural Massachusetts, and makes her living as a carpenter. She has given numerous readings in New York City and had a play produced there. Her work has appeared in Ikon, Conditions, and other magazines, as well as in a number of anthologies including Naming the Waves: Contemporary Lesbian Poetry.

CAMILLE NORTON'S work has appeared in the Georgia Review, the American Voice, Trivia: A Journal of Ideas, and Word of Mouth: Short-Short Stories by Women. She won a Grolier Prize in Poetry in 1981 and a Stegner Fellowship in Poetry in 1985. She is a teaching fellow in English at Harvard University. She lives in Jamaica Plain, Massachusetts.

LOU ROBINSON'S writing has appeared recently in Trivia, Conditions, Quarterly, f(Lip), Tessera, Trois, and in three short story collections. A chapbook of her fiction, Extremes of High and Low Regard, has also been published. Her novella Napoleon's Mare won the 1991 Fiction Collective competition. She lives in Ithaca, New York, and works at Cornell University Press.

GAIL SCOTT is the author of Heroine and Spare Parts and Spaces Like Stairs, co-author of La Théorie, un dimanche, and cofounder of Spirale and Tessera. She has published fiction as well as texts on women and writing in the anthologies Fatal Recurrences, A Mazing Space, and In the Feminine.

NTOZAKE SHANGE has written numerous plays, novels, and collections of poems, including for colored girls. . . , Nappy Edges, A Daughter's Geography, Betsey Brown, Riding the Moon in Texas, and Sassafrass, Cypress, and Indigo. She has written several performance pieces for music and dance and is the recipient of two Obies, one for her adaptation of Brecht's Mother Courage. She is a Guggenheim Fellow, a Chubb Fellow, a Fellow of the National Endowment for the Arts for Playwriting, and the Macdowell Colony. She has taught at a number of colleges and universities, among them Rice University and Villanova.

SALLY SILVERS is a New York City-based choreographer and performer who has made group and solo dances since 1980. She is most known for her explorations of unconventional activity and structure designed to open up possibilities for movement as an art form. She has taught composition and improvisation nationally and in Europe and has collaborated with film-makers, writers, and improvising musicians. Her theoretical writing and scores have appeared in the *Drama Review* and other journals.

RENATE STENDHAL was born in Germany, grew up in Berlin, and studied at the University of Hamburg. In Paris, she cofounded COLTRA, an experi-mental theater group that produced the first feminist play in Paris—Mod Donna (1972). Throughout the 1970s she worked as a cultural correspon-dent in Paris for German radio and press. In 1979, with Danish artist Maj Skadegaard, she created multimedia shows on women's liberation. One of these, *In the Beginning . . . of the End* was filmed by the National Film Board of Canada and won the Prix de la Critique at the Paris Avantgarde Film Festival in 1983. She is the translator of numerous works into German by Gertrude Stein, Audre Lorde, Adrienne Rich, and Susan Griffin. With Kim Chernin, she is the coauthor of *Sex and Other Sacred Games*. In 1989, she published a photobiography of Gertrude Stein. She lives in Berkeley.

ROSMARIE WALDROP'S recent books of poetry are *The Reproduction of Profiles* and *Peculiar Motions*; she has also written the novels *The Hanky Panky of Pip-pin's Daughter* and *A Form/ of Taking/ It All*. She has translated Edmond Jabes's *Book of Questions*, Jacques Roubaud's *Some Thing Black*, and *6 Austrian Poets* (with Harriet Watts). She lives in Providence, Rhode Island, where she and Keith Waldrop run Burning Deck Press.

ANNE WALDMAN was an assistant director and director of the Poetry Project at St. Mark's Church-in-the-Bowery from 1966 to 1978. With Allen Ginsberg, in 1974, she founded the Jack Kerouac School of Disembodied Poetics at the Naropa Institute in Boulder, Colorado. Among her many publications, she has published over more than twenty-five pamphlets and books of poetry and edited numerous magazines and anthologies, including three antholo-gies of writing from the Poetry Project. She is a celebrated "performance poet," working extensively with dancers and musicians, and has performed her work in India, Nicaragua, and Prague, as well as across the United States, Canada, and Europe. She has taught at the New College of California and the Institute of American Indian Arts. She directs the Department of Writing and Poetics at the Naropa Institute.

BETSY WARLAND'S collection of essays, poems, articles, and prose, *Proper Definitions*, was published in 1990. She has published several books of poetry, including her collaboration with Daphne Marlatt, *Double Negative*. She is editing an anthology of U.S., Canadian, and Quebec lesbian writers on their own work. She coedited f(Lip) and *Telling It: Women and Language Across Cultures* and lives on Salt Spring, an island on the West Coast of Canada.

ELLEN ZWEIG is a performance/installation artist, a writer, and a theorist. Her work in all of these fields concentrates on images on the Other and the discourses between us and them. She has presented work in Europe and the United States, has received two NEA grants, and is working to complete a collaborative project with Meridel Rubenstein and Steina and Woody Vasulka about Edith Warner, who lived near Los Alamos when the atom bomb was being made. Zweig's other projects include a permanent installation of a camera obscura for the Exploratorium in San Francisco, continuing works on the series of performances *Ex(Centric) Lady Travellers*, and the organization of a Performance Studies Program at Franklin and Marshall College.